TEXTBOOK
ON
ALCOHOLISM AND DRUG ABUSE
IN THE SOVIET UNION

E. A. BABAYAN and M. H. GONOPOLSKY

TEXTBOOK
ON
ALCOHOLISM AND DRUG
ABUSE
IN THE SOVIET UNION

Authorized
by
the Chief Board for Educational Establishments, USSR
Ministry of Public Health, as a Textbook for Medical School
Students

INTERNATIONAL UNIVERSITIES PRESS, INC.

New York • New York

Library of Congress Cataloging-in-Publication Data

Babaían, E. A.
    Textbook on alcoholism and drug abuse in the
Soviet Union.

    Translation of: Uchebnoe posobie po narkologii.
    1. Alcoholism--Soviet Union. 2. Drug abuse--Soviet
Union. I. Gonopol'skii, M. Kh. (Marks Khaímovich)
II. Title. [DNLM: 1. Alcoholism. 2. Mental Health
Services--USSR. 3. Substance Dependence. WM 274 B112u]
RC56.5.B2413 1985   362.2'92'0947   85-18086
ISBN 0-8236-6470-8

Manufactured in the United States of America

Contents

Synopsis

This book explains the organizational principles of the Soviet substance abuse ("narcological") service, describing the duration and methods of therapy provided. Light is shed on the clinical, social and legal aspects of drug abuse, including alcoholism, abuse of substances legally defined as narcotics ("narcomanias"), as well as those not recognized as narcotic under the law ("toxicomanias").

This study aid is intended for medical school students who are training to become assistant drug therapists ("feldsher-narcologists") and medical nurses at institutions with substance abuse services.

The book contains four figures, four tables and five diagrams.

Reviewer: Prof. V. E. Rozhnov, Head of the Psychiatry Chair at the Central Institute for Advanced Medical Training, USSR Ministry of Health.

Foreword

A consistent and determined campaign against heavy drinking and alcoholism has been organized in the Soviet Union. In recent years the concepts of habitual drinking and alcoholism have become more clearly defined. However, until 1975 the treatment of this group of patients was solely the concern of the mental health care network. This prevented the concentration of efforts and necessary facilities for the organization of comprehensive care to patients suffering from alcoholism.

At present a narcological service is vigorously being developed in the country, with paramedical personnel playing a prominent role. Such persons are tackling serious tasks within their competence toward detecting, treating and preventing alcoholism, promoting health education in this field, and improving the microsocial climate.

Until now the experience in this work by paramedical personnel was rather limited and rarely generalized. In addition, the narcological service system has its own specific features which call for analysis, scientific substantiation and recognition in the literature. Thus, the many paramedical workers already engaged in narcology, or just starting work in this field, feel an acute need for a textbook to guide them through the clinical and organizational straits of narcology. Moreover, intensive research in recent years has resulted in the formation of a theory of alcoholic disease, its pathogenesis, different stages, and chief methods of treatment and prevention.

These factors have prompted the authors of this textbook toward the first attempt to generalize the experience thus far accumulated by the country's substance abuse service, and to analyze and outline its prospects for further development and improvement. Attention

xi

has been given to organizational, methodological and medico-legal questions as well as to those of diagnosis, treatment, prophylaxis and expert examination. Our hope is that others will be helped in mastering the new discipline of "narcology."

Introduction

For many years, medico-prophylactic care to patients suffering from alcoholism and drug abuse in the Soviet Union had been provided by special drug treatment rooms and departments within the psychiatric care system. Some of the functions in providing specialized narcological care were fulfilled by Institutions of the USSR Ministry of Internal Affairs, especially compulsory treatment in "work-therapy preventoriums" (WTP) or assistance in detoxification and sobering of persons in a state of heavy drunkenness.

After a number of decisions by the Central Committee of the Communist Party of the Soviet Union (CPSUCC) and the USSR Council of Ministers had established concrete tasks for improving narcological care to the population (including measures for early identification, greater treatment effectiveness, and prevention), in 1975 the Collegium of the USSR Ministry of Health passed a proposal to create an independent narcological service. Its mandate was to tackle all problems associated with heavy drinking and alcoholism and to provide medico-prophylactic aid to persons suffering from alcoholism and drug abuse (i.e., narcomanias and toxicomanias). This decision made it possible to create, along with the psychiatric service, a new, independent narcological service representing a unification of efforts. Not only the institutions and departments within this system, but also the narcological facilities functioning in the mental care system and those of the general medical network would be involved together.

The narcological service of the Soviet Union is conceived as an interrelated structure of narcological institutions and departments of public health organs and of other ministries and agencies, in particular, the USSR Ministry of Internal Affairs. Such a structure provides the foundation for a step-like system of medico-prophylactic, medico-social and medico-legal care, having hospital, semihospital, outpatient and industrial facilities. It would allow medical workers, while taking into account the individual features of the patient and his microsocial environment, to utilize all the divisions of the service to ensure the identification of persons suffering from alcoholic disorders, inducing them to undergo treatment and providing comprehensive care.

The organization of the smoothly functioning narcological service can be traced to Order No. 131 of the Minister of Health of the USSR on February 5, 1976. That Order introduced a new type of institution into the nomenclature of medical facilities of the USSR Ministry of Health—the "narcological dispensary." Statutes of the Narcological Dispensary were elaborated to define its specific tasks and functions. For this much preliminary work had to be done to study, analyze and generalize relevant legislative rules and acts as well as the views of local public health bodies, individual institutions and specialists. A Council of Public Inspectors was created under the Board for Introducing New Medicinal Drugs and Medical Technology, USSR Ministry of Health, whose opinions and conclusions on medical and legal matters also underlay the Statutes of the Narcological Dispensary.

Because of the specific features of narcological practice, the Statutes have a number of distinctions from the Statutes of the Neuropsychiatric Dispensary. First of all, one should single out the section determining the dispensary's relations with nonmedical institutions, for example, the facilities of the USSR Ministry of Internal Affairs, and with public organizations of both local and national levels (e.g., the Red Cross and Red Crescent Society).

To distinguish from the Statutes for traditional dispensaries (for instance, neuropsychiatric), the Statutes of the Narcological Dispensary stipulate that the dispensary can and should move many of its units (narcological consulting rooms, departments) closer to the population—into medical units, into premises situated in the grounds of industrial and agricultural enterprises, into general outpatient clinics and, in some cases, even into the premises of sobering-up stations.

Until recently the positions of psychiatrist-narcologist and assistant feldsher-narcologist did not exist in our country, although in fact a narcologist was appointed in neuropsychiatric dispensaries from among the psychiatrists. Now the positions of psychiatrist-narcologist (a doctor) and feldsher-narcologist (doctor's assistant) have been established by order of the USSR Ministry of Health. At the same time, curricula were drawn up for training such specialists, and internships in neuropsychiatry were established for training narcological personnel. The matter of the accreditation of the aforementioned groups of specialists was also resolved. Moreover, the study of narcology has been introduced into the curricula of higher and secondary medical training establishments. It should be noted that when deciding on personnel matters, the requirements not only of medical institutions were taken into account, but also of institutions within the system of the USSR Ministry of Internal Affairs (WTP for alcoholics). Specialized medium-echelon medical training departments for feldsher-narcologists were established in every Union Republic. All narcology specialists are eligible for all the fringe benefits established for psychiatrists (added salary allowances and additional paid leave).

Special importance is attached in this light to the training of para- or secondary narcological personnel, including feldshers—assistants of the psychiatrist-narcologists.

Keeping in mind the above-mentioned tasks, this textbook provides clear definitions on the subject of "narcology," sheds light on the epidemiology and basic forms of organizing the control of alcoholism, narcomanias and toxicomanias, and also on some consequences of the aforementioned diseases.

Acknowledging the importance of organized help to the population in combating alcoholism, this problem is pushed to the fore. A detailed examination is made of the system whereby such help is organized and the role of the different agencies, ministries and departments. Particularly, a leading place is given to the country's newly organized narcological service and to the position to be occupied by paramedical personnel in the different stages of this organization.

The clinical part of the textbook acquaints students with the etiology, pathogenesis and specific clinical manifestations of alcoholism, narcomania and toxicomania in relation to age and sex. It also considers combinations of the main disease with mental, somatic and neurological diseases, the specific features of higher nervous activity in alcoholism and the pathological anatomy of these diseases.

Great attention is given to the treatment of alcoholic ailments. Therefore, the basic principles of treatment are examined in great detail; the different stages and individual forms and methods of therapy are described. Psychotherapy is singled out as a leading method. Therapies are provided for psychoses and intoxications, for handling narcomanias and toxicomanias, and for breaking the tobacco smoking habit.

A special section of the textbook emphasizes the prevention of alcoholism, narcomanias and toxicomanias on a broad plane of deontology, health education and improving the microsocial environment.

Various kinds of expert examinations of alcoholic intoxication, forensic-psychiatric, military service, and labor examinations occupy a special place in the narcological service, and a whole section of the book is devoted to these questions.

The appendix to the book includes a list of the abbreviations used and an index of legal documents and methodological materials pertaining to narcology that are now in force.

Each section of the book concludes with review exercises and problems containing in concise form the basic questions that should be primarily mastered by the student. This will allow the instructor to concentrate attention on key issues of each section.

The course is illustrated with clinical examples, tables, diagrams and drawings.

PART ONE

GENERAL

Chapter 1

Alcoholism, Narcomanias, Toxicomanias and the Subject of Narcology

When addressing the problem of narcology, it is essential to form an idea about the structure of the groups of people with whom the psychiatrist-narcologist or paramedical worker are concerned. For the purpose of clearly defining the tasks facing the narcological service, the psychiatrist-narcologist and paramedical workers, and for the individualization of these tasks according to the groups of the population to be handled, beginning from antialcoholism propaganda and to the administration of specialized medical care, it is important to know the population of the district concerned—its occupational composition, cultural standards, age groups, as well as its attitude toward the consumption of alcoholic beverages. With regard to the latter indicator, the population is conditionally divided into 5 groups. However, one should bear in mind that there are no clear-cut borderlines between the groups singled out; they undergo dynamic change, and attitudes to alcohol are variable. Nor is such singling out in any way sociologically relevant.

The first group in the population does not use alcoholic drinks at all. This group includes a considerable number of women, some men, the sick, and children. It may so happen that upon recovery many sick people will start using alcoholic drinks; a certain number of teenagers will start drinking upon coming of age. Other persons who had

3

not used alcoholic beverages, either by conviction or because they just did not fancy them, may with time change their attitudes.

The second group of the population consists of persons who for one reason or another, frequently out of curiosity, want to taste or in some cases to experience their effect, or compare some beverages with others, to drink, or, to be more precise, taste alcoholic beverages. This group is called the experimenters.

The third group are those who use alcoholic drinks episodically, regularly, or according to a definite pattern—the users. Of course, persons from the first group, the non-users of alcohol, may join the group of users, bypassing the "experimenters" group.

It should be stressed that the experimenters drink to satisfy their curiosity on the taste, smell or nature of the effect produced, whereas the users, whether drinking episodically, regularly or according to a definite pattern, drink the beverages for known and expected gustatory, emotional or other effects.

The fourth group of the population consists of alcohol abusers. This group is made up mainly of former users (although it is not ruled out that this group may consist of individuals from the first and second groups).

The fifth group of the population are those suffering from chronic alcoholism; it is composed of alcohol abusers.

The scope of the psychiatrist-narcologist's competence and his particular duties depend in every case on the group to which he is attending. The primary concern of the psychiatrist-narcologist and his assistant (the feldsher-narcologist) is the handling of persons belonging to the fourth and fifth groups. This does not mean, however, that health education should not reach members of the second and third groups as well as those who are generally nondrinkers. At any time they may change their attitudes to drinking, especially in the absence of appropriate antialcoholism propaganda. From the juridical standpoint it should be stressed that the use of alcoholic beverages is not illegal, no matter which of the above enumerated groups an individual may belong to.

If we apply the same system to the classification of groups according to attitude toward narcotic drugs, the entire population consists, as a rule, of individuals who do not use narcotics. There is only a small number of experimenters who deem it permissible to try the effect of one or another narcotic drug. From these a third group may gradually emerge, consisting of persons using narcotic substances—users, and it is from this third group that a certain number of drug addicts evolve.

From the medical and legal standpoint, one should distinguish among users those who use narcotic substances legally, with a physician's prescription for health reasons, and those who use such drugs illegally, for other than medical indications. Unlike the use of alcoholic beverages, every case of nonmedical use of narcotics, experimenting included, should be regarded as abuse and, from the legal point of view, as a reprehensible act. The duties of narcological service personnel include health education with the purpose of discouraging experimentation or the use of narcotics, preventing addiction (narcomania), and in case of narcomanias, giving needed treatment.

When assessing the groups of people needing narcological care, it should be stressed that all persons suffering from alcoholism and narcomanias (or toxicomanias) are certainly in need of medical care. This gives rise to a rather difficult legal question. Most of these persons wish to undergo treatment and actively cooperate in the therapeutic process. Yet a small number reject voluntary treatment, mainly because they do not consider themselves to be sick. In such a case, it becomes necessary to define clearly the medical attitude toward such a person. Should we comply with the patient's point of view and leave the sick person to his fate, indifferently watching his destruction, or should we administer treatment against his wishes? From the medical point of view the latter path is the truly humane one, but it goes without saying that the wish of the psychiatrist-narcologist alone is not enough for resolving the matter, and appropriate legal acts are necessary. Of course, there are a number of fundamental and specific differences in the approaches to the organization of treatment for these two groups, which are so different in their legal aspects, although their methods of therapy are the same or have much in common.

Medical aid to persons suffering from narcomanias and toxicomanias, in contrast with the therapy given chronic alcoholics, is specific first of all in that therapy tactics largely depend on the characteristic effect of the particular narcotic substance causing the morbid state of narcomania or toxicomania. Therefore, when organizing the treatment of persons suffering from narcomanias and toxicomanias, the character of the narcomania or toxicomania concerned (morphine-induced, barbiturate, hemp drugs, etc.) must be taken into account. Yet the general system of treating alcoholism, narcomanias and toxicomanias must certainly combine both inpatient and outpatient treatments.

SOME QUESTIONS OF TERMINOLOGY IN NARCOLOGY

Many medical terms are associated with legal acts and cannot therefore be arbitrarily used based on the medical criterion only. When using them one must take into account the legal criterion defined by the above mentioned acts. This becomes especially important when the terms refer to medicinal drugs and when they concern problems of narcology, where they are associated not only with Republican state legislation, but also with international law.

An investigation of the question of terminology demonstrated that specialists frequently use terms that fail to reflect the totality of the legal, social and medical aspects of the problem. The terms used most frequently reflect only medical and clinical aspects, and this is unacceptable for narcology. One must bear in mind that such terms as "narcotic drug," "narcomania," though used in narcology, are not so much the property of medical workers, as of lawyers, sociologists and public figures. They are used from the legal and social points both in international treaties and conventions and in national legislations.

The term "narcotic drug" in itself contains three interdependent criteria: medical, social and legal. Medical—when the drug, substance, or medicinal form concerned renders a specific effect on the central nervous system (CNS) (e.g., stimulating, sedative, hallucinogenic), which is the reason for their nonmedical use; social—when such nonmedical use assumes a scale that becomes socially significant; and legal—when, proceeding from these two mentioned prerequisites, the appropriate authority (in the Soviet Union, the Minister of Health of the USSR) recognizes this drug as a narcotic and includes it in the nomenclature of narcotic drugs. The absence of even one of these criteria denies grounds for qualifying the medicinal drug or chemical (e.g., synthetic, biological, vegetable) as a narcotic, even when the substance or medicinal drug may become an object of abuse and may cause a corresponding morbid condition. A number of terms are used in the criminal code, and the application of such a term to a narcological phenomenon also entails the exercise of the corresponding clause of the criminal code.

In addition, the matter of terminology is of exceptional importance where international conventions are concerned. When using the term "narcotic drugs," the question of including it in the established order must be considered, placing it into the appropriate Schedules of the Single Convention on Narcotic Drugs, 1961. This means to take into account the legislative acts entailing limitation of production of these substances, determining volumes of production with international control organs, and also incorporating regular UN information on questions of the production, consumption, export and import of these substances. As is known, substances recognized as narcotic are subject to laws of exports and imports only within the framework of the 1961 Single Convention on Narcotic Drugs, with the application of a system of mutual information by the Parties and the UN control organ.

Proceeding from international and national law, in particular Soviet law, a substance or medicinal remedy may only be called a "narcotic drug" when it has been legally recognized as narcotic. The law ultimately recognizes a substance as narcotic when it renders a corresponding effect on the CNS, is the cause of its repeated use for other than medical purposes, and assumes a scope which becomes socially significant. However, the legislative act of legally recognizing a substance as a narcotic does not always immediately coincide with the establishment of the phenomenon that is brought about by the abuse of the substance concerned. Moreover, new substances or medicinal drugs may for a long time fail to manifest themselves as substances causing harm on a socially significant scale.

The term "narcomania" is defined not only, or rather, not so much from the clinical point of view as from the medico-legal and social and is *applicable only to abuse of illicit substances or medicinal drugs that have been recognized as narcotic under the law*. Such application necessitated the introduction into the terminology of an additional conception for the clinical definition of *abuse of substances or medicinal drugs not recognized as narcotic under the law*, i.e., "toxicomania," a term essential for determining the nosological form of the disease. It is fitting to point out that the terms of reference for the discipline of narcology traditionally cover not only problems associated with narcomanias, but also those of toxicomanias and alcoholism, while care for persons suffering from these conditions is organized in the same institutions and divisions of the public health system.

A number of foreign countries, e.g., France, have introduced such new terms as "alcohology" and "alcohologist" in order to distinguish the problems associated with narcomania from those connected with alcoholism. They have not been accepted in the Soviet health system.

The concept "narcotic drug," just like the term "narcomania," may be used upon the recognition of a corresponding substance as a narcotic, and, on the contrary, these terms cannot be used to refer to a substance excluded from the group of narcotic drugs.

Following the legal act of recognizing a substance as a narcotic, the group of patients previously given the diagnosis of toxicomania is transformed into a group of narcomania patients. It must be said that in distinction from other diseases, narcomania and toxicomania, being social phenomena, allow for the transformation of the diagnostic terms without any change in the clinical picture.

The same considerations should be used for studying the terminology associated with alcoholic beverages and alcoholism. Alcoholic beverages cannot be recognized as narcotics and alcoholism cannot be included in the category of "narcomania." The difference between alcoholic beverages and narcotic substances or between alcoholism and narcomania is considerably greater than between narcomania and toxicomania. The latter are distinguished from the legal and social points of view only, whereas alcoholism and narcomania are distinguished also by a number of quite substantial medical criteria. For example, physiologically human blood always contains from 0.01 to 0.03% of endogenous alcohol even when no alcoholic beverages have been used, which cannot be said about narcotic medicinal drugs and other narcotic substances.

Strelchuk points out that free ethyl alcohol exists in small quantities in the organisms of man and animals. It is still unknown, however, whether it is a metabolic intermediary or is a result of bacterial fermentation in the intestine. The concentration of endogenous alcohol may vary in different individuals, but it may increase in response to various stimuli, hypoxia in particular. The normal alcoholic content in the human organism is probably 0.018-0.03%, though some authors indicate a higher level.

The discovery in recent years of physiologically active polypeptides of a narcotic character, such as encephaline and endorphines in some parts of the CNS, does not rule out the conclusion that there are actually no narcotic substances in the organism, since these polypeptides exist in the receptor apparatus and not in the blood; moreover, structurally they do not resemble narcotics and their concentration is extremely low.

There is a special enzymatic structure in the human organism which splits alcohol in the process of metabolism. Several ethanol oxidation mechanisms have been described, two of which are alcohol dehydrogenese (ADH) and microsome ethanol oxidation systems (MEOS). Other mechanisms may also influence the level of ethyl alcohol in the human organism, including those which form glucuronides and sulfate-bearing compounds and also fatty acids esterification mechanisms.

Thus, when using the terms "alcoholic beverages" and "narcotic substances," one should bear in mind that from the medico-legal and social points of view these substances are classified under different categories (Babayan, 1975) (see Tables 1 and 2).

Such clearcut distinctions are of the utmost importance from the standpoints of international and national law and in effectively organizing the work to combat alcoholism and narcomanias. They are also important when providing health education. Possible confusion about these substances may in turn cause moral damage to some persons

TABLE 1

A Comparison of Narcotic Substances and Alcoholic Beverages

Alcoholic Beverages	Narcotic Substances
1. Belong with foodstuffs.	1. Belong with medicines or chemicals.
2. The use of most alcoholic beverages is related to their taste qualities, which is typical of foodstuffs.	2. Their use is never related to taste qualities.
3. A number of alcoholic beverages are added as flavoring substances to confections (chocolates, cakes, liqueurs, rums, cognacs, brandies, etc.), which also confirms their nutritional nature.	3. Narcotic substances or narcotic medicinal drugs are never used for these purposes. Adding them to foodstuffs would be criminal.
4. Some alcoholic beverages (vodka) and pure alcohol are added in small doses to syrups, soft drinks and other food products as preservatives to prevent fermentation and spoilage.	4. Narcotic drugs are never used for these purposes nor can they be, because of their chemical composition. Such use is inadmissible.
5. Use is permitted, they are on free sale. Their use is not unlawful.	5. Obtainable only on medical prescriptions; not permissible to addicts. Use without prescription is illegal.
6. No restrictions or single doses are stipulated under the law.	6. Single doses and the volume of a single dispensation are drastically restricted. The prescription is a strictly accountable document.
7. Production is determined by planning and trading organizations. There are no restrictions at the international level.	7. Production is strictly limited by the USSR Ministry of Health and the Standing Committee on Narcotics Control; relevant international conventions restrict output and consumption at the international level.
8. Consumption is determined by the consumer himself.	8. The consumer has no right of decision whether to use narcotic drugs; the decision is made by the physician only.

TABLE 1 (continued)

Alcoholic Beverages	Narcotic Substances
9. Use is not punishable under the law.	9. Illicit use without a physician's prescription is a criminal offense.
10. Citizens may keep them in the home without special permit (storage is legal).	10. Storage without special permit is a criminal offense.
11. Alcoholic intoxication is a frequent cause of criminal actions.	11. Most frequently an addict commits a crime or in order to obtain narcotics.
12. Before committing a crime the criminal frequently brings himself to a state of drunkenness in the hope of excusing his crime or for building up "courage."	12. Cases of addicts using narcotics and committing crimes in a bid to excuse their actions or for building up "courage" are unknown.

TABLE 2

A Medical Comparison of Alcohol and Narcotics

Alcohol	Narcotics
1. Physiological content in the blood is 0.01-0.03%.	1. Unless administered there is no physiological presence of narcotic substances in the body.
2. Physiologically the human organism contains special alcohol-splitting enzymes (e.g. catalase).	2. The organism has no special enzymes for splitting narcotic substances.
3. Alcoholic beverages contribute to the energy balance (1 gram of alcohol generates 7 calories).	3. Narcotic drugs do not contribute to the energy balance.
4. It is advisable to restrict the use of alcohol for reasons of health. This mainly refers to the prevention of alcohol abuse (the use of alcoholic beverages by children, pregnant women, breastfeeding mothers and sick people is absolutely impermissible).	4. Health education endeavors not to rouse interest in narcotic substances and is conducted among certain categories of people (drug addicts) and is aimed at discouraging the use of narcotics. Physicians are recommended to use utmost restraint and caution when employing narcotics for therapeutic purposes. Their use without medical indications is prohibited.

or encourage a tendency toward leniency of administrative and punitive measures in response to drug addicts and narcotics control; it may also complicate relationships between medical workers, the patient and the public.

Chapter 2

Emergence, Spread and Organization of Control of Alcoholism, Narcomanias and Toxicomanias

From prehistoric times people were apparently able to make some kinds of intoxicating substances, as indicated by surviving ethnographic and archaeological evidence. It is also suspected that at that stage the use of intoxicating substances was of a collective, tribal character and only later became individualized. The ancient Greeks worshipped Dionysus, the god of wine, whose Roman counterpart was Bacchus. Rites in his honor were accompanied by frenzied orgies, and the Bacchic ritual was always associated with song and dance and the drinking of wine.

Along with the division of society into classes and the rise of religions, the use of alcohol assumed much broader scope. Production relationships underwent change, methods of manufacturing alcoholic beverages improved, and the experience of using them increased. Simultaneously, the negative sides of alcohol use became apparent, such as diseases, mental and physical degradation, congenital pathologies, crime, etc. Even in the distant past these problems compelled people to take steps toward putting an end to excessive drinking.

Thus, a decree issued in ancient China prohibited the use of alcoholic beverages. In ancient Egypt we saw disapproval of persons who abused alcohol. In ancient Sparta slaves were deliberately induced to drink to excess in order to demonstrate to young Spartans the baneful effects of alcohol. In India women using alcoholic beverages were severely punished. Various bans on alcoholic beverages were imposed from time to time in Rome and Athens.

The spread of alcohol use in the Middle Ages was promoted, in all probability, by the circumstance that nearly all Western Europe at that time was in a state of internecine wars, which brought terror and destruction for some, enrichment and luxury for others. The church also helped the spread of drunkenness, encouraging it in the period of various religious festivals, though many religious dogmas, for example, in Islam, and certain trends in Christianity (Evangelism), condemned the use of alcohol. Judaism allowed the use of alcohol only during festivals and in moderation.

Alcoholism spread further with the development of bourgeois society and the enhancement of capitalist relationships. Some employers, anxious to boost labor productivity, strove for the introduction of prohibitive and restrictive measures against alcoholism; others, engaged in the making and sales of alcoholic beverages, on the contrary, opposed this in every possible way.

In the late 19th and early 20th century in Denmark the annual consumption of alcoholic beverages per capita population above the age of 20 came to 67 liters. In Belgium, "a country of taverns," as it was called at that time, with a population of 6 million, the average consumption was 46 liters of alcohol per citizen (with the exclusion of women and children). In Switzerland it was 11 liters per adult, in Britain about 8 liters.

The highest alcohol consumption has been observed in large cities and capitals. In France the "alcoholic expenditure" has come to 1.5 billion francs, made up of lost workdays, losses due to absenteeism, the maintenance of the mentally ill, suicides and accidental deaths. During the same years Germany spent from 10 to 12% of its budget on alcoholic drinks (wine, beer). In Great Britain 39 million citizens spent 3.5 billion pounds sterling on alcoholic beverages. The Belgian Minister of Justice stated that expenditure on alcohol in the country increased by 50% in half a century and that the country's population actually "drank away" all the railroads, canals and military facilities. During the same years the Secretary of State of the United States published figures showing up to 1.8 billion dollars of the total budget were being spent annually on alcohol.

Spending on alcohol has also become a heavy burden on the family budget. Thus, in the early 1970s the share of spending for alcohol in percentage to the total family budget was 4.3 in Great Britain, 5 in the United States, 5.2 in Finland, 6.7 in Switzerland, and 6.1 in Sweden. The harm to society from alcohol is gradually becoming even more apparent, and in some countries various forms of combating alcoholism—moral-ethical, prohibitive and restrictive—have made their appearance.

In the early 19th century (1808), temperance organizations appeared which set themselves the task of explaining to people how harmful the use of alcohol was. Subsequently, temperance societies launched more organized work along these lines, particularly among young people. In the United States and Switzerland, obligatory antialcoholism education was even introduced in the schools. In Germany and Britain temperance societies (the British Temperance League) carried out cultural and enlightenment work, exerted influence on their governments forcing them to adopt legislation aimed at controlling alcoholism, and opened cheap tea houses and canteens. Not only did the teetotalers in the United States carry out moral instructions among the population, but they were able to pressure the government into enacting a number of prohibitive and restrictive measures.

Toward the late 1830s the activities of these societies in the United States resulted in some two million people taking the pledge to abstain from alcoholic beverages. In 1851-1856 these societies were able to obtain the legal introduction of prohibition on the sales of hard liquor (whiskey, vodka) in 16 states. The sale of alcoholic drinks to young people was limited on certain days (for example, on payday) and over certain periods (army recruitment, during spring sowing and autumn harvesting).

In Sweden, where in the mid-19th century alcoholism assumed alarming dimensions, the lack of a state monopoly on wines and spirits

prevented the introduction of restrictive legislation, and for that reason the so-called "Goteborg system" (after the city of Goteborg) was
introduced. According to this system, personal profit from the sale
of alcoholic beverages was made impossible. Wholesale trade in alcoholic drinks was permitted to anyone wishing to undertake it, while
the right to retail trade was granted to joint stock societies bound
under contract to a definite sales quota and an established percentage
of profit (6%). Actually all the profit accrued to the state treasury to
be spent for the control of alcoholism, for pensions to invalids, for
allowances to urban and rural communities.

The Goteborg system produced quite hopeful results. By 1921,
crime, court summonses, prostitution, total mortality and the incidence of alcoholic psychoses diminished from 10 to 3%. Sweden's
neighbors Norway and Finland soon thereafter introduced similar
restrictions, which produced still better results since they were conducted consistently and according to plan. With time the Goteborg
system underwent some changes in a number of countries. Thus, in
Sweden itself it was replaced in 1919 by the Bratt system under which
the head of a family residing in a certain territory was entitled once
a month to a certain alcoholic ration (up to 4 liters of vodka). In cases
of family festivals and celebrations, an additional quota of alcoholic
beverages was granted.

In the early 20th century still another restrictive system emerged
in Norway, Denmark, Finland, The Netherlands, Germany and Switzerland. This system relegated the right of deciding such questions as
the opening and closure of alcoholic beverage sale outlets to local
bodies of self-administration. However, in this case all kinds of alcoholic beverages could be purchased in unlimited quantities in a
neighboring region or country.

Prohibition on hard alcoholic beverages was introduced in Belgium
and France, and in Norway on beverages with over 12% alcohol content. Such restrictions proved inadequate, since they led to the usage
of beverages of lower strength but in considerably larger quantities.

Peculiar forms of alcoholism control appeared on the British Isles.
After nearly all of the country's Justices of the Peace, roused by the
alarming spread of intemperance among the population, petitioned

the British Parliament, in 1736 they legislated for heavily taxing liquor. Infringement entailed a fine or corporal punishment. This, however, at once prompted the appearance of illegal distilleries and illicit sales of alcoholic beverages even in pharmacies, where alcohol was dispensed on prescriptions, and there was a rise in crime. One hundred years later the government repealed this law that encouraged the brewing and sales of beer.

All the above described forms of alcoholism control proved to be half measures, at best restricting the use of hard liquor for some time but failing to tackle the problem of improving the population's health. Therefore, different countries were compelled to realize the need for a complete prohibition of the production and sales of alcoholic beverages. The first to introduce such a system was the United States, which in 1855 did so in two states. In 1917 the US Congress passed legislation introducing prohibition throughout the country. Once it came into force in 1919 the illicit production and sales of alcoholic beverages began. An entire bootlegging empire came into being.

Mortality caused by alcoholism, which somewhat dropped in the first year of prohibition, by 1925 almost reached its former level. As a result, in December 1932 the US Congress decided to repeal the law on prohibition. In 1936 the society of Alcoholics Anonymous was organized consisting of persons suffering from alcoholism. This society is functioning to this day and has active membership. Similar societies run on the same principles have been created in a number of other capitalist countries.

In 1912 Iceland adopted a law on the complete prohibition of the production, sales and imports of alcoholic beverages. But in 1923, under the pressure of Spain who threatened to stop importing Icelandic fish unless it opened its market to Spanish wines, prohibition was lifted. In 1926 prohibition also was ended in Norway under the pressure of Spain, France and Italy, who threatened to end the purchase of fish unless Norway would purchase their wines and liquors.

The Finnish parliament banned trade in alcoholic beverages back in 1907. The czarist government repealed this law, however, a complete ban on the production and sales of alcoholic liquor was reintroduced in that country in 1919.

There are indications that even Hippocrates described psychoses associated with the use of alcohol, and in Byzantium there were special infirmaries for the treatment of alcoholics. It is known that in 1879 and 1888 the British Parliament passed a Habitual Drunkards Act under which such persons were sent to special institutions for treatment.

The first decade of the 20th century was characterized by the development of various forms of medical aid to alcoholics in all countries. Thus, functioning in Germany in 1909 were a number of infirmaries giving therapy to alcoholics. In Prussia alcoholics were given treatment in special infirmaries and mental hospitals. Treatment in these infirmaries was either voluntary or compulsory. Special infirmaries also were opened in Britain. In addition, alcoholics were treated in mental hospitals and wards of general somatic hospitals in consultation with psychiatrists. At the same time, information and guardianship bureaus were opened in some cities for the identification and registration of alcoholics. Though very few, such institutions under different names functioned in a number of other European countries too. Persons with psychoses and pronounced symptoms of alcoholic degradation were hospitalized in mental and general somatic hospitals where they were subjected to detoxification, general supportive treatment and psychotherapy.

Alcoholism became particularly rife in the 1950s. According to the Finnish Fund for the Study of Alcoholism, the production of alcoholic liquor in the world between 1960 and 1968 increased as follows: beer by 41%, wine by 15%, hard alcoholic beverages by 40%.

Regarded as the main wine consumers today are France, Italy, Chile, Switzerland and Yugoslavia. A lot of beer is consumed in such countries as Czechoslovakia, West Germany, Belgium, the United States, Austria, Great Britain, Switzerland and Sweden. Countries believed to be the highest consumers of strong alcoholic beverages are Yugoslavia, Switzerland, Austria, West Germany and the United States.

The New York Statistical Yearbook informs us that by 1971 the world output of wine was 29 billion liters, beer 63 billion liters, and alcohol 850 million decaliters, which means an average annual output of about 5 liters of absolute alcohol per every dweller of the globe, or 2.4 liters of liquor, 8.3 liters of wine and 17.6 liters of beer, which is 17% higher than in 1960.

By 1970 the per capita consumption of alcohol (in liters of absolute alcohol) in different countries was as follows: in France 18.6, Italy 17.5, West Germany 13.2, USA 9.5, Hungary 8.8, Czechoslovakia 8.4, Yugoslavia 7.3, Romania 6.6, and East Germany 5.9.

Along with the growth of alcoholism, there is a steep rise in the crime rate and road and industrial accidents, and a growing total mortality of the population. All this is a source of concern for the health and governmental bodies of several countries, for the World Health Organization (WHO), the United Nations, and a number of other organizations and agencies. By 1975 several committees and organizations studying drug addiction and alcoholism were functioning in the framework of international organizations alone: the WHO Expert Committee on Drug Dependence, a number of departments and sections of UNESCO, the International Council on Narcotics Control, the International Council for Controlling Alcoholism and Drug Addiction. All of these organizations, councils and committees, by studying the various aspects of the general problem of drug addiction and alcoholism (scientific, epidemiological, organizational, etc.), have contributed much valuable material in recent years and given recommendations that are useful components of the common measures to control alcoholism.

National committees, leading and coordinating the efforts of various organizations to control alcoholism, are functioning in Britain, Austria, the Netherlands, West Germany, France and Sweden. The same countries have enacted legislation aimed at the prevention and treatment of alcoholism, including regulatory measures toward compulsory treatment.

In France, compulsory treatment following a court decision is carried out at a dispensary or a "reeducation center." In Britain the national health system comprises special asylums, and there are reform institutions under the Home Ministry. The legislation of France, Great Britain, the United States and other countries envisage heavier punishment for committing unlawful actions in a state of drunkenness, for example, giving liquor to minors and selling spirits to persons in a state of intoxication or convicted earlier for drunkenness. In Sweden, practically all alcoholics are under the observation of the courts and the police.

The majority of countries have specialized antialcoholism hospitals or outpatient clinics (West Germany, Switzerland). In individual states of the United States there are special programs for the treatment and rehabilitation of alcoholics in specialized, government, university and private clinics (e.g., drug therapy, group and individual psychotherapy, and other forms of therapy). Upon their discharge these persons are under supervision of social workers.

Some countries (France, The Netherlands, Sweden and others) have institutions that are not headed by physicians to which alcoholics turn of their own free will, spending at least one year undergoing reeducation and psychotherapy. Some of these institutions charge a fee; others are supported by charitable funds.

Psychotherapy involving the active participation of the patients' relatives is given an important place in Denmark, France and Britain. Most countries have various public organizations like temperance clubs for combating alcoholism. Serious attention is being given in recent years to the training of paramedical personnel to handle persons suffering from alcoholism.

Certain strides in the organization of antialcoholism work has been made in the socialist countries. They have national committees for controlling alcoholism: in Bulgaria, the National Temperance Committee; in Poland, the Social Committee for Controlling Alcoholism, etc. All the measures carried out in these countries are supported by legislative acts. In Yugoslavia and Poland such legislation was passed in 1959. It envisages compulsory treatment also. For example, in Yugoslavia such treatment is given depending on the gravity of alcoholism by dispensaries, hospitals, correctional colonies; in Poland, at infirmaries of the close and open type. Alcoholism is regarded as a socio-medical problem; hence, the legislative acts and participation of the patients' relatives in therapy programs, the organization of an institute to study alcoholism and drug dependence (Poland), and the organization of independent antialcoholism establishments within the public health system.

In ancient times on the territory of what is now Russia people drank homemade beer, ale and honey. In the Middle Ages, just as in Western Europe, drunkenness was widespread in Russia. On the one hand, there was a demand for and production of alcoholic beverages, while on the other, pitiful attempts to prevent the spread of drunkenness. The priesthood encouraged drinking in every way while the Metropolitan Photius in 1410 banned the drinking of beer before dinner. Sylvester's code of household proprieties (16th century) admonished a son and a daughter-in-law not to drink to excess and keep an eye on the servants.

The first attempts to control alcoholism in Russia date back to 1652 when an Assembly on taverns, acting on the advice of the Patriarch Nikon, decided "to sell a man one cup-full four days a week, but to end the sales of liquor one hour before the liturgy." But no more than seven years had passed before a new decision was issued according to which the sale of spirits was permitted "in order to bring a profit to the great sovereign's treasury."

Ivan III issued a government decree prohibiting "abominable drinking." Under this decree the lower classes of the population could drink only four times a year. The privileged estate was not to perform its duties in a state of alcoholic intoxication. When off duty they were permitted to drink alcoholic beverages. In the reign of Peter I penalties for drunkards were introduced—they were beaten with sticks and put in pits. Academician Miller on orders from Peter I prepared a plan for opening a special workhouse "for the mental correction of sick people, harlots and drunkards."

In the mid-16th century a stronger alcoholic beverage — vodka—appeared. Its production was organized at special distilleries and drinking houses; "Czar's taverns" were opened with the encouragement of the authorities because of the large revenues they yielded. In the 18th century the czarist government for the first time granted the right for liquor sales to individual entrepreneurs. These leaseholders, prompted by high profits, sought to step up the output of alcoholic beverages and to find a market for them. There were cases when the prices of wine and vodka were lowered for a time or dispensed free, and after people came into the habit of heavy drinking, the prices were raised again.

Exhausting labor, which squeezed out of man all physical and mental strength, was conducive to the spread of drunkenness. The lack of bright prospects in life dragged a man still deeper into the morass. In his book *The Condition of the Working Class in England*, Friedrich Engels wrote:

> The working-man comes from his work tired, exhausted, finds his home comfortless, damp, dirty, repulsive; he has urgent need of recreation, he must have something to make work worth his trouble, to make the prospect of the next day endurable. His unnerved, uncomfortable, hypochondriac state of mind and body arising from his unhealthy condition, and especially from indigestion, is aggravated beyond endurance by the general conditions of his life, the uncertainty of his existence, his dependence upon all possible accidents and chances, and his inability to do anything towards gaining an assured position. His enfeebled frame, weakened by bad air and bad food, violently demands some external stimulus; his social need can be gratified only in the public-house, he has absolutely no other place where he can meet his friends. How can he be expected to resist the temptation? It is morally and physically inevitable that, under such circumstances, a very large number of working-men should fall into intemperance. And apart from the chiefly physical influences which drive the working-man into drunkenness, there is the example of the great mass, the neglected education, the impossibility of protecting the young from temptation, in many cases the direct influence of intemperate parents, who give their own children liquor, the certainty of forgetting for an hour or two the wretchedness and burden of life, and a hundred other circumstances so mighty that the workers can, in truth, hardly be blamed for yielding to such overwhelming pressure. Drunkenness has here ceased to be a vice, for which the vicious can be held responsible; it becomes a phenomenon, the necessary, inevitable effect of certain conditions upon an object possessed of no volition in relation to those conditions. They who have degraded the working-man to a mere object have the responsibility to bear. But as inevitably as a great number of working-men fall a prey to drink, just so inevitably does it manifest its ruinous influence upon the body and mind of its victims. All the tendencies to disease arising from the conditions of life of the workers are promoted by it, it stimulates in the highest degree

the development of lung and digestive troubles, the rise and spread of typhus epidemics.[1]

In 1895 the Czarist government introduced a state monopoly on the trade of alcoholic beverages.

It is known that revenues from the sales of liquor made up one-third of Czarist Russia's budget. It was not for nothing that it was called a "drunken budget." Whereas before the introduction of the wine monopoly the per capita annual consumption of vodka in Russia was 0.62 bucket, in 1913 the figure increased to 0.66 bucket.

In the 1850s-1860s there appeared temperance societies in Russia. Such a society was organized in the Ukraine in 1874. Society members were to abstain from alcoholic beverages. They took the pledge not to drink in a church ceremony and if they violated the pledge, they received moral chastisement.

However, the temperance societies were very soon proscribed since their activities occasionally resulted in lower profits for the leaseholders and tavernkeepers and, consequently, for the treasury to which the lion's share of the profits accrued. Toward the end of the 19th century the temperance societies were permitted again, and 200 city, parish and factory societies of this type were organized, but their activities were much less aggressive than in the period of their origin, and in fact they were hampered by a lot of formality. Referring to temperance societies, F. Engels wrote that they have done much, but could hardly change anything, since what was a few thousand teetotalers among millions of drinkers.

Apart from these societies, since 1894 there existed an official organization—the Trusteeship Board for People's Temperance. Such Boards attempted to raise the hygienic standards of the population and opened tea-houses, canteens, libraries and reading rooms. Together with the priesthood they issued special literature. But the people, being virtually illiterate, could not benefit from the printed matter made available to them.

In 1907, a group of deputies to the State Duma (Assembly) tabled

[1] Engels, F. (1973), *The Condition of the Working-Class in England.* Moscow: Progress Publishers, pp. 141-142.

a bill aimed at combating drunkenness. The bill was to become law
in 1909; however, it was not enacted before the start of the First
World War. Concerns associated with military operations pushed the
question of drunkenness into the background, but not into oblivion.
Choosing the easiest way, in 1914 the Czarist government issued a law
prohibiting the sales of alcoholic beverages. In Russia, just as in other
countries which introduced prohibition, the first two years afterward
were marked by a decrease of heavy drinking and a drop in the
number of people suffering from alcoholic psychoses; there was also
a drop in the mortality rate with a rise of wellbeing among the working
classes, and particularly, the peasantry. However, illicit distilleries
were quickly set up, together with the smuggling of alcoholic beverages and the use of diverse substitutes. The initial ostensible drop in
heavy drinking soon assumed the former scope, while the use of
substitutes inflicted still greater harm to health than vodka made by
licensed distillers did.

In the overall efforts to control drunkenness in Russia, one should
note the activities of progressive public circles. Thus, the Russian
Society for Protecting the People's Health included a Standing Commission on Alcoholism Control, which published 12 volumes of proceedings and doubtlessly made a definite contribution to the control
of alcoholism.

Of great importance were scientific congresses which discussed
various aspects of alcoholism. Central among them were congresses
of Russian psychiatrists. The first was held in the winter of 1887 in
Moscow, and it discussed the matter of the early detection and treatment of persons suffering from alcoholism.

The Second Congress of Russian Psychiatrists in 1905 proved an
important landmark in the history of organized alcoholism control in
Russia. It discussed the building of state and provincial hospitals that
would contain alcoholism wards.

The Third Congress of Russian Psychiatrists was held at the end
of 1909 and beginning of 1910, and its last session was held jointly
with the First All-Russia Congress on Combating Drunkenness. By
that time unique experience in the work of alcoholism outpatient
clinics had been accumulated in Russia. The Congress drew attention

to alcoholism among women, to the improvement of the microsocial environment and suggested the enlistment, in addition to psychiatrists, of physicians of other specialties for antialcoholism work, and urged the training of young doctors to do alcoholism therapy.

The Pirogov Congresses also played a progressive role. The 8th Pirogov Congress suggested the treatment of alcoholics as outpatients, and when necessary, their hospitalization. The establishment of colonies was recommended in the form of settlements maintained at the expense of the state and the community.

The 9th Pirogov Congress (1906) examined clinical problems—the early detection of the initial forms of alcoholism, its treatment, and evaluation of therapeutic measures. The Congress suggested state measures to control alcoholism, such as the establishment of enlightenment centers at outpatient clinics, and the creation of conditions essential for providing work therapy and "culture-therapy" at infirmaries "for chronics and dipsomaniacs."

Of particular interest was the 12th International Medical Congress held in Moscow on March 12, 1897, when psychosis of alcoholic etiology, for the first time described by the outstanding Russian psychiatrist, Korsakov, was classified under his name. Based on a proposal by Ignatyev and Erisman, a section on alcoholism was organized to examine the question of placing alcoholics in special infirmaries and establishing guardianship over their property.

It may be stated, therefore, that in a short historical period (from 1887 to 1910), congresses of psychiatrists and general practitioners in Russia discussed various medico-diagnostic and organizational questions that doubtlessly proved very useful in the subsequent development of a system of antialcoholism measures.

Prerevolutionary Russia had no proper organization of medical care for alcoholics. There existed only a few infirmaries, outpatient clinics only, mainly maintained by the funds of charitable societies in Yaroslavl and Moscow. In St. Petersburg an alcoholism institute was organized by the outstanding psychiatrist V. M. Bekhterev, which included both inpatient and outpatient departments. However, during the First World War all these institutions had practically ceased to function.

Prohibition was still in force in Russia following the Great October Socialist Revolution, yet alcoholism was on the increase because of the use of various substitutes and self-distilled spirits. The governments of the Russian Federation and the Ukraine launched resolute measures to control illicit distillation of spirits, which in the Ukraine was subject to trial by military tribunal and merited the maximum penalty. Amidst the gravest food crisis a great quantity of valuable food products was wasted for illicit distillation. Instances of poisoning with lethal substances increased. All this resulted in the fact that from 1922 to 1925 the permitted sale of vodka increased from 20 to 40%.

With the exception of psychotic cases, no medical care was given to alcoholics. Since 1923 alcoholics began to be received at narcological stations and dispensaries. Then independent narcological dispensaries were organized, but they did not function for long. In 1928 the mental services were reorganized. Since 1928 in Leningrad and 1932 in Moscow, the psychiatric and narcological dispensaries were merged and outpatient care to alcoholics was rendered at psychoneurological dispensaries. Inpatient treatment was given at mental hospitals. The year 1929 saw the foundation in Moscow of the country's first clinic for the treatment of acute alcoholism, and in 1932 a colony for lasting treatment was established at the settlement of Medny.

Also organized in the 1920s was a society for combating alcoholism, but conditions apparently had not yet ripened for a radical improvement of the situation and the society's activities gradually dwindled. On September 11, 1926, the Council of People's Commissars of the USSR passed a decision on the compulsory treatment of alcoholics who represented a social danger. However, this kind of treatment was not widespread at that time. In the years following the Second World War and up to 1958, research work was launched in the country to study the pathogenesis, clinical aspects and methods of treating alcoholism, and alcoholics were treated in the mental care network.

The Communist Party of the Soviet Union and the Soviet Government are giving tremendous attention to combating various legacies of the past, including alcoholism. Thus, during the very first years of Soviet power (March 1919), the 8th Party Congress laid down in the Party Program that "... the RCP [Russian Communist Party] poses as its immediate task . . . the control of social diseases (tuberculosis, venereal disease, alcoholism and others)."[2] In 1920, conversing with Klara Zetkin, an outstanding figure in the international Communist movement, Vladimir Lenin said: ". . . the proletariat is an ascending class. It has no need of intoxication that would either stun or excite it. It needs no intoxication by alcohol. It dares not, nor does it wish to forget the vileness, filth and barbarity of capitalism, it draws the strongest incentive to struggle from the situation of its class, from the communist ideal. It needs clarity and once again clarity. This is why . . . there must be no weakness, no dissipation and destruction of forces. . . . The future of the youth concerns me deeply. For it is part of the revolution."[3]

The question was raised again at the 15th Party Congress in 1927. The same matter was discussed at the 8th Congress of the Trade Unions, which set down in a resolution that "a war should be declared on alcoholics for every one of them is an enemy of the working class."

A 1958 decision of the Central Committee of the Communist Party of the Soviet Union (CPSU CC) and the USSR Council of Ministers, "On Stepping Up the Drive Against Drunkenness and on Putting in Order the Sales of Strong Alcoholic Beverages," carries on the policy outlined by the Party in the first years of the Soviet State aimed at eradicating drunkenness and preventing alcoholism. It settles a number of questions, such as restricting the sales of alcoholic beverages, and makes it incumbent on public health bodies to improve antialcoholism work.

In response to this decision, psychiatric research institutes established departments to study alcoholism, to theoretically substantiate the clinical facts and formulate the teaching on alcoholism as an independent nosological form with clear-cut borders, symptoms, course, prognosis and specific treatment.

Works by Zhislin (1920), Sluchevsky (1933), somewhat later by Rapoport, Kantorovich, Strelchuk, and Banshchikov, Myasishchev,

Portnov, Zenevich, Lukomsky, Rozhnov, Morozov and others came to play an important role in these investigations. At the same time organizational forms of treating alcoholism underwent approbation.

The first work-therapy preventorium (WTP) was opened in our country in 1964 in Kazakhstan. In 1966 a psychoneurological hospital and narcological stations began functioning in the Dnepropetrovsk Region. In the same year a network of narcological departments at industrial enterprises was created in the Moscow Region.

In May 1972, the CPSU CC and the USSR Council of Ministers passed a decision "On Measures to Step Up the Drive Against Drunkenness and Alcoholism." This document is distinguished from the earlier ones in that it poses clearly and broadly the basic questions of the general problem of alcoholism and outlines diverse measures to combat it. In a short period of time, up to the end of 1975, narcological consulting rooms and departments were organized at industrial enterprises in many cities of our country, and an experimental narcological dispensary was opened in Karaganda (Kazakhstan) and a number of other places. It then became apparent that an independent narcological service ought to be created in this country to shoulder all responsibility for providing medical care to persons suffering from alcoholism. A peculiar concluding note in this discussion was sounded at the 6th All-Union Congress of Neuropathologists and Psychiatrists (December 1975), which decidedly urged the creation of an independent narcological service. In April 1978, the USSR Council of Ministers once again passed a decision on additional measures to step up the drive against drunkenness and alcoholism.

During the years of Soviet power, the implementation of organizational, medical and social measures to combat drunkenness and alcoholism has gone on purposefully and simultaneously. It is briefly described in the following four periods in the development of a system of narcological care to the population of the USSR.

The first period: 1917-1941—lifting of prohibition, first narcological dispensaries organized, treatment of alcoholism and alcoholic psychoses in the mental care network; attempt to organize compulsory treatment of alcoholism.

The second period: up to 1958—theoretical elaboration of the social and medical aspects of alcoholism; the treatment of alcoholics in the mental care network.

The third period: up to 1972—introduction of a number of legislative acts for combating drunkenness and controlling alcoholism in connection with a decision of the CPSU CC and the USSR Council of Ministers; the further theoretical and practical elaboration of questions pertaining to the pathogenesis, clinical aspects and treatment of alcoholism; approbation of the activities of narcological institutions; development of compulsory treatment within the system of the USSR Ministry of Internal Affairs.

The fourth period: from 1972—introduction into life of the Decision of the CPSU CC and the USSR Council of Ministers "On Measures to Step Up the Drive Against Drunkenness and Alcoholism"; Commissions for Combating Drunkenness and Alcoholism are organized under the Soviets of People's Deputies, at enterprises, in institutions and establishments of the national economy; organization of a narcological care service within the system of the USSR Ministry of Public Health.

As is known, the problem of drug addiction is a social problem. In prerevolutionary Russia narcomanias were widespread in areas of Central Asia in connection with the habitual use of narcotic drugs, particularly the smoking of opium. The use of cocaine and other narcotics was widespread in large cities.

The day-to-day use of narcotics in Soviet Central Asia and in other regions where this took place was eliminated completely in the very first years of Soviet power after the October revolution. It was due, first of all, to the new social conditions created for the population. Since that time narcomanias have not presented a serious social and hygienic problem in the USSR. This can be attributed to the overall social and economic conditions as well as to the special measures of the Soviet Government.

Unemployment has been completely eliminated in the Soviet Union; the people's economic and cultural standards are steadily rising; such social phenomena as prostitution, beggary and vagrancy have been done away with. All this helps in preventing the spread of narcomanias. Still another important factor preventing the development of drug abuse in the USSR is the concentration of the pharmaceutical industry and the pharmacy network in the hands of the state. The state system of public health is allowed to carry out effective measures toward the prevention and treatment of drug addictions.

The Soviet Union has been and is vigorously combating drug addiction and the illicit traffic in narcotic drugs not only at the national, but at the international level. Being a party to nearly all international treaties on the control of narcotic drugs, the Soviet state diligently complies with their provisions. This country's well-organized borderline and customs service virtually precludes any smuggling of narcotics across the border. The production, storage and dispensation of narcotics is under constant control of appropriately authorized state agencies.

The study of drug addiction in the USSR gives grounds to believe that addicts are mainly chronically sick people and invalids who had systematically taken narcotic preparations, such as morphine and codeine, because of their basic disease, and have become addicted.

There is occasional use of narcotic drugs obtained from some wild-growing species of hemp. In recent decades not a single case of heroin addiction has been recorded in the USSR, with heroin being long prohibited for production and use in this country. Nor is there any cocaine or LSD addiction, or use of other hallucinogens or amphetamines. Soviet legislation enforced the strictest criminal responsibility for violating the rules of storage, manufacture, sale and use of narcotic drugs. The legislation also imposes criminal penalties for abetting the use of narcotics. A particularly aggravating circumstance is the involvement of minors.

As to medicinal narcotic drugs, these have always been dispensed on special prescriptions by physicians and for medical purposes only, in accordance with USSR Ministry of Health orders. The prescription forms have serial numbers and are subject to special accounting, and medico-prophylactic institutions regularly account for the number of prescriptions made out for narcotic preparations. Both at pharmacies and in medico-prophylactic institutions, narcotic drugs are stored under special conditions in safes according to authorized instructions, and their movement and expenditure is regularly checked. The manufacture of narcotic substances is under complete state control and is limited to medical and research needs only. The cultivation of Indian, South-Chui, South-Manchurian hemp and opium poppy is absolutely prohibited.

In accordance with USSR Ministry of Health orders, all medical and pharmaceutical institutions are obligated to report, according to established form, any primary applications received from addicts to narcological institutions (dispensaries) near the addicts' residence. This information is used to place them on the registry and accessible for the necessary therapy. This allows for the timely detection of addicts and for providing treatment at an early phase of the addiction. The unsatisfactory practice of issuing addicts with a narcotic "ration" has been long prohibited in the country.

The Soviet Union is a Party to the majority of International Conventions and Protocols on narcotic drug control, including the Single Convention of 1961, which superceded all former international treaties on the question, and the 1971 Vienna Convention on Psychotropic Substances. It consistently fulfills all of its obligations under these conventions.

In many countries during the past decade there was an increase of narcomanias associated with the use of so-called "psychotropic preparations," placed under international control according to the 1971 Vienna Convention. Amphetamines, hallucinogens, LSD and other lysergic acid derivatives have been found to be especially dangerous in this regard. The group of narcomanias associated with the use of soporifics have long been observed by physicians in the majority of countries. (Due to timely and rigid measures of control, there is no such problem in the USSR.)

The WHO Expert Commission had frequently discussed the question of road accidents caused by the use of soporific and psychotropic preparations by drivers of motor vehicles. Not a single case of this kind has been recorded in the Soviet Union. However, for purposes of prevention, the USSR Ministry of Health issued a special order that calls for caution when prescribing psychotropic preparations and soporifics to drivers. If such persons must use soporifics or psychotropic preparations because of illness, they undergo treatment while given leave of absence from their jobs, with the preservation of their wages or salaries in the prescribed manner according to their sick leave certificate.

Article 17 of the 1961 Single Convention stipulates that "The Parties shall maintain a special administration for the purpose of applying the provisions of the Convention." In accordance with this Article, a Standing Committee on Narcotics Control was created in the USSR under the USSR Ministry of Health. In accordance with Article 6 of the 1971 Convention on Psychotropic Substances, this Committee is entrusted with all the functions of controlling the implementation of the Convention. According to regulations enacted in the USSR, all psychotropic substances of the Schedules of the 1971 Convention were put in the nomenclature of narcotic drugs and placed under control, with all of the rigid measures covering them.

Thus, the Standing Committee on Narcotics Control exercises a universal approach to the problem of narcotic and psychotropic substances. This Committee is independent from the producer, trading organizations and consumers, and exercises the right of controlling the volume of production of narcotic and psychotropic substances. Serving on the Committee are outstanding specialists—physicians, pharmacists, pharmacologists, chemists, and top officials of the USSR Ministry of Health, the USSR Ministry of Internal Affairs, the USSR Ministry of Foreign Trade, the Customs Board and the USSR Ministry of the Medical Equipment Industry. During its sessions the Committee may hear all ministries and departments concerning questions connected with the production, sales, imports, exports and use of narcotic drugs, as well as the organization of medical care for drug addicts. The Standing Committee on Narcotics Control conducts its work in accordance with regulations authorized by the USSR Ministry of Health.

The Committee publishes schedules of medicinal drugs and other substances regarded as narcotics under the law. Decisions of the Standing Committee on these questions are binding on all. Besides, the Standing Committee compiles a classification system and library of all the Conventions, UN sessions and legislations of other countries throughout the years. Coordination of the Committee's activities with the work of the special Board for the Introduction of New Medicinal Drugs and Medical Technology and the USSR Ministry of Health allows them to resolve promptly questions pertaining to timely control. The Board for the Introduction of New Medicinal Drugs and Medical Technology has at its disposal expert committees, such as the Pharmacological Committee and a Committee for Studying the Side Effects of Medicinal Drugs. One of its functions is to provide up-to-date information about all substances and medicinal drugs hazardous from the viewpoint of being addiction-forming. The data are utilized for their placement under control and inclusion in the nomenclature of narcotic substances. Not infrequently such information is already received from the above-mentioned committees during the clinical trial of new preparations, which allows for the adoption of immediate control measures.

It is not accidental that there are no addictions at all to amphetamines and psychotropic preparations in the USSR since the Pharmacological Committee and the Committee for Studying the Side Effects of Medicinal Drugs proposed, and the Standing Committee on Narcotics Control of the USSR Ministry of Health decided, to place these substances under corresponding controls. Their distribution was permitted on medical prescriptions only, while such substances as LSD and other lysergic acid derivatives were banned from production and human administration as early as in 1967. The Standing Committee on Narcotics Control under the USSR Ministry of Health together with the Board for the Introduction of New Medicinal Drugs and Medical Technology carries out regular check-ups and inspections of medical and scientific institutions in the Union Republics and regions on all questions concerning narcotic drugs and the implementation of the provisions of Conventions. On the basis of the proposal of he Standing Committee on Narcotics Control, the nomenclature of all combined preparations comprising these or other narcotic substances was revised, and the substances curtailed accordingly.

Before issuing a license for the production, storage or dispensing of narcotics to the population and for research and medical purposes, the Standing Committee on Narcotics Control, USSR Ministry of Health, checks the institutions, pharmacies or factories requesting such a permit and issues an appropriate license only upon being satisfied that production and storage conditions preclude any illicit leakage.

Every year the Chief Pharmaceutical Board, USSR Ministry of Health, and research institutions submit substantiated and well-calculated requests for narcotic substances. The Committee discusses them at its sessions and makes amendments, and only upon the receipt of a permit is the industry entitled to dispense the quantity indicated in the permit for research and medical purposes.

In accordance with Article 36 of the Convention and its other sections, depending on the gravity of the crime, Soviet legislation provides adequate punishment for violating the rules for manufacture, sales, storage and application of narcotic substances. The relevant legislation and legal acts are being perfected regularly on proposals from the USSR Ministry of Health and other agencies along with the Standing Committee on Narcotic Control, USSR Ministry of Health.

An important requirement of the current Convention is the matter of organizing the identification and treatment of drug addicts. Article 38 points out that the Parties shall give special attention to the creation of conditions for the treatment of addicts and provide appropriate effective measures of therapy.

This country has a narcological service whose tasks include, along with the identification and treatment of alcoholics, the detection and treatment of persons suffering from narcomanias. Every identified addict is promptly put on the register and an information card is filled in about him, to be sent to the Standing Committee on Narcotics Control, USSR Ministry of Health. (Such cards serve the Standing Committee for Narcotics Control as the basis for dawing up government reports to the UN Commission on the state of drug addiction in the country.) For effective treatment drug addicts are hospitalized in special wards of narcological departments and given necessary treatment.

It should be noted that an obligatory requirement for the proper initiation of therapeutic measures is hospitalization for purposes of examination and treatment of all primary detected addiction cases without exception. The duration of hospital treatment for primary patients, as well as in cases of pronounced abstinence symptoms in patients admitted for a second time in a calendar year, must be adequate (at least 60 days). However, the physician may prolong the duration of treatment according to medical indications.

Chapter 3

Epidemiology and Some Consequences of Alcoholism

The prevalence of diseases in a society is characterized by two basic conceptions: incidence and morbidity.

By *incidence* is meant the ratio of the number of those who contracted a disease for the first time in their life in the given year (never before registered, so-called new patients) in relation to the total population.

However, as a rule alcoholism and narcomanias develop gradually. The time between the initiation to alcohol or a narcotic and the appearance of morbid symptoms may be counted in days, months or years. Besides, either because of reluctance or ignorance, many fail to apply for medical aid, which obscures the true incidence. The number of first visits to the doctor by patients may be considered close to the actual incidence, given a broad network of narcological and psychiatric institutions and well organized registration over a long period (15-20 years). Otherwise it would be more correct to designate it as incidence according to number of first visits.

By *morbidity* is meant the number of patients (old and new) on the files of narcological or neuropsychiatric institutions. This definition should be qualified by the term "registered."

In order to enable the comparison of data for different localities, countries or periods of time, it is advisable to conduct calculations in intensive indicators, with the standard index calculated per 1,000,

10,000 or 100,000 population. When calculating incidence and morbidity indices one should indicate the group of people they refer to: the total population, adults, children (0-14 years), or some particular age group, for example, 25 to 30 years, males, females, individual persons affected by alcoholism or narcomanias.

If we turn to international statistics we shall see that one out of every 16 persons using alcoholic beverages becomes an abuser. According to Strelchuk one or two out of every five to six heavy drinkers become chronic alcoholics.

In the majority of industrialized countries the rate of alcoholism increased more than 35 times in as many years (from 1930 to 1965). A comparison of mental morbidity and alcoholism indices shows that from the beginning of the 20th century and till now the growth rate of alcoholism is five times higher than the growth rate of mental disorders.

The growth of morbidity indices in a country is directly related to the quantities of alcoholic beverages consumed. However, one should bear in mind that during the same years the detection of patients has improved just as the overall cultural standards of the population and methods of treating alcoholism, which increased the number of sick people turning for medical aid. The growth of alcoholism runs parallel to the increasing rate of hospital admissions.

In the United States, primary admissions for alcoholism within 17 years (1940 to 1957) increased from 3.4 to 6.4, and for alcoholic psychoses, from 2.9 to 3.9 per 1,000 population. In France between 1900 and 1959, hospital admissions increased from 7 to 28 per 1,000.

Peculiar tendencies in the prevalence of alcoholism have been noted among women. According to WHO data, a century ago the ratio between male and female alcohol abusers was 10:1. At present this gap has been bridged nearly by half and is 5:1 (in Britain, 2:1; USA, 5.6:1; West Germany, 10:1; Finland, 15:1; Sweden, 23:1). In the United States women account for nearly 20 percent of chronic alcoholics.

Studies indicate that approximately 50% of female alcohol abusers start drinking before the age of 20. More than half are single, widows, or divorced; 65% of them have only primary or incomplete secondary education. Those occupied in trade and food supply and distribution come first, women workers engaged in servicing and running the transportation system come second. In the last 25 years there was also a relative increase in the number of women admitted to hospitals for alcoholism.

The question arises of the cause of such a catastrophic increase in female alcoholism. There is no single answer. The causes are many, including tradition, imitation, striving toward self-assertion in society, mental instability and inadequate will power. Women frequently begin drinking at the insistence of their husbands, under the influence of bad company when going through difficult life situations, because of an unsettled personal life, or when alcoholic beverages are available at work. Some scientists suggest that the phenomenon is also associated with the consequences of the Second World War.

Along with a growing prevalence of alcoholism among adults, there appears the problem of active dissolution of the younger generation. Thus, in recent years alcoholism increased three times among the youth of Sweden and Switzerland. There is a catastrophic rise of alcoholism among children and young people in West Germany. In the United States 14% of senior school children drink 52 times a year, actually every weekend. It is noted that up to three million teenagers are strongly drawn to alcohol, and they account for about 5% of persons afflicted with alcoholism.

The consumption of alcohol by the younger generation is also growing in this country. The results of a sociological study including senior school children and students showed that in the 8th grade 75% of boys and 40% of girls had already tasted alcoholic beverages. By the time they finished the 10th grade the indices were higher—90-95% of boys and girls already knew the taste of wine. Thus, by the age of 15 to 19 years the majority of young people have tasted alcoholic beverages. So the question arises: Who, after all, encourages them to do so? The same group of subjects replied to the above question, as follows: parents and close relatives in 20% of the cases; schoolmates, 25%; adult acquaintances, 12%. Thus, in 52% of cases these are members of the family, relatives or school friends, i.e., those who would be expected to protect the teenagers against this vice. A further question concerned the students' attitude to drunkards. The absolute majority replied that they despise heavy drinkers who, they feel, are unpleasant and arouse disgust. There were also those who voiced absolute indifference and tolerance to this vice.

Compared to capitalist countries, the consumption of wine and hard liquor in the Soviet Union has increased negligibly, while the consumption of strong alcoholic beverages even decreased by 20%.

The incidence and morbidity of alcoholism in different geographic and economic zones of the country differ depending on many causes, in particular, the ability of being identified, the prevalence of drinking attitudes, and antialcoholism propaganda. The incidence rates fluctuate from 0.13 to 0.98 per 1,000 population in the towns and from 0.01 to 0.52 in the countryside. The higher incidence for towns in all probability means shortcomings in the organization of narcological services in the countryside.

Morbidity indices are at the level of 6-10 cases per 1,000 population. The male to female ratio is 10-8:1. Among the males, town dwellers predominate over villagers five times on the average; alcoholism among town-dwelling women is also four to six times higher than in the countryside.

The lowest alcoholism morbidity figures are registered for the ages under 20 and above 50 years. The highest indices are recorded in the 40 to 49 years age group. Female alcoholism morbidity is recorded ten years later than for males. According to family status, persons afflicted with alcoholism are more frequently divorced, single, or widowed.

Incidence is higher among people with an elementary or incomplete secondary education. Most of them have low cultural standards, though the number of better educated alcoholics has increased in recent years. According to occupation, predominant among males are workers, mainly engaged in physical labor, in industry, construction, on the transport, and some clerical workers. Among females this correlation, as has already been mentioned, is reversed. Recent years have witnessed a slight increase in the number of hospital admissions for psychosis and nonpsychotic forms of alcoholism.

Let us now consider some consequences of the use and abuse of alcoholic beverages. According to a WHO report, more than 100,000 people are killed every year on the roads in different countries. For every death there are 35-40 persons who sustain injuries, and 78% of these road accident victims are males in a state of alcoholic intoxication.

A comparison of the different causes of mortality reveals that road transportation is more hazardous to men than all the infectious diseases taken together. In the United States, for example, 38,702 persons died in 1952 as a result of road accidents, and only 24,256 succumbed to various infectious diseases. In 1971 the United States lost 55,000 people killed on the road, 30,000 of them because of driving an automobile in a state of drunkenness. A similar situation also prevails in other countries. For example, the British believe that 25% of those driving their own cars and 80% of professional drivers constantly drive while under the influence of alcohol.

Addressing a plenum of the USSR Supreme Court, the Procurator-General of the USSR noted that throughout 1974 a large number of drivers in this country were brought to court for driving an automobile in a state of drunkenness.

It was noted at the plenum of the USSR Supreme Court, which discussed problems connected with alcohol-related offenses, that while there is a tendency toward a general drop in the crime rate in this country, the role of alcohol, rather than diminishing, is on the increase. More than half of all offenses are alcohol-related. A study of grave offenses demonstrates that the role of drunkenness involves up to 75-90% of all cases.

Heavy drinking and alcoholism inflict considerable economic losses in different countries. These stem from industrial accidents, a drop in working capacity, spoilage in production, and absenteeism.

In the United States temporary disability in heavy drinkers is four times higher than in other employees. Alcoholism comes fourth among total incidence of disease involving disability, coming annually to 30 million workdays. Every alcohol abuser loses an average of 22 workdays a year. The material loss to the country comes to 352 million working hours. In Britain cases of disability among heavy drinkers amount to 13 days per year. In a control group the figure came to only 5.8 days.

Studies conducted in recent years demonstrated that the incidence of disease involving temporary disability in a group of alcohol users is 1.9 times higher (cases and days) than in a control group. The incidence indicators for all nosological forms is two to three times higher, and the rate of domestic injuries is 7.8 times higher among drinkers.

Scientists have calculated that with moderate use of alcohol, labor productivity drops by 4-5%, and in cases of abuse, by 15-30%. On the day following payday, output drops by 26-30% beneath the normal level. According to figures for several countries, decrease in labor productivity, absenteeism following payday, holidays and days off by heavy drinkers has become a kind of "law."

The toxic effect of alcohol on the human organism is well known. I. V. Strelchuk and others believe that mortality in alcoholism depends on the quantity and frequency of alcohol use and on the average accounts for 1-2% of all deaths. Alcohol has a deleterious effect on the nervous system and mental capacity, causing polyneurites, encephalopathies, epileptiform seizures, psychoses, and changes of personality. Then there is liver pathology; it is believed that in 20-25% of cases cirrhosis of the liver is due to alcoholism. The cardiovascular system and the gastrointestinal tract are also affected. The incidence of bronchitis, pulmonary emphysema is 3-4 times higher among alcoholics. Alcoholics make up 30-40% of tuberculosis patients, and they are more likely to contract infectious diseases and suffer from various forms of vitamin deficiency.

It should be regarded as an established fact that the life expectancy of alcoholics is about 20 years shorter and does not exceed 55 years on the average. Moreover, in 20% of cases this is due to accidents or premature death. It can be stated therefore that the postwar years in industrialized countries saw an increase in alcohol consumption, a growth of alcoholism incidence and morbidity, a "rejuvenation" of drinking groups and an increase of drinking in women. The harmful consequences of alcoholism become increasingly apparent among heavy drinkers—road accidents and domestic injuries, temporary and permanent disabilities, the undermining of health.

EXERCISES FOR REVIEW

1. State the medical-related division of the population depending on attitude to alcoholic beverages; the concepts of narcomania, toxicomania, alcoholism, polynarcomania, complicated narcomania, the transformation of narcomanias into alcoholism; the legal, socio-legal and medical distinctions between alcoholic beverages and narcotic drugs.

2. Describe alcoholism control measures—moral, ethical, prohibitive, restrictive and medical in the USSR and in some other countries.

3. Outline the concepts of incidence, morbidity, various epidemiological indices, and some consequences of heavy drinking and alcoholism.

CHAPTERS 1-3 QUESTIONS

1. A person is tasting different alcoholic beverages out of curiosity. Which conditional group of the population would you place him in? What could be his probable fate in the conditional grouping of alcohol users?

2. In order to celebrate his birthday a citizen buys a few bottles of alcoholic beverages. Could he buy some narcotic drugs in order to treat his friends? What are the distinctive features of narcotic drugs and alcoholic beverages?

3. In order to control alcoholism some people suggest the introduction of prohibition. What has been the experience of introducing prohibition, in which countries, and why was it repealed? What measures have generally been used for controlling alcoholism in different countries?

4. A consistent campaign to control alcoholism has been waged in the Soviet Union for many years now. Give the periods that can be singled out and their characteristic features.

5. Every year one person per 1,000 of the adult population is put on the register of a narcological dispensary with a diagnosis established for the first time in his life. What is the name of this statistical index and how does it differ from the index of morbidity?

6. The number of alcohol-related road traffic accidents has been growing in recent years. Why is it so, and what are the basic social, domestic and medical consequences of heavy drinking and alcoholism?

Part Two

Organization

Chapter 4

The Narcological Care System

In accordance with the 1972 Decisions of the Central Committee of the Communist Party of the Soviet Union (CPSU CC) and the USSR Council of Ministers' "On Measures to Step Up the Campaign against Heavy Drinking and Alcoholism," the USSR Ministry of Health issued an order which outlined the basic attitudes and trends for public health organs and institutions in their activities toward organizing antialcoholism measures (USSR Ministry of Health Order No. 694 of August 24, 1972).

An uchastok (health district) psychiatrist-narcologist (USSR Ministry of Health Order No. 1180 of December 26, 1975) was added to the nomenclature of medical positions, an internship in neuropsychiatry was restored in medical institutes, narcology subjects were expanded at the institutes for advanced medical training, and certification in the specialty of physician-narcologist was introduced. The position of feldsher-narcologist was also established.

In February-March 1976 the "narcological dispensary" was added to the nomenclature of public health institutions (USSR Ministry of Health Order No. 131 of February 5, 1976), and staff complements for medical and pharmaceutical personnel were authorized for narcological dispensaries, departments, and consulting rooms (USSR Ministry of Health Order No. 270 of March 18, 1976). A number of documents were issued defining the main trends in the development and forms of activities of the narcological organization, including orders on obligatory minimum chronic alcoholism treatment courses (USSR Ministry of Health Order No. 928 of September 21, 1976), as well as statutes and regulations concerning the uchastok psychiatrist-narcologist and narcological consulting rooms (March 19, 1976), the feldsher-narcologist, i.e., assistant psychiatrist-narcologist manning the feldsher-narcological room (July 22, 1976), the Standing Commissions for Alcoholism Control under health organs (institutions) (March 11, 1976), the narcological dispensary (August 20, 1976), and others.

All these documents ensured real opportunities for organizing the country's narcological service. The health organs and institutions (narcological and neuropsychiatric) function as the organizing core of an integral system comprising not only neuropsychiatric institutions and other individual structural units of the general medical network, but also some institutions of the USSR Ministry of Internal Affairs, bodies of justice, a number of subdivisions in the system of the national economy, public organizations and standing commissions of the Executive Committees of the Soviets of People's Deputies.

Essential for smooth interaction, cooperation, mutual information and reporting is a harmonious organizational structure of the narcological care available to the population. The narcological care system consists of five elements (see Diagram 1), all of which function simultaneously or in sequence, depending on the tasks set before them.

COMMISSIONS FOR COMBATING DRUNKENNESS

In 1972 and 1973 "Statutes on Commissions for Combating Drunkenness" were authorized under decrees of the Presidia of the Supreme Soviets of the Union Republics.

The Statutes cover a number of questions within the competence of these commissions—first of all, coordinating the activities of state agencies and public organizations to combat drunkenness, and also the elaboration and implementation of measures to prevent and stop drunkenness.

The Commissions for Combating Drunkenness are set up under

the Executive Committees of district, city, regional Soviets of People's Deputies and under the Councils of Ministers of the Union Republics. When necessary such commissions may be organized with the permission of the Executive Committee of a regional Soviet under the executive committees of village and settlement Soviets of People's Deputies.

The composition of the Commissions is authorized by the Executive Committees, and serving on them are Deputies to the Soviets, representatives of trade unions, the Young Communist League and other public organizations, work collectives, managers of enterprises and construction organizations and also staff members of public health, educational institutions, trading enterprises, organs of the Ministry of Internal Affairs, cultural-educational and other institutions.

The Commissions fulfill administrative functions, being empowered within their terms of reference to make decisions that must be implemented by officials at all state institutions, enterprises, public organizations and citizens. All institutions and officials are duty bound to inform the Commissions within ten days on the implementation by them of the Commission's decisions and orders.

In their work the Commissions rely on volunteers—representatives of plant and factory, local trade union committees, YCL committees, voluntary public order squads, street house committees, and other public representatives. Appointed from among these volunteers are public inspectors whose functions include working with alcohol abusers, labor discipline infringers, disturbers of the peace, and those who have undesirable influence on children. In this work the public inspectors should maintain close contacts with industrial narcological posts.

Because of the specifics of antialcoholism work, the Commissions for Combating Drunkenness keep in touch with other commissions of the executive committees of the Soviets, for example, the Commissions for the Affairs of Minors, Administrative Commissions, and others.

The Commissions should periodically inform public organizations and work collectives about their activities. The commissions are empowered to elaborate measures toward preventing drunkenness, al-

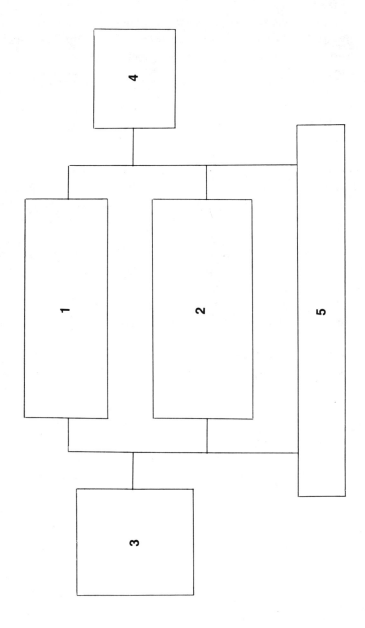

Diagram 1. The Narcological Care System.

The Narcological Care System
(Separate Territorial Units: Republic, City, District)

Legend

1. Commission for Combating Drunkenness and Alcoholism Control under the Councils of Ministers of the Union and Autonomous Republics, Regional, District, and Settlement Soviets of People's Deputies.
2. Ministry of Public Health, Regional, City, and District Departments of Public Health. Standing Commissions for Alcoholism Control. Institutions of the narcological, psychiatric, and general somatic network.
3. Narcological care in the national economy. Commissions for Combating Drunkenness and Alcoholism Control, and Medical institutions.
4. Organs of justice and institutions of the Ministry of Internal Affairs.
5. Organizations and societies engaged in health education and improving the microsocial environment.

coholism, and alcohol-related offenses, and to ensure that health education is conducted at enterprises and establishments aimed at stopping drunkenness.

The Commissions check up on the work of the organs of the Ministry of Internal Affairs and public health in identifying and registering alcoholics, and on their implementation of the necessary treatment, including supportive therapy; they also check up on the work of the WTP in the system of the Ministry of Internal Affairs and on the sobering-up stations, and give assistance to the management of these institutions. Commission members constantly check up on the work of public catering and wine trading establishments and hold hearings to which they invite top officials of the network concerned.

It is the Commissions' practice to hear reports by the heads of enterprises, organizations, institutions, and collective farm chairmen on what has been done toward preventing drunkenness. When necessary, they also make recommendations to the appropriate organs and departments for censuring those heads of institutions, organizations and enterprises who fail to conduct adequate antialcoholism work.

When necessary they table various questions connected with stepping up the campaign against drunkenness and alcoholism control for deliberation by the Executive Committees of the Soviets of People's Deputies. They are empowered to plead before courts of justice to send chronic alcoholics to WTP, to limit the legal rights of persons afflicted with alcoholism, and to curtail parental authority.

The Statutes envisage that the Commissions for Combating Drunkenness under the Councils of Ministers of the Union Republics coordinate all the work aimed at preventing drunkenness, alcoholism and alcohol-related offenses in their respective republics and also control and provide methodological assistance to corresponding Commissions of the regional, district and city executive committees of the Soviets of People's Deputies.

The following divisions may be created within the Commissions: for health education work and antialcoholism propaganda, for the registration and public observation of persons abusing alcohol and suffering from alcoholism, for medicoprophylactic work, for checking up on the observance of prescribed rules of alcoholic beverage sales, etc., by trading and public catering establishments.

The medical aspect is merely one of the Commissions' many activities in the overall problem of combating drunkenness and controlling alcoholism. Without joint efforts coordinated with other ministries and departments, the health organs and institutions would be unable to resolve many of the questions pertaining to the treatment and prevention of alcoholism and drug addiction. The broadly empowered Commissions for Combating Drunkenness are the organs through which medical workers may extend their influence and reach the interested persons and organizations.

REPUBLICAN MINISTRIES OF HEALTH—STANDING COMMISSIONS ON ALCOHOLISM CONTROL. NARCOLOGICAL, PSYCHIATRIC AND GENERAL SOMATIC FACILITIES

The work of organizing alcoholism control in the public health system is headed by Standing Commissions (see Diagram 2) set up at ministries, at regional, city and district health departments. The heads of these health departments or their deputies act as the Commissions' chairmen.

The Standing Commissions constitute a kind of organizational-methodological center, leading and directing the work toward alcoholism control in the respective republic, region, city or district. Being concerned with medical questions they maintain close contacts with the Commissions for Combating Drunkenness and Alcoholism Control of the Councils of Ministers of the Union Republics, of the Soviets of People's Deputies, of the interested ministries, departments, individual enterprises, building sites, and farms at the corresponding levels of republic, region, city or district. The size of the Commissions is not restricted and, therefore, depending on the administrative level, they may include psychiatrist-narcologists, psychiatrists, physicians of other specialties, and staff members of health education centers, the Red Cross, and Red Crescent Societies.

The Commissions check up on the fulfillment and observance of decrees, orders and decisions aimed at improving antialcoholism work among the population, give assistance to health bodies and institutions and other departments in organizing and implementing prophylactic and therapeutic measures, provide guidance in health propaganda, and generalize and disseminate beneficial and praiseworthy practices.

The narcological service, an integral part of the country's public health system, comprises narcological institutions and narcological subdivisions of the psychiatric and general somatic specialties.

The basic narcological institution is the *dispensary*, an organizational-methodological and medico-prophylactic center for administering specialized care to people afflicted with alcoholism, narcomanias and toxicomanias (see Diagram 3). Conscious of the need to bring narcological care as close as possible to the population, the dispensary may deploy part of its structural units—consulting rooms, stations, departments—in the psychiatric and general somatic network or on the premises of other institutions and enterprises.

The staff units of uchastok psychiatrist-narcologists have been included in the establishment of a narcological dispensary or, when such an institution is lacking, into the establishment of the psychiatric and

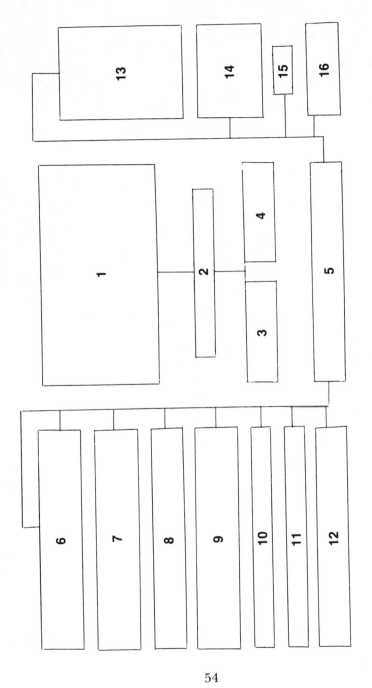

Diagram 2. Narcological Care within the Public Health System

Narcological Care within the Public Health System

Legend
1. Ministries of Public Health of the Union Republics; Regional, city, district departments of public health; Standing commissions for alcoholism control; Chief narcologists, psychiatrists, specialists—public health department inspectors in narcology and psychiatry.
2. Narcological dispensary.
3. Mental care network.
4. General somatic network.
5. Health education and improvement of the microsocial environment.
6. Industry, construction, agriculture. Commissions for combating drunkenness and alcoholism control.
7. Narcological departments at industrial enterprises, in construction and agriculture.
8. Narcological consulting rooms at enterprises (doctor-narcologist).
9. Narcological station of medical unit at enterprises (feldsher-manned narcological station).
10. Narcological post at enterprise.
11. Health education center.
12. Red Cross and Red Crescent Society.
13. Ministries of Internal Affairs of the Union Republics—Boards of Internal Affairs of regions, cities, districts; Organs of justice.
14. Specialized medical asylums (medical sobering-up stations).
15. Work Therapy Preventorium (WTP)
16. The "Znaniye" ("Knowledge") Society.

general somatic facility. This is of great importance since many towns and cities in the Soviet Union do not warrant an independent dispensary because of the size of their population (including those employed at industrial enterprises).

No less important is the introduction of the position of psychiatrist-narcologist into the establishments of rural district hospitals where, together with the psychiatrist or psychoneurologists, they can extend care to mental and drug addicted patients in rural areas.

The basic unit established in the outpatient narcological network is the uchastok (health district) psychiatrist-narcologist, and the basic structural subdivisions in the outpatient department of a dispensary are the consulting rooms of the uchastok narcologists (see Diagram 4). However, unlike the duties of other uchastok physicians, the workload of the uchastok narcologist includes personal reception of patients, visits to patients at home, and a considerable effort toward health education and the organization and administration of the nar-

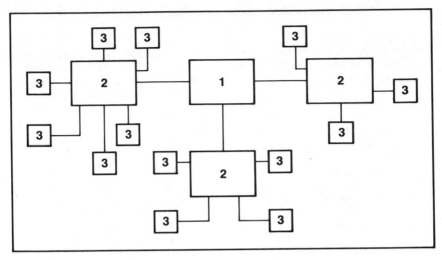

1. Narcological consulting room of psychiatrist-narcologist.
2. Narcological station (feldsher).
3. Narcological post.

Diagram 3. Key Diagram of Narcological Health District (Narcological Team)

cological feldsher stations and posts at factories, institutions and on the farms.

Regulations concerning the uchastok psychiatrist-narcologist and narcological consulting rooms specify the wide range of duties to be performed by this specialist. Above all, this includes the detection and diagnosis of alcoholism or drug addiction, making decisions on priority treatment, either outpatient or inpatient, the administration of basic and supportive therapy courses during a five-year period of dynamic observation, and checking up on the state of registration.

Apart from this the uchastok psychiatrist-narcologist participates in the work of expert examination commissions and commissions for combating drunkenness and alcoholism control, regularly keeps in touch with the organs of the militia for the recognition of alcoholics at medical sobering-up stations; is concerned with the functioning of work therapy preventoriums, and with organizing the treatment of persons discharged from these institutions, etc.

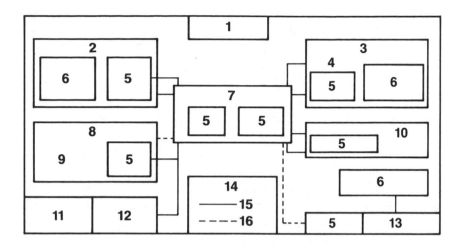

1 Narcological hospital.
2 Agriculture.
3 Industrial enterprises.
4 Medical unit.
5 Narcological consulting room.
6 Narcological departments at
  industrial enterprises.
7 Narcological dispensary.
8 OTP (Occupational-Therapy
  Preventorium).

9 Medical sobering-up station.
10 General somatic network.
11 Psychiatric hospital.
12 Narcological department.
13 Neuropsychiatric dispensary.
14 Conventional symbols.
15 Administrative subordination.
16 Methodological guidance.

Diagram 4. Model Diagram of Narcological Care Service in District Attached
to Narcological Dispensary

A large amount of work toward the planning, organization and methodological guidance of the entire narcological network is carried out by the dispensaries' organizational-methodological rooms. A dispensary's outpatient department must provide all the medico-diagnostic work needed by the patients, and a prominent place in its structure is given, therefore, to diagnostic laboratories and, in large dispensaries, to specialists (internists, neuropathologists, etc.) and medical rooms for special and active methods of treatment and psychotherapy (i.e., hypnotherapy).

The narcological dispensary is also a center of expert examination work to determine alcoholic intoxication and to select persons for treatment and labor reeducation at WTP or the correctional labor colony (CLC) in order to serve one's sentence for offenses committed while receiving treatment for alcoholism and drug addiction.

Meticulous maintenance of dynamic registration by every dispensary is highly important in view of the obligatory five-year period of supportive therapy to be given on an outpatient basis. This work is to be conducted by visiting nurses under the constant control of feldshers and psychiatrist-narcologists.

Work-Therapy Workshops (WTW) are run under special regulations for handling drug-addicted patients and, as a rule, alcoholic patients after having recovered from an alcoholic psychosis, are organized in the narcological dispensaries.

Another form of narcological care is the semi-hospital—the night preventorium. It is most expedient to attach these facilities to enterprises' building sites and send the employees of these enterprises for treatment and controlled leisure there. Receiving therapy in the evening enables the patients to combine work at their regular place of employment with treatment and rest.

Important in the structure of a narcological dispensary are the narcological departments that are attached to industrial and building enterprises and to farms; their purpose is the treatment of chronic alcoholics in combination with labor activity. It is also desirable that a narcological dispensary comprise still another inpatient department, with male and female wards for the hospitalization of patients with psychoses (see Diagram 5). The availability of such a department turns the dispensary into a multi-specialized institution with all the auxiliary diagnostic and therapeutic rooms and services. The departments should operate on carefully thought out plans and schedules, with a rational combination of treatment, work therapy, rest and recreation, elements of self-administration with absolutely strict observance of the prescribed regulations. It is highly desirable from the moment of admission to distribute the patients according to the principle of possible relapses by separating primary admissions from repeat cases.

As stipulated by the USSR Ministry of Health Order No. 291 of March 23, 1976, the obligatory 45-day minimum duration of treatment must be observed without fail. This refers to all alcoholics who volunteered for treatment or those hospitalized in a psychotic state. But narcotic addicts, according to the USSR Ministry of Health Order No. 928 of September 21, 1976, must receive treatment for at least 60 days.

For many years narcological care was provided by the psychiatric network, which has gained ample experience in handling these groups of patients. At present the psychiatric service with its broad network of institutions must give wide assistance in the organization of all kinds of antialcoholism work.

Outpatient neuropsychiatric institutions (dispensaries, polyclinics, consulting rooms), along with the recognition of mental patients, will also put on their files persons suffering from alcoholism, toxicomanias and narcomanias. In many localities, before specialized narcological dispensaries are opened there the narcological consulting rooms will function mainly within neuropsychiatric dispensaries; therefore, they will have to provide the required complex of therapeutic measures. In localities where neuropsychiatric and narcological institutions will function in parallel, prompt exchange of information should be organized between them concerning detected patients, particularly mental patients who concurrently suffer from alcoholism or narcomanias. Such patients may take treatment both in the neuropsychiatric and in the narcological dispensaries.

Recent years have seen the spread in the Soviet Union of the unit of the psychoneurologist, and in some Union Republics with vast territories and small populated areas, that of feldsher-psychoneurologist. These units will be retained, and they, too, where possible, will be used for the detection, treatment and the provision of supportive therapy to alcoholics and drug addicts.

A certain number of persons afflicted by alcoholism, toxicomanias and narcomanias, particularly those with alcoholic psychoses, will be hospitalized in mental health institutions. Naturally, this calls for proper continuity of treatment and observation of such patients. With

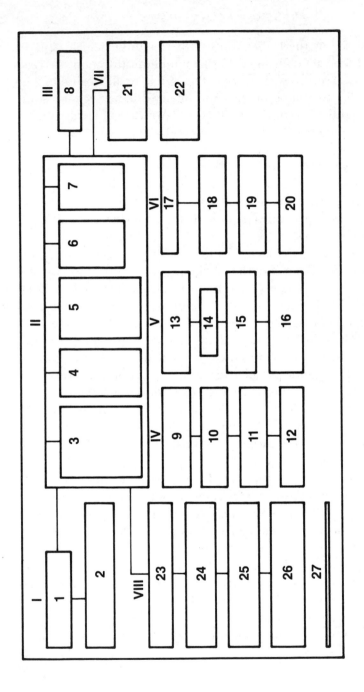

Diagram 5. Narcological Dispensary (Republican, Regional, City, District)

Narcological Dispensary
(Republican, Regional, City, District)

I

1 Registration.
2 First visit consulting room (Reception).

II

3 Narcological consulting rooms of the uchastok psychiatrist-narcologists (including those catering to teenagers).
4 Consulting rooms of internist, neuropathologist, psychologist.
5 Narcological consulting rooms in the psychiatric and general somatic network.
6 Consulting rooms of specialist physicians.
7 Room for drunkenness examination.

III

8 Hospitals.

IV

9 Clinical laboratories.
10 Biochemical laboratories.
11 EEG and ECG laboratories.
12 X-ray room.

V

13 Day hospital.
14 OTW (Occupational-Therapy Workshop).
15 Night-time preventorium.

16 Department at industrial enterprise.

VI

17 Hypnotherapy room.
18 Active therapy methods room.
19 Medical procedures room.
20 Physiotherapy, balneotherapy.

VII

21 Organizational-methodological department.
22 Administrative office, archives.

VIII

23 Narcological consulting rooms at enterprises in the national economy.
24 Narcological stations manned by feldsher-narcologists.
25 Hospital department at enterprises in the national economy.
26 Narcological posts.
27 DISPENSARY DEPARTMENTS: I. Reception, II. Outpatient care, III. Hospital care, IV. Diagnostics, V. Industrial-labour, VI. Therapy, VII. Organizational-methodological, Administration, VIII. At enterprises in the national economy.

the exception of emergency cases, for example, of psychoses, one should strive to hospitalize all such patients through the uchastok psychiatrist-narcologist.

The general somatic institutions, constituting a ramified network employing a great number of physicians and paramedical workers of different specialties, should also be used at different stages in the organization of narcological care. This concerns, first of all, the detection of persons suffering from alcoholism and narcotic addictions. Because of various concurrent diseases, such patients are frequently under the observation of internists, surgeons, dermatologists, and other specialists. Whenever alcoholism or drug addiction is suspected, the proper procedure for such specialists is to fill in Registration Form No. 281 and send it to the uchastok psychiatrist-narcologist for establishing the final diagnosis and, when necessary, putting such a patient on the register.

Resort to the facilities of the general somatic network is particularly important in localities and populated areas where current staff complements preclude the employment of psychiatrist-narcologists or even feldsher-narcologists. In order to bring narcological care maximally close to the population, it is recommended that narcologist's and feldsher-narcologist's consulting rooms be established in general somatic (outpatient) polyclinics. This will make it possible to keep in touch with physicians of other specialties. Besides, some alcoholics and drug addicts would seek medical care, even for alcoholism, at the general outpatient clinic rather than at a narcological or neuropsychiatric dispensary.

It is advisable to open narcological departments at large general somatic hospitals and narcological wards at hospitals with a small number of beds (city or central district hospitals). Such specialized wards will make it possible to admit a greater number of people needing hospital treatment, in order to nip relapses in the bud and arrest psychoses.

ORGANS OF JUSTICE; ORGANS OF THE UNION AND REPUBLICAN
MINISTRIES OF INTERNAL AFFAIRS; COURTS OF JUSTICE;
MEDICAL SOBERING-UP STATIONS; WORK-THERAPY
PREVENTORIUMS

Different questions pertaining to alcohol abuse are reflected in various legislative acts and codes of the USSR and of the Union Republics.

In connection with the introduction of compulsory treatment and labor reeducation of persons suffering from alcoholism and drug addiction, the Presidia of the Supreme Soviets of the Union Republics issued decrees setting the duration of treatment in the WTP of the USSR Ministry of Internal Affairs at two years. Compulsory treatment is not a punitive measure implying a criminal record. The patient retains all civil rights; this includes his job (provided he had not been dismissed before the court hearing), seniority, his dwelling, pension, etc.

According to explanations by the Plenum of the USSR Supreme Court of September 26, 1975, No. 6, the duration of compulsory treatment is decided individually by a court of justice on the basis of recommendations by medical commissions. The judiciary is entitled to decide on a preterm discharge from a WTP upon representation by medical commissions and the management of an institution or enterprise.

The organs of the Ministry of Internal Affairs are charged with major and serious duties within the narcological care system. These involve, first of all, putting an end to excessive drinking and alcohol-related disturbances. Here an important role is relegated to the medical sobering-up stations. Their tasks include the temporary isolation from society of a heavily intoxicated citizen and the administration of detoxicating measures. Though administratively the medical sobering-up stations are subordinate to the organs of the Ministry of Internal Affairs, their tasks are much wider. They may maintain narcological consulting rooms or narcological stations where medical workers make contact for revealing new cases of the disease and serve as the primary center for conducting therapeutic, health education

and reeducation work. Special WTPs are also organized for drug
addicts. The rules concerning admission, upkeep and other legal
norms are regulated by the same orders and state legislation as the
WTP for alcoholics.

For example, special WTPs are singled out within the system of
the USSR Ministry of Internal Affairs and those of the Union Republics specializing in the treatment and labor reeducation of women.
Everything concerning the prescription of treatment, the stages of
certification, the courts of justice as well as their maintenance and
treatment is similar to male WTP. However, specific features of female
alcoholism require special approaches to some of the organizational
and therapeutic matters.

Under the articles of the Criminal Code of the Union Republics,
in addition to punishment, persons who had committed a criminal
offense may be prescribed compulsory treatment for alcoholism
(when indicated). Such treatment is given at a CLC and, though its
basic principles are similar to those adopted for WTP, a number of
specific features are connected with the special regulations involved.

Narcological Care in the National Economy. Commissions for Combating Drunkenness and Alcoholism Control at Industrial and Building Enterprises and in Agriculture

The narcological care system attaches much importance to ex-
tending care to heavy drinkers and alcoholics employed in the national
economy. The narcological care system at an enterprise, on a building
site, in a motor transport establishment, at an institution, or on a
collective or state farm is organized on the following principles: a
narcological post is manned by volunteers, a narcological station is
manned by staff personnel (feldsher-narcologists), and a narcological
consulting room is served by a psychiatrist-narcologist.

The narcological post is the initial element in the narcological
service. The volunteers manning a narcological post come from
among the work collective, being most closely in touch with alcohol

abusers during daily work, and sometimes at home. A narcological post is set up at enterprises (sectors, workshops), building sites, transport establishments, in housing cooperatives, secondary and higher educational establishments, technical schools, state and collective farms, from among the active members of Red Cross and Red Crescent Societies, trade unions and other public organizations.

Narcological post service is a social assignment from one's collective. The task of the narcological post is to reveal alcohol or narcotics abusers, keep an eye on those who receive treatment to break the drinking habit, and carry out primary registration of alcoholics and health education toward raising the population's health standards (pin up posters, hand out leaflets, booklets, etc.).

Uchastok psychiatrist-narcologists and narcologists employed by enterprises or feldsher-narcologists direct the work of the narcological posts (holding periodical seminars, daily check-ups on activities). Every narcological post keeps a ledger. Inspections of narcological posts ought to be held periodically.

Narcological stations are headed by feldsher-narcologists. Such stations are set up at industrial and construction enterprises, at motor transport establishments, and in agriculture.

The narcological consulting room of a psychiatrist-narcologist may be organized within the medical unit of an industrial or construction enterprise, and at motor transport establishments with sufficiently large numbers of workers and employees.

The work of the psychiatrist-narcologist employed at enterprises and institutions of the national economy is many-sided. He must organize and guide the work of the feldsher-narcologists and of the volunteers manning the narcological posts. He must participate in the work of the commission for combating drunkenness at the enterprise where he is employed, or under the district (city) Executive Committee of the Soviet of People's Deputies. He also must maintain close contacts with the district officers, district stations, and children's rooms of the militia. For conducting antialcoholism propaganda he must constantly keep in touch with health education centers, with the "Znaniye" ("Knowledge") Society and the local branches of the Red Cross and Red Crescent Society.

A significant place in the activities of the psychiatrist-narcologist will go to psychohygienic and prophylactic work at the enterprise and institution itself. The main occupation of this physician, however, will be the detection of initial forms of disease, conducting of diagnostic and therapeutic work, and organizing supportive and arresting therapy.

In 1972 the Secretariat of the All-Union Central Council of Trade Unions and the Collegium of the USSR Ministry of Health acclaimed the working experience of narcological departments at industrial enterprises and recommended its broad utilization. In 1975 the Statutes on the Narcological Department and a Model Agreement was published.

The Statutes say that the narcological departments are structural units of narcological (mental) hospitals and narcological (neuropsychiatric) dispensaries intended to provide inpatient care to persons afflicted with alcoholism, ensuring their obligatory involvement in labor by way of work therapy.

The Model Agreement regulates legal relationships between the contracting parties. It is noteworthy that premises for the departments are granted by the enterprises, which also pay for the work done by those under treatment according to current rates and output. Forty percent of these wages and salaries are remitted to a special assets clause of the appropriate health institutions, and the remaining part of the wages minus taxes are remitted to the narcological (neuropsychiatric) institutions for payment to the patients.

Apart from obligatory labor activity, the patients admitted to narcological departments receive a full course of detoxification, general strengthening exercise and therapy. It is advisable to limit the duration of stay at this department to two-three months. Following their discharge, all those treated are transferred for observation to the narcological-neuropsychiatric outpatient network.

The best and most active industrial workers, employees and pensioners are elected by open vote to serve on the commissions for combating drunkenness and alcoholism control organized at the enterprises, institutions and in the countryside. Enterprises with a small number of workers and employees may set up posts for assisting regional and city commissions.

The main task of the commissions is the prevention of heavy drinking and moral looseness, the conducting of prophylactic work and, when necessary, the implementation of compulsory measures in regard to drunkards; at the same time the commissions organize and guide all antialcoholism work at their enterprise or institution, broadly enlisting for this purpose the medical workers available.

The commissions are endowed with considerable powers since they may initiate such measures as the imposition of a fine, deprivation of awards, rejection of applications for granting a better home, demotion, suspension of payment or appointment of guardianship, and tabling of documents for compulsory treatment.

On agreement with Party and trade union bodies, the commissions may check up on labor discipline and the education and propaganda work in their collectives, may suggest measures to remove factors conducive to drunkenness, etc. Keeping in touch with the personnel departments of enterprises and institutions, the commissions also assist in the job placement of persons who have been treated for alcoholism at narcological consulting rooms or WTP and in effecting transfers to other jobs.

HEALTH EDUCATION AND IMPROVEMENT OF THE MICROSOCIAL ENVIRONMENT; HEALTH EDUCATION CENTERS; THE UNION OF RED CROSS AND RED CRESCENT SOCIETIES; THE "ZNANIYE" (KNOWLEDGE) SOCIETY; TEMPERANCE CLUBS

Communist education of the people presupposes uncompromising struggle against drunkenness and alcoholism. Therefore, this work is an important element in the overall set of measures aimed at improving the health of the population. Health education centers are called upon to be the organizing pivot in such work.

The Red Cross and Red Crescent Society also carries on antialcoholism work among the masses, and this has been laid down in the Society's Rules. It is from among active members of this Society's local organizations that narcological posts at industrial enterprises are mainly drawn, and they should be instructed and widely used for holding group and individual talks and discussions right at the working place, during brief breaks and even at leisure.

The medical section of the All-Union "Znaniye" Society constantly carries out antialcoholism propaganda addressed at alcoholics themselves and their immediate environment. The various forms of antialcoholism propaganda include lectures, question-and-answer sessions, readers' conferences, and meetings with those people who, following treatment, abstain completely from the use of alcoholic beverages. Articles in the press—the newspapers, magazines, and also wall newspapers and satirical posters should be used more widely.

The different groups require individual approaches, and propaganda should therefore be organized with definite purpose, always trying to evade stereotyped methods, keenly responding to the interests of the audience. Great care should be given to preparing antialcoholism propaganda materials for radio and television programs.

Recent years have seen the establishment and consolidation of temperance clubs, such as "Anti-Bacchus," "Health" and others, in a number of our country's cities. These are associations of former alcohol abusers, now recovered and engaged in the propaganda of temperance.

Enlightenment work is vigorously conducted by a number of ministries, departments and public organizations within the system of general educational measures, for example, the USSR Ministry of Education, the Ministries of Higher and Specialized Secondary Education of the Union Republics, the Young Communist League, trade union and other organizations. Members of the narcological service should actively utilize these methods of influencing the masses of youth, and the people in general.

The life of an alcoholic is closely bound up with his relatives, friends and colleagues who are not always capable of rendering a positive influence. Because of ignorance, thoughtlessness or other reasons, such people are often unable to create a healthy, temperate climate around an alcoholic undergoing treatment. Hence the narcological service's serious task of improving the microsocial environment.

Chapter 5

Legislation Pertaining to the Control of Alcoholism and Drug Addiction

Different questions connected with alcohol and narcotics abuse are reflected in the various legislative acts and codes of the USSR and the Union Republics. The Model Internal Regulations for the workers and employees of state enterprises and institutions authorized by the State Committee of the USSR Council of Ministers for Labor and Wages, and the All-Union Central Council of Trade Unions (January 12, 1957) say that a worker or employee absent without a good reason is liable to disciplinary censure, and even dismissal. Here, reporting for work in a state of drunkenness is likened to absenteeism (Article 23).

Article 17 of the Fundamentals of Labor Legislation of the USSR and of the Union Republics stipulates that a labor agreement may be dissolved by the management for absenteeism without a good reason, including reporting for work when not sober (Clause 4).

Article 16 of the Civil Code of the Russian Federation and other Union Republics restricts the legal capacity of citizens abusing alcoholic beverages and narcotic drugs. Under the law such persons are liable to be placed under guardianship and they may enact property transactions, including the disposal of their incomes, only on the agreement of their guardians. Once the abuse of alcoholic beverages or narcotic drugs is given up, the court may abrogate the limitation of legal capacity and lift guardianship.

The Civil Code of the Russian Federation stipulates that eviction from an apartment without granting another dwelling may be effected in regard to persons who, despite warnings and public admonition, continue to disturb the peace, violate rules of socialist behavior, or damage the premises. We now know that the perpetrators of such acts turn out most frequently to be alcoholics and drug addicts.

A decree of the Presidium of the Supreme Soviet of the Russian Federation requires responsibility for drinking alcoholic beverages in public and for disturbing the peace of citizens. Punishment for this may be a fine, delivery to a medical sobering-up station and an official warning.

The Code on Marriage and the Family of the Union Republics can enforce possible deprivation of parental authority of one or both parents when they shirk their duties toward the upbringing of children, abuse their parental authority, display cruelty in regard to the children and expose them to harmful influences by their immoral, antisocial behavior or when the parents are chronic alcoholics or drug addicts (Article 59 of the RSFSR Code on Marriage and the Family).

A number of articles of the Criminal Code of the Union Republics provide for punitive measures against persons committing criminal offenses in a state of alcoholic intoxication. Though these articles appear under different numbers, they are essentially the same.

Article 12 of the Criminal Code of the Russian Federation (RSFSR) stipulates that a person who committed a crime in the state of drunkenness shall not be exempt from criminal responsibility. Irrespective of the punishment imposed, the court may decide on compulsory treatment of persons convicted of crimes who are found to be suffering from chronic alcoholism or drug addictions. The compulsory treatment of these persons is carried out at places of detention or in special institutions.

Commentaries to the Criminal Code of the RSFSR indicate that the commission of a crime by a person in the state of drunkenness is regarded as an aggravating circumstance. Articles 5, 6, 7 of the Decree issued by the Presidium of the RSFSR Supreme Soviet on June 19, 1972, prescribe punishment for involving minors in gambling, heavy drinking or other actions harmful to society and the minor concerned. The same Decree of the RSFSR Supreme Soviet qualifies as illegal the manufacture and sale of hooch and also of other home-made strong alcoholic beverages, the infringement of restrictions on the sales of alcoholic beverages, and the driving of transport vehicles in the state of drunkenness. All the enumerated offenses warrant different degrees of punishment, including the deprivation of freedom for a term of one to five years.

More severe punishments are exacted for crimes related to the use of and trafficking in narcotic drugs. Briefly, they may be defined as follows: the stealing of opium, morphine, cocaine, promedol, codeine, poppy capsules and other narcotic substances; the illicit manufacture, sales, storage or acquisition of narcotic drugs; infringement of the established rules of manufacture, storage, dispensing, accounting, transportation, and dispatching of narcotic substances; illicit dispatch of narcotic substances in the mails or in luggage; sowing of opium, oil poppy, and hemp without appropriate permits; use or acquisition of narcotic drugs without medical prescription; maintenance of dens for the use of narcotics; and inducement of minors to the use of narcotic drugs. Persons committing any of the aforementioned actions shall be held criminally responsible and deprived of liberty for a term of one to ten years.

For improving continuity and conducting outpatient supportive therapy upon discharge from a WTP, special registration forms have been established allowing for dynamic observation of those concerned (Orders of the USSR Ministry of Health and the Ministry of Internal Affairs of the USSR and the Union Republics No. 955/270 of October 5, 1976).

Chapter 6

Medical Personnel in the Narcological Care System

The medical workers providing all the necessary care at every level of the narcological service may be divided into three large groups: physicians, paramedical workers, and junior medical personnel. Depending on the main forms of medical services we also distinguish between the medical workers occupied in the outpatient and the inpatient network.

Employed in the outpatient network (the polyclinics, narcological or psychiatric dispensaries, general somatic outpatient departments, medical units of industrial enterprises, at construction sites and in agriculture) are uchastok psychiatrist-narcologists, feldsher-narcologists, medical nurses (uchastok, visiting, treatment-room nurses, laboratory assistants, diagnostic and consulting-room nurses, registration nurses, statisticians, head nurses or sisters) and junior medical personnel (matrons or attendants of uchastok physicians' consulting rooms, diagnostic and treatment rooms and departments).

In order to bring narcological care as close as possible to the population, the units of uchastok psychiatrist-narcologists are established by taking 0.2 of staff unit per 10,000 workers of industrial, construction, transport enterprises, and 0.1 staff unit per 10,000 of the remaining adult population of a given city or settlement.

Every staff unit of an uchastok (district) narcologist is provided with an uchastok nurse and a half-unit (in terms of salary) of a visiting nurse, and one feldsher-narcologist per 5,000 industrial, construction and transport (motor and urban public transport) enterprises and organizations. The staff units of paramedical workers of the diagnostic and treatment rooms and of departments are calculated according to their number and workload. Junior medical personnel are engaged in attending all the consulting rooms and laboratories; there is also one attendant per two consulting rooms of the uchastok psychiatrist-narcologist.

Employed in the inpatient narcological network (narcological hospital or department, narcological dispensary, mental hospital, general somatic hospital, neuropsychiatric dispensary, medical departments at industrial enterprises, building sites, or in agriculture) are staff narcologists (psychiatrists), consultants in particular fields (neuropathologists, therapists and others), and also specialists in different kinds of diagnostic examination and treatment (laboratory assistants, physiotherapists, and others). In the inpatient departments of narcological dispensaries or psychiatric, neuropsychiatric and general somatic institutions, the positions of secondary medical personnel are calculated to provide one round-the-clock post per 30 patients, and in the narcological departments at industrial enterprises, per 45 patients. The medical nurses of departments and treatment room nurses must be on duty in every department. The paramedical personnel of diagnostic and treatment rooms are distributed according to the availability of such rooms.

If the narcological department has 60 beds or more, the position of a matron is established, and for every 50 patients a round-the-clock post of attendant or junior medical nurse is established. The units of paramedical workers at the work therapy workshops, day hospitals and night preventoriums are introduced according to staff requirements.

Since the specific work of narcological institutions is regarded as hazardous, persons under the age of 18 are not employed in them. Before being hired all would-be staff members of the narcological service must pass a medical examination, which is to be repeated every year.

At hiring and every subsequent year all personnel are specially instructed about the working conditions, the special features of observing and servicing the patients, internal rules and regulations, the rights and duties of narcological service personnel; the attendance is registered in a special ledger.

Schools and universities with regular seminars are established for improving the personnel's special knowledge and skills. Classes are conducted one to two times a month for a 9-10 month period every year. The curriculum is required to be constantly updated according to the latest achievements of science and practice.

Chapter 7

The Paramedical Worker in the Narcological Care System

Persons suffering from alcoholism (stages I, II, III), narcomanias and toxicomanias are placed on the register of a narcological institution or other facility (dispensary, consulting room of psychiatrist-narcologist at neuropsychiatric dispensary, medical department, etc.). In cases in which a patient's complaints suggest habitual heavy drinking without symptoms of alcoholism, the question of placing such a person on the register is decided by the physician; however, such patients can and must be given treatment in either decision.

During the first visit by a patient seeking narcological assistance the registration nurse fills in an individual outpatient card (Registration Form No. 25) based on his identification document. Subsequently, the physician makes entries on the card during every contact with the patient.

The individual cards are filed in alphabetic order and according to territorial division and kept in the registration department of the narcological dispensary or narcological consulting room. At the same time during the patient's first visit, a control card of dispensary observation of a psychiatric (narcological) patient (Reg. f. No. 30-PS) is filled in. The card consists of two parts: the main part remains at the institution of registration, and a tear-off slip is dispatched to a psychiatric statistical center according to place of residence.

Upon recovery, movement from the territory concerned, transfer for observation to another medical institution, absence of information within a year, or in case of a patient's death, a statistical slip is filled in so that the neuropsychiatric (narcological) patient is removed from the dispensary register (Reg. f. No. 30-A-ps).

Both registration forms (Nos. 30-PS and 30-A-ps) intended for dynamic registration are kept in the consulting rooms of the uchastok psychiatrist-narcologist of the narcological, neuropsychiatric dispensary, general somatic outpatient clinic, central district hospital, medical department or medical room, etc.

Due to the specific features of alcoholism and drug addiction, persons suffering from these afflictions should be kept on the register for a long time and must regularly take courses of supportive treatment. Such patients may develop psychoses or commit socially dangerous acts which is why continuous observation of this group of patients for a period of five years is prescribed under the Order of the USSR Ministry of Health "On Authorizing Obligatory Minimum Treatment Courses for Chronic Alcoholics." The same Order defines the main therapeutic measures to be administered each year that the person is on the register, which consist of an uninterrupted, continuous therapeutic cycle.

In the outpatient part of the narcological service the secondary medical workers are represented by the uchastok and visiting nurses. The uchastok (district) nurse is the physician's first assistant. She should be familiar with the community of the district, its boundaries, its enterprises, transport and building organizations, and the institutions situated in its territory, and keep in touch with the narcological stations manned by feldsher-narcologists. The uchastok nurse must also know the main groups of patients on the register and assist the physician in maintaining dynamic registration, strictly watching over the correct movement of Reg. f. No. 30-PS through the compartments of the five dynamic-registration groups.

In order to maintain constant observation of a patient not only within the annual registration cycles but during the therapeutic courses and other daily treatment courses, therapeutic registration is recommended. This kind of registration is distinguished for its efficiency and dynamic character. It allows the attending medical worker (physician, feldsher-narcologist, medical nurse) to check-up directly on the implementation of the required therapy at any point in the course of treatment. More specifically, a "Medical Prescriptions Sheet" is used when prescribing courses of treatment or individual procedures to a patient. These sheets are kept in the small sections of a single drawer of the registration file, and are divided into 25 compartments according to the number of working days in a month.

When prescribing treatment, the physician fills in the "Prescriptions Sheet" and inserts it into the compartment for that day of administration. The paramedical worker prepares the necessary medicines every day according to these sheets. Upon the actual administration of the procedure, it is marked off on the sheet and inserted into the compartment of the day the patient is expected to receive the next procedure.

After treatment (course or individual prescriptions) the sheet is attached to Reg. f. No. 25 (individual outpatient card).

On assignment from the uchastok narcologist the visiting nurses maintain constant observation of the patients. They visit them at home, take note of their domestic surroundings, call on the production collectives to get in touch with management and public organizations in order to bring about an improvement of the environment and, when necessary, arrange a transfer to another job.

The priority tasks of visiting nurses include rendering social assistance to the patients, their families and relatives; protecting their rights; and helping them to settle family difficulties, housing problems, etc. The visiting nurses work with persons discharged after a course of treatment at a WTP or CLC toward receiving supportive therapy. There are special forms of notification which allow both public health bodies and Ministries of Internal Affairs of the USSR and of the Union Republics to check up on the treatment of these groups.

Many persons afflicted with alcoholism, toxicomanias and narcomanias begin to believe that they are completely recovered and do not want to take systematic therapy courses throughout the prescribed five-year period; they frequently change their place of residence and employment, evade medical workers, fail to visit the doctors and cheat medical personnel during treatment. All of this requires additional time and effort, the involvement of the police, administrative bodies, public organizations, and the standing commissions for combating drunkenness of the Executive Committees of the Soviets of People's Deputies, of industrial enterprises, building sites and organizations.

There may be several types of hospitals admitting narcological patients: those for patients with alcoholic psychoses, for alcoholics, for drug addicts, for patients in whom alcoholism is aggravated by concurrent diseases (e.g., tuberculosis), and lastly, narcological departments or wards in general somatic hospitals. In such cases, hospital patients are given a certificate of standard form—it is absolutely prohibited to issue a sick leave certificate to them.

Patients with alcoholic psychoses are admitted to the hospital according to indications, irrespective of the wish of the patients themselves or their relatives, particularly if their condition is dangerous to others or the patients themselves. It is a different matter when hospital treatment of alcoholics and drug addicts is considered. In such cases some of them do not wish to go to a hospital. Their reasons are many: some assert that they will give up drinking themselves, others do not consider themselves to be alcoholics at all—"I drink just as everybody does," they tell the doctor; still others are apprehensive about being admitted to a narcological or psychiatric hospital; others do not want to be placed on the register with the subsequent five-year obligatory treatment course; lastly, there are those who belatedly experience feelings of shame for their behavior and are anxious lest they damage their career or public image.

The choice of the method of treatment lies with the physician. It is he who decides whether the patient should be hospitalized or given outpatient treatment. Whatever the case, however, it is essential that the patient undergo treatment willingly, with the desire to recover. An important role here goes to paramedical personnel because this attitude is not easily inculcated and occasionally it takes a long time and the help of relatives, friends and colleagues to convince the person concerned. Thus, psychotherapy[1] should begin well before drug treat-

---

[1] Psychotherapy is a complex of therapeutic measures based on influencing a person's mental sphere by word (which may include suggestion, rational, group and other kinds of psychotherapy).

ment and must accompany the latter at every stage of the protracted course of inpatient, outpatient, supportive and antirelapse treatment.

The internal regulations in narcological departments are of a special kind. It is recommended that patients be admitted to the department according to territorial zones, yet a variant is feasible when certain departments admit patients in psychotic states only. After arresting the psychoses such patients are transferred for further treatment to other departments. Then there are departments for treating primary patients, repeat patients and those with tuberculosis. In a single territorial department it is also advisable to have several sections—for admitting patients with psychoses, for persons in the initial (generally in the second to third week) stage of treatment, and for stabilizing therapy.

Regulations in the first section must be strict, with close observation of the patients, which should correspond to those established for mental hospitals. In the second section the regimen becomes more relaxed, and in the third it may follow the "open-door" principle. In these sections a council of patients is elected so that there are elements of self-rule, albeit under the close supervision and guidance of the medical personnel. It is particularly important to establish a carefully thought-out system of observation by secondary medical workers. Such a regimen must be based on:

1. a psychotherapeutic climate of mutual trust and respect between medical personnel and patients;

2. support and help to primary patients from the convalescents;

3. unquestionable and conscious fulfillment of all medical prescriptions;

4. obligatory occupational activity, physical activity;

5. inculcation of temperance attitudes, preparation of an appropriate psychological climate in the family and at work;

6. increasing health knowledge and education aimed at instilling an aesthetic taste for literature, the arts, and sound attitudes to life.

In narcological departments functioning on the principle of two-step services, the patient receives most of the medical care from the physician and paramedical worker. The function of junior attendants is merely to provide sanitary and hygienic functions to the patients.

In this connection one should bear in mind the specific features of the regime in narcological departments and the mental state of alcoholics and drug addicts. Notwithstanding elements of self-rule and relative freedom, the entire therapeutic climate in the department should be distinguished for high professional psychotherapeutic standards along with constant firmness, tidiness, exactness in observing the demands of the regimen, treatment and occupational therapy.

One should remember that during abstinence the patients seek access to alcoholic beverages, something that may be possible in unstructured situations. There are some who are reluctant to take medicines, particularly antabuse. They cheat the medical personnel, hide the tablets under their tongue, or even learn to induce vomiting following the administration of their medicine. For these reasons it is better to administer medicines in the form of powders or solutions, to always inspect the oral cavity, and to closely watch particularly suspicious patients.

Depression may develop in these patients, some of whom may make suicidal attempts. Rare hypomanic states also may occur. The behavior of the majority of patients follows the psychopathic type—they behave capriciously, quarrel with their neighbors in the ward or with medical workers, advance all kinds of demands and are never satisfied, may become sullen, refuse medicines and, at times, refuse food.

Abstinence in drug addicts proceeds more severely, with asthenia lasting much longer, and steep shifts of mood and dominant depression. These patients are even more persistent in their striving to get narcotic drugs by any means.

These and many other forms of patient behavior call for increased vigilance and attentive observation on the part of the personnel. In hospitals nurses daily record the patients' behavior and verbalizations in special ledgers. These records call for keen observation and high professional standards.

General somatic departments may also have a few narcological beds, which should be situated in a separate ward placed in charge of the same team of medical nurses who work in close collaboration with the psychiatrist-narcologists. Paramedical workers also keep an eye on the participation of the alcoholics and drug addicts in occupational activities, and particularly, in their job placements in industrial enterprises and on building sites. At first this requires their retraining and looking for opportunities to acquire new skills that could be utilized locally. The medical nurse in these cases should have good organizational ability and be a real helper to the physician or vocational guidance counselor.

A distinction of the narcological service from many other forms of patient care is the prominent place of the feldsher-narcologist. According to the Statutes for the feldsher-narcologist manning the feldsher-narcological station, he is the organizer of narcological services at the industrial, building and motor transport establishments and in agriculture. The feldsher-manned narcological station functions as one of the outpatient facilities of the unified narcological service of a city (district, region) and is fully subordinated to it in all organizational-methodological and medical matters (see Diagram 3).

All the work of the narcological station is conducted under the constant organizational-methodological and medical-consulting control of the psychiatrist-narcologist (of the uchastok or narcological consulting room). Meanwhile the functions of the feldsher-narcologist are sufficiently broad—he is entrusted not only with the identification, registration and observation of patients, but also with the administration of the active supportive treatment of alcoholics prescribed by the psychiatrist-narcologist (general roborant, detoxification, sensitization, and other types of therapy). Taken into account here must be the terms of active treatment and observation over a three-year period and passive registration and supportive antirelapse treatment for another two years, as established under the aforementioned Order of the USSR Ministry of Health. Treatment may be given at the premises of the narcological station, and some kinds of therapy (supportive, etc.) right at the enterprise or institution.

The feldsher-narcologist visits his patients at home, sees to it that they regularly and accurately follow the physician's instructions concerning the supportive therapy and promptly notifies the physician in cases of failure to do so. In all this work the feldsher-narcologist relies on the narcological posts, keeping in daily and effective touch with them.

Diverse types of work require that the feldsher-narcologist maintain close contact with the Commissions for Combating Drunkenness and Alcoholism Control, with the administration and public organizations of enterprises and institutions, with the district militia officers and voluntary public order squads. The feldsher-narcologist must be immediately involved in all measures to control drunkenness and alcoholism carried out in his respective zone, and together with personnel departments, to help in the job placement of his patients. In cooperation with the Commissions for Combating Drunkenness and Alcoholism Control he must provide mentorship with respect to alcohol abusers. The feldsher-narcologist is expected to constantly engage in health education work and contribute to the improvement of his patients' microsocial environment both at work and at home.

The feldsher-narcologist differentiates health education programs according to the group of population to which his audience belongs (the collective work of an enterprise, individual alcoholics, the families of alcoholics). In all these cases the best effect is produced by conversations conducted in a tone of confidence and trust, but without slipping into excessive familiarity.

At the narcological station the feldsher-narcologist maintains the essential registration documents, which includes, first of all, the outpatient card filled in for each patient. These cards are filed according to groups of dynamic registration and indicate dates of visits, any disruption of regimen, or evasion of treatment. A procedure sheet is inserted in the outpatient card which records all drug prescriptions. Special attention in registration and treatment should be given to persons discharged after hospital treatment who continue as outpatients. A special file is maintained for persons discharged from the WTP.

Registration ledgers of identified patients and health-education work are also maintained at the narcological station. At dates prescribed by appropriate authorities the feldsher-narcologist supplies various registration data concerning the functioning of the narcological station.

Chapter 8

The Paramedical Worker in the Narcological Institutions of the USSR Ministry of Internal Affairs

Vigorous measures toward combating drunkenness and controlling alcoholism are carried out within the system of the USSR Ministry of Internal Affairs. Here a specially important role is delegated to the medical sobering-up stations and the WTP.

Medical sobering-up stations are special institutions attached to organs of the Internal Affairs Ministry intended for rendering medical aid to persons in a state of medium or grave intoxication. They are also expected to carry out preventive and antialcoholism work. The number of feldshers and medical nurses employed at a medical sobering-up station depends on its size. One of them is the head feldsher, who is in charge of sanitary-hygienic work and treatment.

The main tasks of the station's medical personnel are as follows:

1. to carry out a careful primary examination of the clients;

2. to single out persons requiring a stay at the sobering-up station in connection with the degree of drunkenness or somatic disorder;

3. to determine the degree of drunkenness and administer measures necessary for rapid sobering up;

4. to exercise caution so as to prevent possible somatic complications during treatment or as a result of intoxication, or other causes;

5. to always maintain high sanitary-hygienic standards;

6. to identify persons afflicted with alcoholism and ensure their placement on the register of narcological or neuropsychiatric institutions; and

7. to conduct heath education work with every client.

Upon coming on duty the medical personnel should visit the clients undergoing sobering up and examine them so as to compare their observations of the client with the entries in the admissions log, then report their findings to the chief or his deputy and to the inspector on duty.

Upon admission, new clients should be carefully examined to determine their somatic state and to look for possible injuries and traces of bruises or wounds.

Persons in a state of mild drunkenness or, on the contrary, in a state of acute and grave intoxication or alcoholic psychosis, should not be brought or admitted to medical sobering-up stations. Nor should persons with head injuries or other injuries requiring surgical care be admitted, nor persons with symptoms of acute, subacute diseases of the internal organs or with symptoms of infectious diseases. Results of client examination, particularly all the detected small injuries and traces of bruises should be described in a special report and log. If necessary, after rendering first aid to persons with injuries, they should be taken to medical institutions.

The degree of drunkenness should be carefully determined because the administration of medical treatments, their sequel and intensity, are dependent upon this assessment. One should always also bear in mind that drunkenness frequently camouflages a number of injuries and diseases, sometimes even those hazardous to life. These include brain hemorrhages, myocardial infarctions, traumatic injuries to the head and internal organs, conditions requiring resuscitation, or additional poisoning with different narcotics or other substances (hashish, morphine, soporifics, atropine). Any of these conditions complicate the picture of intoxication and require urgent medical care.

Every patient, separately and together, irrespective of the circumstances that brought him or her to the sobering-up station, should be exposed to psychotherapy and health education. These measures are implemented jointly by medical workers and the militia. They should be vigorous and specialized according to age, sex and occupation. Juveniles and teenagers should immediately be separated from adult patients, particularly from the "regulars." Having learned the occupation of the client, when conducting health education one should emphasize the harmful effects of alcohol in his particular occupation.

Next, it is necessary to distinguish "accidental" clients admitted to the sobering-up station for the first time from "regular guests" at these institutions. Notifications are filled in for repeat clients which are sent to the narcological, neuropsychiatric dispensaries and consulting rooms, where they are checked against the patients' files. If the person concerned is on the narcological register and a recurrence occurs, he is promptly summoned or brought for treatment. In all other cases the patient should be carefully examined and, if alcoholism is identified, placed on the register and subjected to treatment.

In cases when the patient is no longer in remission, or in instances of binge drinking, the sobering-up station by itself is not enough for coping with symptoms of the abstinence syndrome. Therefore, it is very important to identify immediately such persons and to send them to a narcological or neuropsychiatric institution for observation. Thus, the medical sobering-up station is the place where new cases of disease are detected, and drinkers are earnestly exposed to health education for the first time.

Among alcoholics there is a group who reject voluntary treatment although, being sick, every one of them is an active disseminator of alcoholism. In this connection, compulsory treatment at WTP has been in operation since 1964.

When deciding the matter of compulsory treatment, two criteria, the social and the medical, should be considered:

(1) The *social criterion* is composed of the following basic indications: infringement of behavior norms in public and in the family; baneful effects on the upbringing of children; failure of educational and administrative measures; and restriction of legal capacity.

(2) The *medical criterion* is composed of the following indicators: chronic alcohol abuse; failure of previous treatment or its rejection; and grave cases of alcoholism of stages II and III.

With regard to administration and functions, the WTP are very special institutions. Maintained within the system of the USSR Ministry of Internal Affairs, organizationally they are subordinate to the boards of internal affairs. In structure, internal regulations in a WTP are basically in line with the regulations prescribed for other institutions of that Ministry. At the same time, in the implementation of its therapeutic functions, a WTP is methodologically and medically controlled by health bodies, i.e., narcological and neuropsychiatric institutions.

The main tasks of a WTP are as follows:

1. isolation of heavy drinkers for a period of 1 to 2 years;
2. protection of the society from potential law offenders;
3. instigation of proceedings to limit legal capacity;
4. creation of healthier family relations, particularly regarding the raising of children;
5. general health improvement and vigorous treatment of alcoholics;
6. labor and moral reeducation of the inmates;
7. ensuring abstinence from alcohol or narcotic drugs following discharge from the WTP; and
8. maintaining solvency of WTP and economic benefits accruing from the inmates' labor.

Since the preventoriums maintain a work-therapy regimen there is a number of contraindications to admission to WTP. These are with reference to age (persons under 18, men over 60 and women over 55) and disease (grave somatic illness, mental disorders). Such patients are sent to neuropsychiatric hospitals for urgent admission.

A ruling on compulsory treatment may be issued by the courts on the appeal of relatives, neighbors, house managements, public organizations, enterprises and institutions, or the militia. District militia officers collect the documents necessary for a court hearing and deliver the would-be WTP inmate to the medical examination board at the narcological, neuropsychiatric or other medical institution.

The medical examination boards, chaired by a psychiatrist-narcologist or psychiatrist, should include such specialists as internist, surgeon, dermatologist, and others. The same boards examine criminal offenders whom the court, apart from pronouncing sentences, considers for compulsory treatment of alcoholism. The quality of treatment at the WTP depends on the performance of the board. Some preventoriums lack facilities for conducting a number of laboratory examinations. Therefore, they (Wassermann test, X-ray examination, ECG, etc.) should be carried out while being examined by the boards. Such an examination makes it possible to start treatment at once upon admission to the WTP, without the preterm discharge of some of the inmates because of somatic contraindications.

In summary, the boards formulate their decision in a special way. The courts rule on compulsory treatment within a ten-day period, while militia bodies, also within ten days, must deliver the designated person to the appointed institution. The medical departments of the preventoriums should provide all the necessary treatments in the WTP. The medical department should have beds amounting to 10% of the total number of places at the WTP, narcologist consulting rooms, a hypnotherapy room, active treatment rooms, laboratories and an isolation ward.

Up to 10% of the inmates may be excused from work by the physician according to medical indications, while the other groups are treated as outpatients. Taking into account the closed character and special demands of the WTP, treatment plans are drawn for the patient's lasting stay at the preventorium. In this connection, therapy is subordinate to the following basic demands: (1) lasting treatment; (2) combined general roborant and active alcoholism treatment; (3) the utilization of psychotherapy and health education at every stage of treatment; (4) reshaping of moral and ethical norms; and (5) labor education.

The general roborant alcoholism treatment is subdivided into three stages. The first, adaptive stage, is the stage of detoxication and overall health build-up, lasting from two to six months. For treating narcomanias longer terms must be prescribed since intoxication and asthenic symptoms persist for a longer time and are usually deeper than in the case of alcoholism. The second is the basic stage of active alcoholism therapy. The duration is determined according to the prescribed stay at the WTP and covers, on the average, one half to three quarters of the total term. The third, conclusive stage, is preparatory for discharge and represents the last quarter of the term. It provides supportive therapy and works toward the consolidation of temperance attitudes. One of the obligatory kinds of therapy here is labor reeducation and occupational employment on different jobs (within and outside the zone).

Upon having received adequate drug medication, and having proved by their work and behavior the development of correct attitudes, inmates may be discharged before term after serving half of it (provided it is over one year). Special medical examination boards at the WTP discuss this matter together with the management and send their recommendations to a court delegated to resolve the situation. This group of inmates should not include those who served an earlier term at a WTP, were sent for treatment from a CLC, or failed to observe the therapeutic regimen, etc. Such cases—refusal of treatment, the drinking of alcoholic beverages, breaking out—do occur at the WTP. In such cases educational and administrative measures are taken, including being sent to court and sentenced to a term at a CLC.

For better continuity and the administration of supportive outpatient therapy following the discharge from a WTP, special exchange forms of registration have been established allowing follow up of an inmate's progress for two years (USSR Ministry of Health and USSR Ministry of Internal Affairs Order No. 955/270 of October 5, 1976).

In view of the special characteristics of narcomanias, drug addicts are under observation and on the register of the organs of both the USSR Ministry of Internal Affairs and the USSR Ministry of Health. For this purpose a system of mutual information by the institutions of these ministries has been adopted. A registration card in triplicate is filled in for each addict, one of which remains at the institution (agency) which identified the addict, another is sent to the central registry of the Ministry of Internal Affairs (the territorial boards of internal affairs, MIA-BIA), and the third sent to the district (city) department of internal affairs (in cases when the addict has been identified by a narcological, neuropsychiatric dispensary or consulting room), or to the narcological, neuropsychiatric dispensary or consulting room (when the addict had been identified by internal affairs bodies). At WTP for drug addicts the internal regulations meet the requirements of isolation, labor reeducation and therapeutic measures. They are administered taking into account certain peculiarities characteristic of this group, like pronounced symptoms of physical and mental asthenia, reduced capacity to work, or a criminal anamnesis.

There are certain specific features in the WTP for women, since in the majority of inmates one observes an aggravated course, with noticeable deterioration of the personality, frequent shifts of mood, and a negative attitude to treatment. All this requires an attentive approach to questions of treatment and reeducation and particularly careful psychotherapy.

There are cases when criminal offenders are also alcoholics. When the court pronounces sentence on them it simultaneously rules on a term of compulsory treatment for alcoholism at a CLC. The principles of such treatment are similar to what has been described for the WTP, but it is conducted in combination with the strict regimen maintained in the colony.

The medical units of the preventoriums have outpatient and inpatient departments. The inmates are hospitalized upon admission for diagnosing their condition and prescribing treatment in cases of exacerbation or the onset of somatic diseases, or occasionally, for conducting alcoholism treatment.

The main course of treatment is given on an outpatient basis. For this purpose a physician and paramedical worker are attached to every so-called "detachment of inmates," and outpatient cards are maintained for everyone. The medical nurse must carefully maintain the file, regularly summon the inmates for treatment, visit the hostel and production shops, and help the physician in conducting observations over their charges.

Active treatment is conducted both in the inpatient and outpatient departments, for which permanent medical nurses are appointed. They must be capable of recognizing complications that may accompany treatment, for example, collapse, cardiac insufficiency, preinfarction states, vegetative crises, and others. The consulting rooms must be equipped with first-aid kits, and secondary medical workers must be able to administer first aid in cases of such conditions pending the arrival of the physician. An appointed medical nurse must undergo special training for serving in the hypnotherapy room.

It is advisable that feldshers concentrate their work along the following lines:

1. ensuring sanitary-hygienic standards in the dormitories, kitchen and canteen, laundry, the toilets, and production shops;

2. inculcating antialcoholism attitudes;

3. maintaining relations between self-ruled public organizations of the inmates and the dormitory councils; and

4. keeping in touch with the industrial enterprises from which the inmates came to the WTP and to which they are discharged after completing the course of treatment.

Exercises for Review

1. Diagram the narcological service and indicate the place of the basic institutions contributing to narcological care. Describe legal acts and legislation related to alcoholism questions, first of all, those related to compulsory treatment and expert examination. Define the functional duties of the secondary medical personnel of narcological institutions in the health system according to the work performed: of the feldsher-narcologist of the narcological station, of the uchastok, and of the visiting, treatment, ward and other medical nurses.

2. Learn how to regulate correctly and follow up the reg. f. 30-PS, 30-A-ps and other forms, following a model of five-year dynamic and therapeutic registration of alcoholics and drug addicts.

3. Visit, when available, a medical sobering-up station, a WTP of the USSR Ministry of Internal Affairs, a narcological institution attached to an industrial enterprise. Be familiar with the work of paramedical personnel and describe the functional duties of paramedical workers employed at these institutions.

CHAPTERS 4-8 QUESTIONS

1. Consider a feldsher-narcologist manning a narcological station of an industrial enterprise. Is he entitled to prescribe medical treatment to a newly identified alcoholic? What should be his proper tactics in such a situation?

2. While on hospital duty, a medical nurse finds out that one of the patients has been drinking alcohol. What measures should be taken?

3. A patient complains of poor sleep and constantly asks the attending nurse to administer a soporific at bedtime. No such prescription has been made by the doctor. What should be done?

4. During his third year of treatment at a narcological dispensary a patient went on a binge. What is the proper therapeutic tactics in regard to this patient? Into what registration group should the Reg. f. 30-PS be transferred?

5. A patient is undergoing treatment at a WTP of the USSR Ministry of Internal Affairs. Can the Reg. f. 30-A-PS be filled in for him and can he be stricken off the register?

6. A patient has missed an appointment at the narcological dispensary. What ought to be done by the treatment nurse?

7. A patient at work rejects supportive treatment. What should be done by the feldsher-narcologist of the narcological station, and on the basis of which legislation?

8. A feldsher-narcologist is employed at a narcological station. What are his contacts and relationships with the doctor-manned narcological consulting room and with the narcological post?

9. A patient has made his first visit to a narcological dispensary seeking medical care. What are the main things that should be explained to him first of all?

10. A client is brought to a sobering-up station for the first time; for the third time. What should be the attitude of the medical personnel in these two cases?

11. A patient has been admitted to a WTP. What are the tasks facing the medical workers?

12. A person is admitted for inpatient examination to decide on

further treatment at a WTP. He flatly denies any abuse of alcoholic beverages. What methods can be used to find out the truth?

13. During inpatient examination a liver disease has been diagnosed. Can this patient be sent to a WTP? If not, how is he to be treated?

PART THREE

CLINICAL ASPECTS

Chapter 9

Alcoholism

PROPERTIES OF ETHYL ALCOHOL

Ethyl alcohol (ethanol), chemical formula C_2H_5OH, appears as a transparent liquid with a sharp specific odor, readily miscible with water and organic solvents. The relative density of 95% alcohol is 0.808-0.812, its boiling point is 78°C, and it burns with a bluish flame. In medical practice ethanol is used as an external antiseptic and irritant.

Ethanol irritates the mucous membranes and the skin, rapidly penetrates them and is absorbed by the blood, while rendering an anesthetizing effect. It causes hyperemia and increased salivation in the oral cavity. In low concentrations it has an astringent effect, and in large doses, a caustic one.

ACUTE ALCOHOLIC INTOXICATION AND VARIANTS OF DRUNKENNESS

It should be stressed that the specific course and manifestations of different degrees of drunkenness frequently depend on the drinker's personal idiosyncrasies.

Three degrees of alcoholic intoxication are distinguished: (1) mild degree, or simple drunkenness; (2) medium degree, with inhibition of the higher portions of the central nervous system; and (3) severe, in which paralysis of central vegetative centers may occur.

A mild degree of drunkenness following the intake of alcohol is marked by excitation, a feeling of good cheer and euphoria, vigor and a sense of well-being; evaluation of reality and of relations between people is colored accordingly. Sorrow and worry are easily ignored. Anxiety and fear are suppressed, particularly feelings of agitation and tension, which points to the tranquillizing effect of alcohol. Alcoholic intoxication usually resembles a hypomanic state, in which, apart from increased cheerfulness, there is motor disinhibition, disturbance in coordination of movements and precision of actions, acceleration of the rate of thinking, and behavior is determined by the dominant affect. In this connection the cheerful drunk cannot refuse a request, becomes excessively kind and generous, is full of promises. He easily communicates and readily makes acquaintances. A person in the state of drunkenness is conspicuously verbose, seems to open up, and relates his experiences and adventures not infrequently with considerable swagger and exaggeration. He loses the sense of tact and discretion. The drunk, overestimating his potential, becomes boastful and commits rather rash actions. Often one observes affective instability in which euphoria is easily replaced by viciousness, aggressiveness or blubbering sentimentality; feelings of sympathy easily change into feelings of antipathy and hostility.

Dominant during this stage is a diminution of inherent differentiated inhibition which results in disinhibition of vital feelings; there is enhanced appetite and libido and more primitive emotionality. On the whole, the observed picture of drunkenness may be described as the *euphoric form of intoxication.* Dysphoric forms also occur, characterized by a predominantly bad mood, looking for trouble, aggressiveness, finding fault with everything, and suicidal thoughts and attempts.

There are many causes for this wide range of manifestations of simple alcoholic intoxication. The main cause, however, is personal peculiarities. Since alcohol reduces the capacity for active inhibition, it lays bare concealed traits of character. Various formerly experienced, exogenous-organic diseases are also significant, for they may lead to an atypical course of drunkenness, causing rapid intoxication. Also important is the mood and attitude at which alcohol intake takes place. In the case of a merrymaking occasion the onset of drunkenness comes sooner. When wishing to remain in control to preserve sobriety, the onset of drunkenness may be delayed.

Mixed or dysphoric variants of intoxication occur most frequently in chronic alcoholism. It is generally known that the rapidity of onset and depth of intoxication are influenced by the kind of alcoholic beverage used and its ethanol content. Lastly, a significant role in the development of alcoholic intoxication is played by the drinker's mental and physical state prior to alcohol intake.

Alcoholic intoxication of *medium degree* is characterized, first of all, by the inhibition of the higher portions of the central nervous system (CNS). Here we note general torpidity, a slower rate of thinking, an unstable gait. The drunkard's speech becomes dysarthric, with many repetitions. Disorientation in the surroundings may occur, with loss of control over one's own behavior, hence, cynical and abusive language, unconcealed sexuality, loss of any self-consciousness, and indecent exposure for physiological relief.

The *severe degree* of intoxication is a state when grave forms of clouded consciousness, including coma, may occur. In these conditions there may be spontaneous defecation and urination, and epileptiform seizures. Muscular hypotony frequently occurs, the temperature drops, and reflex reactions become extinguished. There may be mydriasis and pendular nystagmus, or even hypesthesia with complete disappearance of painful sensations. The skin becomes pale and cool. Pyramidal signs and oral automatisms may be revealed, the latter characteristic of alcoholic coma. Death may occur from the paralysis of the bulbar centers.

A number of tests are used for diagnosing acute alcoholic intoxication. Persons who have experienced severe states of drunkenness remember nothing about the event, remain asthenic for a long time, are adynamic, and show symptoms of ataxia, dysarthria, and vegetative disorders.

Alcohol disrupts intellectual-mnemic functions. It has been proven experimentally that 10-15 grams of pure alcohol interferes with the performance of various psychological tests, especially the understanding of instructions, remembering and counting. Intoxication is marked by diminishing capacity for calculations; the weakening of combinatory associative processes, visual and auditory comprehension; and the speed of responses.

After the intake of large doses of alcohol the period of simple alcoholic intoxication lasts from 6 or 7 to 12 hours. After intoxication and depending on its degree, there is an onset of amnesia—"alcoholic palimpsests," "patchy memory." Besides, there is asthenia, headache, subdepression, etc. Naturally, the degree of intoxication is determined by the physical and mental status of the drinker, his temperament and tolerance.

A number of somatoneurologic disorders are observed in alcoholism, primarily disturbed coordination, and during further intoxication, automated actions. Handwriting becomes altered and speech becomes unintelligible and blurred, with the omission of the last sounds in words. The gait is unsteady, there is giddiness, particularly in the supine position, with such an objective symptom as nystagmus, whose intensity is directly proportional to the degree of intoxication. Cornea sensibility is reduced, just as is pupillary response to light. Hypesthesias and analgesias may occur.

Considerably altered, depending on the state of drunkenness, is the action threshold of stimulants. The sensations of smell and taste, of heat and cold are dulled, just as the perception of visual and auditory stimulants are. The period of adaptation lengthens, color vision is disturbed, and visual perception in the twilight and of weak color contrasts is impaired, which not infrequently results in motor accidents.

Vascular-vegetative changes are expressed in the predominance of the sympathetic or parasympathetic systems, depending on the constitution. They are manifested in facial hyperemia, a sensation of heat, dilation of peripheral vessels, tachycardia, rise of arterial pressure, more rapid respiratory rate, and later, its slowing. There is increased secretion by salivary and alimentary glands and increased intestinal peristalsis and diuresis.

Atypical variants of intoxication, or complicated intoxication occur in psychopathic individuals, in persons with organic deficiency, and also in parallel with the formation of pronounced stages of chronic alcoholism. In complicated intoxication, vital excitation attains a high degree and is combined with changes of consciousness (stupefaction). The chief affective background is lasting irritability and viciousness, a tendency toward aggression and self-injury. Hysterical behavior with functional fits is also possible. Sometimes there are fragmentary delusions and hallucinations.

Pathologic intoxication is a rare and short-lived, acute psychotic state. It is characterized by the sudden onset of deep disorders of consciousness resembling epileptic twilight mental disorder. Pathologic intoxication occurs after the intake of a small amount of an alcoholic beverage, or more often, against the background of medium-stage intoxication. Here, objective symptoms of intoxication disappear (walking and speech without change), and behavior is determined by inner psychotic impulsive motivations and feelings of anxiety and fear, which may be replaced by wrath and frenzied hatred. These reactions arise because of delirious and hallucinatory experiences. Sometimes the patients' actions in a state of pathologic intoxication lack purposefulness and manifest themselves in the form of pointless acts of attack, defense or escape, resulting in grave cases of antisocial actions. Such actions are committed either with shouting and stereotypic utterances of one and the same words, or in concentrated silence. Twilight, delirious, hallucinatory-paranoid and manic forms are distinguished. In some cases antisocial actions are committed, uncharacteristic of the person when sober.

Alcoholism is a dynamic process with its beginning course and terminal state. As a disease, alcoholism takes shape gradually, by degrees, often quite unnoticeable to other people and the would-be alcoholic himself. This is a period of simple or habitual drunkenness, when alcohol is used from occasion to occasion, but more frequently, in large quantities. Here the drinker seeks pleasure, takes alcohol with increasing frequency, but still periodically, though cases of loss of control over the alcohol intake already occur. Vomiting in the state of drunkenness is not infrequent, yet the vomiting reflex diminishes with time, which is one of the signs pointing to the onset of the disease.

Simple drunkenness in different people proceeds differently, lasting on an average from 5 to 10 years, beginning in males more frequently at an age between 20 and 30 years, and in women between 25 and 35 years. It has been proven that when drinking starts before the age of 20, or strong beverages are used more frequently, the first stage of alcoholism begins at an earlier date and proceeds more malignantly.

At present alcoholism is subdivided into three stages: stage I—initial, mild, neurasthenic; stage II—medium; stage III—terminal, severe, encephalopathic. Of the many existing classifications, the one given below is the most widespread and appears in all the report documents.

Marked changes take place in the human organism throughout the three stages, each having its own regularities in course and prognosis and affecting certain systems, tissues and organs. Among such general dynamic symptoms of alcoholism is the formation and development of mental habituation to alcohol, the establishment and dynamics of physical dependence, changes in reactivity to alcohol intake, disorders of the mental sphere, and pathological changes in the somatic and neurological spheres.

By taking into account the general dynamic symptoms, the first stage may be represented as follows. Its beginning coincides with the disappearance of the defensive vomiting reflex.

Alcoholism, Stage I
(Initial, Mild, Neurasthenic)

1. Mental dependence on alcohol occurs in the form of an obsessive syndrome, leading to diminution of control over the quantity of alcohol consumed.

2. There is no physical craving for alcohol.

3. Reactivity to alcohol undergoes change, expressed in a growing tolerance, altered forms of drunkenness, most frequently observed in the form of palimpsests and going from episodic to systematic alcohol use.

4. A neurasthenic syndrome forms with initial manifestations of disorder in the mental sphere.

5. Somatic symptoms may occur, such as loss of appetite, short-lived gastrointestinal disorders, unpleasant sensations and pain in individual organs. Noted on the part of the CNS are insomnia and vegetative peripheral disorders of the nervous system in the form of local neurites.

Mental craving for alcohol is manifested in the form of an obsessive syndrome. By this is meant the appearance of an obsessive desire to have a drink. Most frequently such desire stems from situational causes (family quarrels, mishaps at work, misfortunes, etc.) or shifts of mood. There is no physical craving for alcohol at this stage of the disease. Alcohol intake is more or less systematic, with an increase of the dose drunk (taken three to five times), but without gross symptoms of intoxication. At the same time, control over the quantity of alcohol drunk is lowered, i.e., there is a rise of tolerance (stability) to alcohol. This points to a change in the body's reactivity, also testified by more frequent palimpsests (forgetfulness regarding individual episodes).

The neurasthenic syndrome is expressed in vegetative-vascular symptoms, neurasthenic and asthenic symptoms and some exacerbation of particular character traits which will lead in the future to pronounced psychopathic manifestations. For the time being, however, individual character traits undergo change.

Persons with stage I alcoholism complain of periodic unpleasant sensations in various parts of the body, pains, or gastrointestinal disorders. Neurological observations reveal higher tendon and periosteal reflexes, sweating, and local neuritis.

Case Illustration Patient: Male, age 23. *Anamnesis*: The patient revealed a normal heredity and an early development without peculiarities. He finished 8th grade, then attended trade school. While studying there in a company of friends he began using alcoholic drinks. He tolerated the drinks well and experienced a pleasant state of well-being and good cheer. When training at the trading school failed to satisfy him, he attended classes unwillingly and often received bad marks. At home he began to have conflicts with his parents because of poor progress at the school. After an intake of alcohol he felt more capable and mishaps seemed easy to overcome. He kept the use of alcohol a secret from the parents. There were periods when he took drinks several days in a row, after which he could abstain for a long time. Yet he began noticing a craving for alcohol in order to improve his mood and forget his troubles. He drank mostly wine, and could drink one and a half to two bottles an evening. Occasionally on the next day he could not remember individual events of the drinking party. He became irritable, with frequent shifts of mood, and tired easily. He would loaf about, unwilling to do anything, but all symptoms disappeared after taking a drink. Upon finishing the trade school he worked as a mason, occasionally absenting himself for one to two days. His craving for alcohol was noticed at work. The Commission for Combating Drunkenness sent him for alcoholism treatment. His somatic and neurological stages were without peculiarities, and only occasionally did he complain of unpleasant sensations in the region of the stomach.

On admission the patient was torpid, listless, and slightly depressed by hospitalization. He recognized his craving for alcoholic drinks, willingly talked about himself and his alcohol use, and was willing to cooperate in treatment.

The following case demonstrates how episodes of alcohol use become more systematic under the influence of various external factors.

The second stage of alcoholism develops six to eight years after the beginning of alcohol abuse.

Alcoholism, Stage II

1. Mental dependence of an obsessive character with loss of control over the quantity of alcohol consumed and with striving for physical comfort.

2. Physical craving manifested by compulsive attraction to alcohol, the presence of the abstinence syndrome, expressed mainly in the somatovegetative aspect, and the need for physical comfort.

3. Changes in the reactivity to alcohol are expressed as the establishment of maximum tolerance, the appearance of amnesias and a change in the physiological effect of alcohol, in systematic intake and pseudo-dipsomaniacal excesses.

4. The neurasthenic syndrome may persist with gradual formation of the syndrome of personality diminution, the exacerbation or appearance of new forms of psychopathic behavior (asthenic, hysterical, explosive, apathetic).

5. Various somatic diseases of the internal organs (gastritis, hepatitis) and systems (cardiovascular, respiratory, urogenital) reveal themselves. Disorders of vegetative functions, polyneurites, and cerebellar and other cerebral syndromes become noticeable.

As the disease goes over from one stage to another, the former symptoms exacerbate, become more gross, only gradually taking shape and being transformed into a new quality. Thus, along with the obsessive attraction to alcohol there appears a compulsion to drink it, while the striving for pleasure of the first stage gives way to the need to obtain a sensation of physical comfort. This is accompanied by the final loss of control over the quantity of the alcohol consumed, the intake of which becomes now systematic. Simultaneously there is growing tolerance to ethanol, and over a certain period of time (two to three years) a peculiar tolerance plateau sets in. This differs according to the individual features of the personality concerned.

The physiological effect of alcohol changes at this stage, gradually leading to pseudo-dipsomaniacal states. The drunkard can physically still consume alcohol, but intermittently—a little in the morning, the same at lunch time, and only by evening can he get excessively drunk. Single palimpsests are replaced by deeper and longer amnesias.

A leading criterion in the second stage is the appearance of physical craving and the abstinence (hangover) syndrome, as described by the Soviet scholar S. G. Zhislin in 1934. It is based on the fact that an alcoholic, as a result of intoxication, develops a permanent need to replenish the organism with certain portions of alcoholic drinks (to obtain physical comfort). Otherwise, a peculiar "hunger" sets in that is expressed in different ways and is at times very severe, with disorders of the cardiovascular and vegetative systems and the gastrointestinal tract. Zhislin regarded the abstinence syndrome as a "minor alcoholic psychosis." Alcoholics tell us that on the morning after heavy drinking they note a lower or higher pulse rate, vomiting, diarrhea, headache, weakness, tremor of the hands and legs; they break out in a cold sweat, then are shaken by strong fever. This is called the so-matovegetative component of the abstinence syndrome. Added to this toward the end of the second and at the beginning of the third stage is a psychic component.

When the hangover syndrome appears it may be removed by non-specific remedies, for example, yoghurt, tomato juice, cucumber or such invigorating procedures as a shower or a bath. But after some time this no longer helps. The only palliative is alcohol. The hangover syndrome is very stable. Treatment may remove it completely or sup-press it but as soon as alcohol is resumed it appears again, even after lasting periods of temperance.

The neurasthenic syndrome persists for some time with gradual changes in the personality, which can be thought of as psychopathic alteration (hysterical, asthenic, explosive or apathetic). Characteristic of the sick person are groundless shifts of mood and outbreaks of irritation. Such individuals like to show off and become boastful. Mood rapidly fluctuates from euphoria to dysphoria. One frequently en-counters alcoholics whose behavior is characterized by a predomi-nantly low-key mood, increased fatigability, irritability and torpidity. They find it difficult to fall asleep and at times are very touchy. These are so-called "asthenic" personalities. They are persons whose behav-ior is characterized by rapid transitions from benevolence and ground-less hilarity to viciousness and wrath. These are difficult people whose behavior at work and in the family makes their own existence and the life of other people intolerable.

Some alcoholics are distinguished in that they lose all interest in their surroundings, become indifferent to their own families and to themselves. This is the "apathetic" form of pathological development of personality.

Somatic diseases, if present, become more severe, and more pro-nounced neurological symptoms also build up in the form of poly-neurites, cerebellar and other cerebral syndromes. It is at this stage in the disease that psychoses may arise.

Case Illustration Patient: Male, age 30, a high-altitude construction worker who was admitted on October 5, 1977, and discharged on

November 20, 1977. *Anamnesis*: The patient's father was alcoholic, but the patient grew up and developed normally, went to school at age seven and showed good progress till the fifth grade. Then his progress diminished, he transferred to night school and began to drink in company. He finished school with difficulty. Working as a fitter, his drinking became more frequent until he could drink not only in company but alone, and his intake of alcoholic beverages reached 1-1.5 liters a day. He lost control over the quantity ingested after the first few drinks, and drinking bouts appeared that lasted from two to three days to several weeks. After being absent he reported for work in a nonsober state and was reprimanded by the management. However, he continued to abuse alcohol. He changed several jobs, never working for long at one place. He became irritable, engaged in conflicts, got involved in a scandal in a state of drunkenness and was punished by 15 days' deprivation of liberty. After heavy drinking he suffered from headaches, nausea, vomiting, poor appetite, torpidity, and lack of interest in his surroundings. This is a smoothing symptom following alcohol intake. He frequently failed to remember events preceding drinking and was demoted to unskilled worker, but although he made several attempts to give up drinking he could not hold out for more than a week. He constantly felt a strong craving for alcohol and landed in a medical sobering-up station unable to remember the circumstances that led him there. On the insistence of the management he was sent for inpatient treatment.

Physical status: Symptoms include increased sweatiness, heart tones rhythmical but dulled, tachycardia, pulse rate 100 per minute, and tongue covered with brown coating. There is no pathology on the part of the CNS. He shows defused red dermographism and pronounced tremor of entire body. *Mental status*: All types of orientation are preserved. His mood is subdued, but he is discontented over hospitalization. When talking to the physician he is disrespectful, abusive, and at times irritable, rude. Criticism is absent.

Summary: This patient's case history shows that alcoholism of stage II developed in a short period of time. This can be explained by early initiation to alcohol. Subsequently he had a pronounced abstinence syndrome, drinking binge, and some personality changes.

The severest form of alcoholism is stage III. It develops eight to nine years after the beginning of alcohol abuse.

Alcoholism, Stage III
(Terminal, Severe, Encephalopathic)

1. Psychic craving for alcohol is due to the need for psychic comfort. Quantitative control is lost, and craving is compulsive.

2. Physical craving is expressed in the need to overcome physical discomfort, particularly manifest in the presence of the abstinence syndrome which expands with the inclusion, in addition to the somatovegetative component, of the psychic one. The craving for alcohol is still impulsive.

3. Reactivity of the organism continues to change; tolerance diminishes and apart from pseudo-dipsomania, there are genuine dipsomaniacal episodes or systematic heavy drinking with low tolerance and absence of situational control.

4. There is a further reduction of personality with noticeable changes of intellectual-mnemic functions. Dementia cancels out individual mental personal traits. Psychoses frequently arise.

5. Somatically, individual organs and systems are certainly affected, in some cases irreversibly (e.g., cirrhosis of the liver, cardiovascular insufficiency). Neurological symptoms exacerbate and there may appear systemic disorders and cerebral syndromes (e.g., Wernicke's disease). Complications are expressed in the form of psychoses.

The syndrome of psychic craving for alcohol changes at the expense of the deepening and increasing physical dependence. The abstinence syndrome expands through the appearance of the psychic component. Alcohol consumption is of the character of true dipsomanias: 3-4 days of continuous drinking of alcoholic beverages with 10-15 days of a so-called "bright interval." It may be the other way around. Dipsomania always begins with the compulsion to drink, while tolerance, particularly daily tolerance, diminishes. The alcoholic drinks the beverages in order to regain physical comfort or at least to remove the depressing sensations of general weakness, malaise and guilt, and rapidly becomes drunk, reaching states of severe intoxication. Inferior substitutes are most frequently used since lesser quantities can produce a higher effect of drunkenness. Amnesias are virtually constant, deep and stable.

Intellectual-mnemic disorders progress. The alcoholic loses interest in social life, becomes indifferent to work and very frequently loses his job, resulting in a parasitic mode of life; in addition, the family, as a rule, falls apart. Alcoholics lose their individuality and pronounced psychopathic manifestations become obliterated, so that most stage III alcoholics resemble one another. They are despondent, indifferent to the surrounding life, and are only interested in satisfying their need for alcohol; in essence, they are demented.

Two kinds of such dementia are distinguished. The first kind initially resembles the "explosive" form of psychopathy, with raging anger and excitability at the least pretext. All these proceed against a background of recklessness and elements of faintheartedness, verbosity and feeble humor.

The second kind is torpid, characterized by apathy and indifference, and sometimes, by a euphoric attitude to the surroundings.

During the third stage of the disease organic symptoms of dementia become noticeable—deterioration of memory and critical faculties, as well as general changes in personality make-up. Psychoses have been recorded in 13% of cases.

Somatically, a general diminution of the organism's resistance is revealed, as a result of which these individuals most frequently die of various intercurrent diseases (e.g., influenza, pneumonia). The diseases of the internal organs and systems are of a chronic and hardly reversible character (e.g., gastric ulcer, cirrhosis, myocardial infarction). On the part of the nervous system, in addition to mental symptoms, grosser ones are observed in the form of movement coordination disorders, strokes, thromboses of cerebral vessels, and vascular crises with subsequent paralyses and pareses.

Case Illustration Patient: **Male**, age 33, employed as a fitter. *Anamnesis*: heredity normal. The father abandoned the family, and the mother brought up the two children, working frequently. The boy grew up without adequate attention and was often left to his own devices. His early development was without peculiarities, but his school progress was poor. He preferred the company of street children with whom he began drinking for the first time, the alcohol being provided by the elder children. He developed a liking for card-playing, losing or winning always considered an occasion for a drink. He concealed the money from his mother. Having finished seven grades with difficulty, he entered an apprenticeship and then worked as a fitter. He continued alcohol abuse, drinking to excess. Due to his absence from work, he was reprimanded by the management. Despite these problems he married and had a child. But there were frequent family quarrels because of drinking and neglect of the family including drinking away his wages and finally, going on a binge for nearly a month. Lucid intervals lasted one to two days. He began to use substitutes, such as eau-de-cologne, and drank small quantities, but constantly. He experienced constant craving for alcohol, lost quantitative control over his alcoholic intake, could not remember anything that happened when drunk. He was frequently delivered to a medical sobering-up station, and occasionally, spent the night outdoors. He began to sell family belongings and begged for money from acquaintances to buy a drink. After divorcing his wife, he drank every day and stopped working. Character changes occurred—angry outbursts, irritability and finding fault with everything. In addition, he repeatedly served 15-day terms of detention for hooliganism. He became absolutely indifferent, with no interests apart from procuring a drink, could not sleep at night, experienced fear, kept looking under the bed and hiding from someone. At this point, he was admitted to a mental hospital.

Physical status: Examination revealed tremor of the entire body, puffy face, scleral induration, and dry, brown-coated tongue. Heart sounds were dull, there was increased heart rate of 120 per minute, and his liver 2 cm below the costal arch. His tendon reflexes uniformly increased, with slight rocking in Romberg's posture. *Mental status*: Orientation was intact. He appeared anxious, kept listening to something and looking around, but his mood was subdued. Although unsociable, he answered questions correctly. He heard his name called and asked neighbors whether they heard it, too. He revealed no critical attitude to his disease.

Summary: This case is distinguished for the rapid sequel of syndromes and the appearance of stage III alcoholism symptoms, with dipsomanias, reduced tolerance, deterioration of personality, and mental disorder.

Thus, alcoholism, just as any other disease, is dynamic, with its own regularities in the sequence of syndromes; the presence of one syndrome, for example, psychic or physical craving for alcohol, cannot take shape separately. The presence of several symptoms is necessary for diagnosis.

Strelchuk distinguishes several types of alcoholism. The first type is characterized by continuous and systematic alcohol intake. The second type has a periodical, cyclic course with bright intervals. The third type is pseudo-dipsomaniacal and proceeds according to the drinking-binge type. The continuous and periodical types occur during every developmental stage of alcoholism. The third type occurs only during the second and third stages.

Chapter 10

Etiology, Pathogenesis and Classification of Alcoholism

Alcohol is, ipso facto, an etiological factor of alcoholism. Alcohol is used by millions of people, yet only 3 to 6% succumb to alcoholism. Alcohol alone, therefore, is not enough for the appearance of the disease; some other additional factors are needed for the onset of alcoholism. Most scientists regard such factors as being social, psychological and physiological. Social factors constitute a whole complex among which one should take into account education, family status, financial status, the individual's position in society, the attitude of the state to alcoholism, etc.

It was formerly believed that drinkers were generally semiliterate people. Recent studies have demonstrated, however, that highly educated people also consume alcoholic beverages. This is prompted by drinking habits and traditions in which friendly reunions and celebrations are habitually accompanied by the drinking of alcoholic beverages. Statistics show that the majority of alcoholics are single and divorced people. It is also known that husbands frequently entice their wives into drinking, and wives, their husbands. Material status in all probability has a role to play at the initial stages of alcoholism, but subsequently, as the disease keeps developing and there are changes in the individual's status in society (slipping down the social ladder with a loss or reduction of income), the alcohol intake does not diminish, although the quality and prices of the beverages do.

110

Of certain significance is the policy of the state in regard to the consumption of alcohol; the more rigid and intransigent the policy, the more difficult it becomes for individuals to become attracted to alcohol. The policy of a country most frequently depends on national traditions (for example, Japanese, Chinese, and Jews drink less than other nationalities) and religious attitudes. Thus, among Moslems, Protestants and some other religious sects, alcohol use is prohibited while, for example, the Russian Orthodox Church itself and its priests, as well as some of its rites, could be said to give impetus to the use of alcoholic beverages.

Psychological factors are also important in the development of alcoholism. Alcohol evokes a feeling of pleasure or euphoria, as well as a state of relaxation or relief. The former property induces a certain group of people toward alcohol as a means of having a good time, of deriving pleasure, of drinking alcohol "to relieve boredom," etc. These are primitive persons, with low interests, unable to find a worthy pastime or accustomed to easily available pleasures. In the latter case, we have individuals who, confronted with a difficult situation and unable to cope with it, seek oblivion in alcohol, a sense of tranquility and an "easy-does-it" approach to life, if only for a time. Of great importance here is the moulding of the personality and the upbringing given the individual in the family and at school; in some cases an individual is accustomed to, and therefore demands, easy pleasure or is so cosseted and overprotected that he is unable to stand up to life's misfortunes.

Some persons, with a distorted perception of the surrounding world, excuse their drinking by being occupationally involved in the sphere of the manufacture, storage or sale of alcoholic beverages. In a number of cases underlying alcoholism in children and teenagers is the wish to imitate their elders; at other times it is a protest against a downtrodden and uninteresting life. A certain proportion of alcohol abusers are psychopathic personalities or mentally ill.

In the ancient past people presumed that from alcoholic parents could be born children with various physical deformities, imbeciles, epileptics, and those who eventually become alcoholics. In the view of some scientists, alcohol may affect the metabolism in the fetal organism which subsequently results in a particular susceptibility to ethanol. Thus, genetic factors do play a predisposing role in the development of alcoholism.

In the genesis of alcoholism great importance is attributed to metabolic disorders. In particular, this concerns a pathologic balance of group B vitamins and vitamin C. Chlorine-sodium imbalance in the blood is also recognized as important. Bearing in mind the frequent shifts in mood observed in alcohol abusers, it is suggested that great significance in the etiology of alcoholism be attached to adrenaline-adrenochrome imbalance.

The recognition of biochemical disorders as an etiological factor is far from universal. Some scientists believe that the changes that take place during the development of alcoholism are the consequence of the disease rather than its cause, i.e., are factors of a pathogenetic character. Of certain importance is the individual's higher nervous activity and temperament. Some people are very sociable and enjoy company, while others, on the contrary, prefer solitude; yet, both may become attracted to alcohol with entirely different motives. In the former, there may be a striving to communicate, whereas in the latter, an attempt to relieve loneliness.

Studies are presently being made into the pathogenesis of alcoholism. Its mechanism is not yet very clear, but one may imagine several basic trends in studying the question. The main symptoms characterizing alcoholism are psychic dependence or a striving toward euphoria, and physical dependence or a striving for physical comfort. The striving toward euphoria indirectly points to an initial background of low-key mood. In chronic alcoholism alcohol's euphorizing effect is diminished, which makes it necessary to ingest additional alcohol doses; in other words, it results in loss of control over the quantity of alcohol consumed.

As the latest investigations have shown, nearly all the alcohol intake is metabolized with the participation of special enzymes present in the human organism and partially produced by the liver. In alcoholism this process is disrupted, just as is the metabolism of biogenic amines. Such substances as noradrenaline undergo serious changes, particularly in the brain and hypothalamus. In the pathogenesis of alcoholism, great importance is attached to disorders of vitamin metabolism (vitamin B_1), and the fluctuation of blood sugar (hyper- and hypoglycemia), which cause a kind of "hunger," in particular, for ethanol, which, in turn, bring about secondary alcoholization. Certain attention is given to the functioning of the vegetative nervous system with the alternately predominant action of its sympathetic and parasympathetic systems. Coming recently to the fore in the pathogenesis of alcoholism are investigations into factors of natural and artificial immunity that may possibly induce an increased production of morphine-like substances, leading to the development of physical dependence.

The chief characteristic of physical dependence is the abstinence (hangover) syndrome. It sets in after recovering from alcoholic in-

TABLE 3
USSR Classification System

Designation of Disease	International Classification Number
Alcoholic psychoses,	292
including:	
alcoholic deliria	291.0
alcoholic hallucinoses	291.2
alcoholic paranoia	291.3
other alcoholic psychoses	
(alcoholic encephalopathy,	
Korsakoff's polyneuritic syndrome,	
Wernicke's disease) and other	
undefined psychoses	291.9
Intoxication psychoses:	
in narcomanias	294.32
in toxicomanias	—
Alcoholism:	303
stage I	303.14
stage II	303.21
stage III	303
Other manifestations of alcoholism	303.9
Toxicomanias, narcomanias	304

toxication or drinking-binge and is frequently tinged with depression. This suggests that the abstinence syndrome is based on pharmaco- genic depression, frequently camouflaged by various somatic and re- active disorders. The desire to remove anxiety, low-key mood, sleeplessness, suicidal thoughts, or such somatic symptoms as feeling worn out or having painful sensations, compels toward repeated al- cohol intake. Underlying this phenomenon is the following: Appar- ently at the time of hangover (depression) there is an accumulation of acetaldehydes (it is known that acetaldehydes are 5-10 times stronger than ethanol) or a depletion of biogenic amines; through the mechanism of antagonism the consumed alcohol arrests the effect of acetaldehyde, improving the mood and creating a feeling of physical comfort.

Different classifications for alcoholism, narcomanias and toxico- manias have been suggested over the years. The following classifi- cation are the ones now used in registration and report documents (see Table 3).

The classification of alcoholism, toxicomanias and narcomanias adopted in the USSR differs substantially from the classification rec- ommended by the World Health Organization.

Chapter 11

Alcoholism as Related to Age

In antiquity, the ancient Greeks prohibited the use of alcohol during a wedding. They believed that after drinking the newlyweds might conceive defective children.

At the beginning of the 20th century the French professor Demmé studied ten nonalcoholic families and ten in which the fathers and mothers were alcoholics and there were drunkards among the closest relatives. The results are shown in Table 4.

The French physician Bourneville wrote that out of 1,000 idiots

TABLE 4
Comparison of Alcoholic and Nonalcoholic Families

Observation Made	Children of Temperate Parents	Children of Alcoholic Parents
Died at an early age	5	12
Mentally retarded	2	8 (idiots)
Epileptics	—	13
Deaf and dumb, deformed, dwarfs	2	10
Nervous disorders	2	5
Healthy	50	9
Total	61	57

supported by public charity, the overwhelming majority were conceived toward the end of the grape harvest, Christmas festivals and
carnivals, when the population was particularly given to drinking. The
majority of demented children suffering from epileptic seizures were
children whose mental retardation was associated with their parents'
alcoholism or their drunkenness at the moment of conception.

Soviet scientists have investigated the pregnancy and delivery in
alcoholic mothers. Their results were as follows: premature delivery
34.5%, toxicosis of pregnancy 26%, stillbirths 25.5%, physical weakness 19%, asphyxia 12.5%, difficult and pathological delivery 10.5%,
birth injury 8%, and physical deformity at birth 3%. Thus, the harmful
effects of alcohol on descendants is obvious. An examination of large
groups of alcoholics (up to 8,000) demonstrated that 38.4% had a
pathological heredity.

Still more impressive data were obtained by I. V. Strelchuk (1973).
In the families of 1,974 examined patients, chronic alcoholism was
identified in 71.3% of the fathers and 10% of the mothers, or in
81.3% of all cases. These data proved irrefutably that the risk of
contracting alcoholism during a lifetime in families with aggravated
heredity is higher than in healthy families, and on the average comes
to 3-5% for males and 0.1-1% for females.

Clinical and epidemiological findings have been confirmed by experimental studies in different animals and birds. Alcohol was given
together with their food to rats over a period of 8-12 months. As a
result, the amount of alcohol in the ovaries of the females became
equal to its content in the liver, while the ovarian tissue itself steeply
changed. Seven generations of mice were fed foods containing alcohol. The number of stillborn, deformed and weak animals in the
progeny markedly increased, many of them dying soon after birth.
Similar investigations in guinea pigs demonstrated that 54 out of 88
newborn piglets died at once after birth.

Tests in which chicken eggs were exposed to alcohol fumes demonstrated that only 80 chicks hatched from 160 eggs, and of these 40
died and 25 were deformed.

It is well known that only one hour after the intake of medium
doses of alcohol, it may be detected in the sperm of males and in the

ovaries of females. Therefore, upon the fusion of the male and female sexual cells poisoned with alcohol, the result will be a defective embryo. It has been proved that drunkenness of the would-be mother at the moment of conception is the most dangerous.

Chronic alcohol use harmfully affects the activity of sexual glands both in males and females. These glands are functioning relatively normally on the average in only 10% of chronic alcoholics, while in 50 to 60%, complete atrophy occurs.

It has been established that children of alcoholics have a special physiological vulnerability or intolerance to alcohol, i.e., increased demand for and sensitivity to alcohol, just as in some people there is a hereditary impartiality to salt, sugar, and other food products. In such persons, even rare use of alcohol may quickly induce the formation of characteristic symptoms of chronic alcoholism: habituation or the hangover syndrome; psychoses with grave consequences may appear in shorter periods after initiation to alcohol.

All this prompts the question: do chronic alcoholics have the moral right to have children? Yes, they do, but only if they stay off alcohol for at least three to five years before conception.

No less important is the period of pregnancy. During gestation when the fetus is completely nourished by the mother, it is absolutely inadmissible to use alcohol; it not only intoxicates the organism of the would-be mother, but to a still greater degree, the unborn baby. Hence the considerable number of premature, stillborn, physically and mentally defective children of drinking mothers. Two examples follow:

(1) N. gave birth to a premature child. The baby weighed 1,600 grams. Because of an inadequate suckling stimulus and frequent refusal of the breast, the baby put on weight slowly and growth was retarded. It began to sit up only by the age of one year and to speak by the age of four. At five years it contracted a severe form of influenza and died. Examination indicated that heredity was not aggravated, but during her pregnancy the mother had developed a craving for homemade beer and continued to drink it while breastfeeding the baby. Upon reconsideration, she started treatment and recovered from her alcoholism, but upon the loss of her baby she was no longer able to bear a child.

(2) A healthy infant weighing 3,600 grams was born into the family of P. The suckling stimulus was adequate and there were no abnormalities in the child's physical and mental development. However, the infant's mother, disregarding advice and admonitions against drinking during breastfeeding, used alcohol in the form of beer in order to produce more milk, and vodka or wine to cheer her up. As a result the boy began lagging behind in development. At six years old he looked like a three to four-year-old child. He was small, thin, slow-moving, uninterested in toys, and would sit silently all day long in a corner.

In distinction from mature age, the development of alcoholism in teenagers and youths proceeds about three times faster, taking from three to four years only, i.e., the process goes on rapidly from the first use of alcoholic beverages to pronounced symptoms of the alcoholic disease. The development rate of alcoholism is influenced by external factors: unfavorable surroundings (family, friends), negative customs and traditions. In the early beginnings of alcohol use, personality and character traits of the teenager or youth and physiological features of the organism are all of great importance.

It is known that the growing child experiences several age crises (stages) when deviations from normal development may be thwarted by presumably trivial causes, e.g., poor nutrition, infectious diseases, or intoxications (e.g., intoxication with alcohol, nicotine), The first crisis occurs at the age of 3-4 years, when the child's brain is not yet anatomically and functionally mature; the second at the age of 7-8, when the nerve cells of the cortex do not practically differ in any way from adults; the third extends in girls from 8 to 17 years and in boys from 10 to 19 years, when cerebral tissue completely develops and sexual maturity occurs. (The last 3-5 years of this time is also called the pubertal period.)

The unhealthy atmosphere pervading the families in which the father or mother drinks influences the immature nervous system of the child. Susceptible to their surroundings, still unable to correctly assess what is happening, children at times perceive their parents' behavior as an example to emulate. In such situations, in addition to witnessing the improper behavior of the father or mother, they not infrequently become the victims of beatings and scandals. In this connection, treatment has to be given to terrorized children who stutter or complain of loss of appetite or, on the contrary, are disinhibited and easily excitable.

The physiological features of the age crises in the pubertal period are a kind of fertile ground for the rapid development of alcoholism. The degree of alcoholism, the frequency, doses, concentration of the alcoholic beverages and reactions of the organism to alcohol intake are also significant.

It is believed that alcoholism more readily develops in teenagers and youths when their personality has been changed by cerebral injury, organic lesion of the CNS, psychopathies, etc. In these cases alcoholism develops more intensively and proceeds more perniciously, rapidly leading to the loss of quantitative control and the appearance of a craving for alcohol, to the development of the hangover syndrome. An aggravation of pathological character traits takes place, and subsequently, such children easily resort to alcohol whenever difficult situations are encountered.

The symptoms of alcoholism in young people may have some peculiarities: the hangover syndrome is of a flickering character, i.e., it may appear after the ingestion of large alcohol doses, is of shorter duration than in adult alcoholics, and is manifested by mildly pronounced somatovegetative disorders.

Personality changes reveal themselves in the affective-volitional sphere, i.e., they evolve according to the psychopathic-like type. Thinking becomes more superficial, with a diminution of judgment and an overestimation of one's own abilities. Developing more frequently than in adults are spastic seizures and alcoholic psychoses. Not infrequently the psychotic changes imitate the schizophrenic process. Youths become cruel, rude, lose contact with their relatives and lose interest in their family. However, upon the discontinuation of alcohol these symptoms may become obliterated or disappear altogether, which points to their alcoholic, not schizophrenic nature. Rapidly developing at this age are symptoms of vitamin imbalance, particularly of the B vitamins group, the early appearance of atherosclerosis of cerebral and retinal vessels, and possible neuralgia of the auditory and facial nerves.

Case Illustration Patient: Male, age 23. *Anamnesis*: heredity unaggravated by mental diseases or alcoholism. The patient started taking alcoholic beverages from the age of 11-12. After finishing seven years of schooling he started working and quickly became accustomed to alcohol, looking for any pretext to have a drink. He soon became extremely irritable, irascible and quarrelsome, and repeatedly found himself in sobering-up stations. The hangover syndrome developed quickly; chronic, stage II alcoholism was diagnosed at the age of 15. He served two years in detention for disorderly conduct. After his release he was employed in timber felling. There he continued to drink, with bouts lasting 10-20 days during which time he was absent from work. He changed employment repeatedly and was sentenced to another year for parasitism. He continued to indulge in heavy drinking systematically. Toward the end of April (the month he was released from prison), he was without drink for two days because he had no money. He slept badly, had nightmares, then began to hear voices, some of abuse, others of protection. Vision became strangely keen. Through the crossed fingers of his hands he could see the surrounding objects as if the hands were transparent. At night he observed horrible beasts, people with deformed faces. Then it seemed to him that he was led to be shot but he escaped his persecutors. He found himself at a railway station. Obeying orders from the voices he jumped into a moving carriage of a departing train, getting off at another station. The voices constantly pursued him. Suddenly he heard the voice of God ordering him to kill somebody. Obeying the order he ran up to a 10-year-old girl and nearly killed her with a bottle, but God averted the murder saying, "Do not kill a child." The girl's shouts attracted people who beat him up; an ambulance and the militia were summoned and he was taken to hospital. In this case early initiation to alcohol led to a rapid development of stage III alcoholism, then to changes of personality, and subsequently, to psychosis.

When developing at a later age, after 45-50 years, alcoholism also has its peculiarities. By this time, the alcoholic's anamnesis is, as a rule, aggravated by a number of somatic diseases: atherosclerosis, cardiovascular insufficiency, metabolic disorders, and the waning function of endocrine glands. These frequently prove to be contributing factors in the development of the clinical picture of alcoholism. At this age the different stages of alcoholism develop at a fast rate. The hangover syndrome, reduced tolerance, and changes of personality consistent with the alcoholic type develop within 3-4 years. These changes in turn may be aggravated by vascular atherosclerosis, craniocerebral injuries and mental disorders of old age.

Spasmodic attacks and psychoses occur more frequently in elderly people. The course of alcoholism in this age is more pernicious, with a higher rate of deterioration and unfavorable prognosis. The poor prognosis is also due to the fact that active alcoholism therapy is contraindicated to such patients because of concurrent somatic diseases, and that after the age of 60 they cannot be sent for compulsory treatment to a WTP. Besides, due to the organism's reduced resistance, these patients frequently die of the various concurrent diseases (influenza, pneumonia, etc.).

Case Illustration Patient: Male, age 72. *Anamnesis*: His father was an alcohol abuser. The patient himself had higher legal education and worked as a lawyer. From the age of 55 he began to display irritability, impairment of memory and a tendency to weep. From the age of 67 (after the death of his wife), he began using alcohol. Two years later a craving for alcohol appeared with rapid loss of control. Bouts lasted for up to a week, and the hangover syndrome was observed. At the time of hangover he is restless, feels weak and sick all over, has a poor appetite and sleeps badly. Occasionally he has nightmares, indefinite fear and inner agitation.

Examination on admission to hospital revealed the following. *Physical status*: heart sounds were dull, blood pressure was somewhat increased (160/90 mm Hg), liver protruded by 3 cm from under the edge of the costal arch. There was general atherosclerosis, sclerosis of the vessels of the heart and brain, and symptoms of alcoholic polyneuritis (sensibility disorders, pain along the nerves in the arms and legs). *Mental status*: underestimation of his morbid condition, noticeable impairment of memory, low-key mood and faintheartedness.

Summary: The patient was detoxified, and given general roborant therapy and rational psychotherapy. Active alcoholism therapy was not prescribed because of old age and poor physical status.

This example showed the process of alcoholization at a late age (67), with rapid development of stage II alcoholism. The patient's condition was aggravated by a severe somatic complication in the form of atherosclerosis and symptoms of polyneuritis, which precluded active treatment for alcoholism and rendered the prognosis poor.

Chapter 12

Alcoholism in Women

Alcoholism in women has some specific features which distinguish it from alcoholism in men. Just imagine a woman under the effect of alcoholic fumes: her face flushed, in red spots or bluish; eyes glittering; hair dishevelled; clothes untidy, or perhaps, even filthy. At first she is lively, gesturing, speaking loudly. In a state of drunkenness, a modest and restrained woman loses these qualities, becomes impertinent and cynical. She takes offense at the least lack of attention to her person. Her mood suddenly becomes elated, and then, without apparent reasons, plunges into despair and dejection.

Steep fluctuations of mood are generally characteristic of female alcohol drinkers. They weep, shout, hurl objects, blame everyone for their misfortunes and bad luck, then become silent, glum and unapproachable, and if their mood brightens, it is for a short period only.

A study involving 3,300 women afflicted with chronic alcoholism established that 33.9% were bad-tempered and pugnacious, 40% tended to get excited, 19% tended to weep at the least pretext, and only 30.5% were relatively calm (Strelchuk). Upon beginning to use alcohol gradually (in company, with friends, when celebrating, etc.), women rather quickly feel attracted to alcoholic beverages. The craving becomes morbid and irresistible. On the next day after alcohol intake their general status is poor; they feel ill, with headaches and unpleasant sensations, and only a new portion of alcohol brings some measure of relief. Thus, there soon appears in women one of the main symptoms of chronic alcoholism—the hangover syndrome.

One should note, however, that the interval from the beginning of systematic alcohol use to the appearance of the hangover syndrome is three to four times shorter in females than in males, lasting, on the average, one to three years.

Case Illustration Patient: Female, age 25. *Anamnesis*: She recalls that her mother led a loose, wild life. Before the girl's eyes passed a string of her mother's so-called "husbands." For the last four years her mother had been living with an alcoholic. Life was, generally speaking, impossible. Since the age of 16 they forced her to drink too, first on holidays, when they had visitors, and then "to keep mother company." Half a year previously she had met a young man and fell in love, but he was called up for service in the Soviet Army. Awaiting her sweetheart's release from the army she would often feel depressed and weep, slept badly, and lost her appetite. In order to cheer herself up she began taking an occasional drink; this lasted for about two years. Upon his return from the military service they met daily, and she was gay and happy. All of a sudden, without any explanation, the young man stopped visiting her. Her mood dropped steeply, she wept a lot, then stopped sleeping at night. Within a year the hangover syndrome formed. In the morning she felt out of sorts, in a low-key mood, suffered from headaches and loss of appetite. Taking 200 grams of wine would make her feel better. Before admission to the hospital she started on a drinking binge and drank for a whole week. Suddenly she heard the voice of her young man calling her by name. Then he began speaking to her, said he would kill her mother, and urged her to run away because she too was about to be killed. Depending on what she had heard, she would run away from home or ardently prayed, begging for mercy. It was in this state that she was brought to a mental hospital.

Summary: This case is interesting in that the patient grew up in a problem family and began to use alcohol at an early age. Unable to cope with the misfortunes of her life, she resorted to drinking alcohol. She is an example of a patient who rapidly developed stage III alcoholism and a mental disorder.

With time a woman may consume less alcohol than before, but the state of drunkenness sets in quickly. Gradually the dose drops to 0.5-0.7 liters of wine, i.e., tolerance to alcohol is reduced. Alcoholism in women frequently proceeds according to the drinking-binge type. The mental framework of drinking women changes quickly. They become rude, egotistic, cruel and cynical, losing their sense of tact and restraint. They are interested in nothing but the satisfaction of their deleterious craving. Many eventually give up working, lead a loose life, or become unproductive derelicts.

Case Illustration Patient: Female, age 50, with eight years of school education and two courses of power-engineering in a technical school. *Anamnesis*: Her two sisters were alcohol abusers by whom she was initiated into drinking. Since 1963 she had been drinking constantly. Since 1965 she began taking a drink "the morning after." She would drink heavily for 2-4 days, then abstain for a week or month. Since 1973 noticeable changes occurred in her character. On the one hand, she became short-tempered and egocentric, on the other, obsequious and fawning. She was also callously cruel to her ill daughter. She was unable to keep a job for long because of careless attitudes, frequent absenteeism, and reporting for work when drunk. At first she drank up to 1-1.5 liters of wine, but at present half a liter is sufficient to make her quite drunk and forgetful. She frequently carries away objects from home to sell for drinking money. On three occasions she underwent treatment, but lucid intervals were brief, and eventually a court ruling sent her for compulsory treatment.

Summary: In this case, there was an unfavorable family situation in which the patient got accustomed to alcoholic beverages, and a rapid development of the disease during which gross changes of personality took place. Treatment was unsuccessful. In some women alcoholic psychoses occur. Their clinical picture is the same as in men, but they have their own distinctions. They proceed more severely, with a tendency to frequent relapses, and they occur after a shorter history of alcohol drinking.

Case Illustration Patient: Female, age 45; was admitted for treatment five times during the last four years. *Anamnesis*: The patient has been an alcohol abuser for eight years. She usually drank alone, occasionally with her friends. She would drink 300-400 grams of vodka, quickly becoming drunk. During the last few years she experienced the wish to take a drink "the morning after." She lived with her elderly parents and four children and worked as a washerwoman. She had been married twice, the first husband having drowned in a state of drunkenness, the second, having left her for another woman. Approximately two weeks before admission to the hospital, she began hearing the voices of her husband and his new wife threatening to kill her. She could no longer eat or sleep. The day before admission she fled from home to save herself from her imagined murderers. She sought protection from the police and was taken to hospital. In the ward she heard voices for three weeks alternatively loud, then soft, which continued to threaten murder. She would hide under her blanket in fear, and at night hardly ever slept. She was rude and cynical to the medical personnel and, having flatly refused treatment for alcoholism, was discharged. Soon she went on a binge again, and again heard voices. The patient believed that her former husband had put a spell on her, having become "the chief sorcerer." When readmitted to the hospital she kept shaking something off her body, saying: "These are small snakes, like devils, sent by the sorcerer or his assistants." It was only during her latest admission that she began treatment for alcoholism.

Summary: Excessive drinking frequently leads to immoral behavior, hooliganism, and crime. It has been learned that from 9 to 12% of criminal offenses by women have been committed in a state of alcoholic intoxication. Alcoholism undermines the physical health of women. Special studies demonstrated that in drinking women aging of the organism sets in early; the face and body fade, teeth fall out, and hearing and vision are impaired. Menstruation sometimes ceases ten years before the physiological norm. Women stubbornly conceal their state for a long time, turning for medical aid very late. Due to the severity of the pathological process and belated attempts at treatment, therapy frequently fails.

Case Illustration Patient: Female, age 62. *Anamnesis*: The patient was an only child in the family. She was a good student, liked to draw, and played the piano. After finishing the seventh grade, she entered an art school. Concurrent with finishing ten years of schooling, she entered an engineering institute. In 1942 she married, but her husband soon left for the front and rarely wrote. Eventually she learned that he had another family. She continued to live with her mother, bringing up a son.

Upon graduating from the institute she worked as an engineer and was cited for good performance. She worked for ten years at the same timberyard, and frequently traveled on lengthy trips. Away from home she began to drink in company. She liked to be able to drink on a par with men; then a neighbor in her communal flat frequently invited her in for a glass of wine. Eventually she began to drink alone. Because of her mother's illness she could not travel on commissions and changed her place of employment. She began drinking one to two glasses of wine during her lunch break. She drank mainly wine, but the desire to take a drink "the morning after" developed quickly. This was noticed at work and she was asked to leave. She changed her place of employment many times, and eventually got involved with a company of men with whom she participated in robbing a store. She served time in detention, then worked as a technician, and subsequently, as a cleaning woman in a canteen. Soon she began picking up empty bottles to sell them for drinking money and indulged daily. She was again convicted for theft. A little wine would quickly make her drunk. She sold things and drank anything that came her way, including eau de cologne and lac varnish. Then she developed weakness in her legs and could not walk without help or without a stick; this was soon followed by weakness in her hands. At times she was unable to bend by herself. She underwent considerable mental degradation, lost interest in her surroundings, and all her thoughts centered on drinking.

Summary: From this history one can see how a person with a higher education undergoes gradual degradation under the effect of alcohol, slips down the social ladder, commits criminal offenses, while belated treatment no longer yields results. This patient was treated for more than five months at a mental hospital, but without success. Mental deterioration in women sets in rather early, with deterioration of memory and of the capacity to assess critically one's own illness. They agree to undergo treatment, as a rule, at the insistence of their relatives and friends, while showing no wish to undergo treatment themselves. Not infrequently the family life of such women ends in tragedy: wives usually live with alcoholic husbands for many years, sometimes all their lives, whereas drinking women are soon abandoned, which still worsens their already unenvious plight.

Chapter 13

Alcoholic Psychoses

The following mental disorders may occur in alcoholism: deliria, hallucinoses, delirial alcoholic psychoses, structurally complex (mixed) acute alcoholic psychoses, alcoholic encephalopathies, alcoholic depressions, dipsomanias.

Deliria, hallucinoses, delirial alcoholic psychoses and encephalopathies are distinguished, according to the speed of their course, as acute, subacute, and chronic. Besides, they have a number of other varieties. For example, delirium has 14 variants, hallucinoses 15 variants, etc. According to the International Statistical Classification of Diseases, Injuries and Causes of Death (8th revision, 1968), alcoholic psychoses have the classification number "9," with the following figures of the number indicating the group of the psychoses (delirium 0, hallucinosis 1, etc.), and course versions. For example, alcoholic delirium (delirium tremens) will appear in case histories and other documents under the number of 9.0.01, etc.

Alcoholic psychoses occur in 13% of alcoholic cases in persons with an average of five to seven-year history of alcohol abuse, most frequently in the second or third stage of alcoholism. It is still unclear why some people who have been using alcohol for years do not develop psychoses while others do. It must be presumed that, given one and the same harmful factor leading to the onset of psychoses, the general state of the organism (e.g., hunger, dehydration), harmful factors (e.g., sleeplessness), intercurrent diseases (e.g., influenza, hepatitis), the type of higher nervous activity, biochemical imbalance, particular vitamin deficiency, vegetative dysfunction and other factors apparently play their roles. Thus, in the presence of a single etiology, pathogenetic mechanisms apparently are basic in the appearance of psychoses.

According to a majority of investigators, *delirium tremens* (trembling delirium) accounts for 76 to 84% of all psychoses of alcoholic etiology. This condition was described in 1813 by the physician Sutton, but the association of the psychosis with drinking was established somewhat later by Russian physicians Charutsky in 1828 and Vitt in 1834. It was believed for a long time that the psychosis is precipitated only by "white vodka"; however, studies indicate that the disease may develop also from the use of wine and beer.

Most frequently the psychosis sets in against a background of forced temperance, in a state of abstinence. Not infrequently the disease is precipitated by such factor as weakening of the organism from pneumonia, influenza, hepatitis, exhaustion, mental injuries or harmful physical factors. These circumstances also aggravate the picture of the psychosis and frequently develop into fatal cases.

The clinical picture of delirium tremens differs depending on the complicating factors, but the main symptoms are sleeplessness, disorientation, illusions, hallucinations, delirium, excitation, and other somato-neurological disorders.

Abstinence from alcohol results, first of all, in poor sleep. Sleep becomes superficial, with nightmares which wake up the patient in fright and horror. Often before falling asleep hypnagogic hallucinations may occur. When the eyes are shut there appear fearsome pictures; when open, at first there may be illusions. For example, a human figure may seem to be crouching in a dark corner, and extraneous sounds are perceived, such as hearing one's name called or voices. Then they may turn into multiple illusions, in which the patient sees entire pictures on walls and ceiling, mostly of a fantastic content.

Illusions are compounded by hallucinations, as a rule, visual delusions. The patient sees small animals—bugs, spiders, flies—which crawl over the walls and ceiling, the bed and other objects, over the patient himself who keeps sweeping them off, shooing them away, or fighting them. Then the hallucinations become still more ample and diverse (see Figure 1). People begin to take part in them, the hallucinations frequently acquiring a fantastic character.

At the same time there appear voices. Because of the patients' absolutely uncritical attitude to the hallucinations, they perceive them as reality. Gradually, on the basis of the hallucinations, there appears delirium, most frequently consisting of delusions of reference, per-

Figure 1. Visual hallucinations in delirium tremens

secution and action. The patients imagine themselves being pursued with intent to murder. Their experiences are so fantastic that they feel as if they are falling into the abyss of the earth or ascending into the heavens, with pictures so fantastic that at times they may be compared to oneiric experiences.

Peculiar orientation disorders develop. These may be disorientation in time, place, in one's own personality; sometimes, however, patients give correct answers about their whereabouts. Questions concerning a sequel of events reveal disorientation due to lapses of memory. Orientation as to one's own personality and comprehension of the surroundings are frequently upset. Against the background of frightening hallucinations and delirium the patients may often indulge in shallow jokes and laugh, i.e., behave in a manner totally incompatible with their emotions.

Most frequently the patients are excited, vigorously struggling against terrible ogres, hiding, attacking, fighting. In such states they become dangerous to other people and themselves. Frequently during episodes of pathologic experiences, to which they are absolutely uncritical, they make suicidal attempts, may inflict bodily injury, or commit violent acts. This is why patients in a state of delirium tremens must certainly be hospitalized and kept under strict supervision by the personnel.

One of the constant signs of delirium tremens is tremor of the hands and body, possibly with other neurological symptoms. Somatically, in addition to physical exhaustion and dehydration of the organism, diseases of the liver, heart, lungs frequently exacerbate; pneumonia and dyspepsia often occur. Ample vegetative symptoms are revealed, with the patients complaining of feeling cold or, on the contrary, that their "insides" are on fire.

Case Illustration Patient: Male, age 36, wrote the following:

"I had my first drink of vodka at the age of nine when I finished the first grade with distinction. On that occasion, my father, who was always drunk, took me along to a restaurant. When I entered the 8th grade the event was again celebrated in a restaurant; after that second visit to the restaurant I did not drink till the age of 16, yet I began smoking hashish and kept at it for one and a half years, until I was put behind bars for five years for a criminal offense. During these years I used alcohol, morphine, 'chifir,' and all kinds of tablets. Upon release I gave up everything for about three months, even smoking. Then I got a job at a plant and worked well. There I met my future wife, who worked in the buffet 'on beer and wine.' I wonder if she loved me, because she reintroduced me to drink. Since than I began drinking every day. After two years at the plant I was fired under Article 47. This really shook me into despair and I began drinking still more. Nor did my wife drink any less. I don't remember how long I was without a job, but when at last I found one, I was soon fired again. I could no longer keep a job for more than two to three months. After a while I was sent for a year to a WTP, and from there I got into a mental hospital. After treatment I was temperate for one to one and a half months, but whenever I came to meet my wife at the end of her shift, I would see all those people drinking there, could no longer hold out and began drinking again. That is how everything began anew. I can't even tell how much I drank every day, but one thing I know: if I did not drink two bottles of wine during the workday, I was unable to work. It's a long time now that I have been drinking 'the morning after' and of late have been drinking heavily.

"Let me tell you how the hallucinations appeared. One day my wife and I went out swimming in a lake. Before that day I, of course, have been drinking for nearly two and a half weeks. We set out drunk, and drank more when we arrived. And so, when I swam to the middle of the lake I was suddenly seized with fear, and someone shouted, 'I'll drown you!' I quickly turned and made for the shore and when I came out of the water I heard horrible laughter and the shout, 'That one scared you, didn't it?'

"Upon getting out of the water I drank a glass of wine and in a few minutes everything passed away. I told no one about the hallucination and continued to swim and drink wine and beer. On the next morning, back at home, I did not drink. About three o'clock in the afternoon auditory hallucinations appeared which frightened me; I was trembling all over and, for some reason, weeping. I begged the neighbors for a bottle of wine, and while walking to the wine store I became covered with sweat and afraid of everything. As soon as I took a drink, everything was fine. But since that day I could not sleep, had not slept for four days. I am unable now to describe what I saw and heard. One thing I know, though, is that I have been underground and talked to devils.

They were strange, with human faces. I was also in the clouds and asked an angel to admit me to paradise. Death came after me but I shooed it off. I cooked dinner, all kinds of dishes. I was cursed at and cursed back. My wife received a lover through the roof, and I chased her with an ax. And at the militia station I held up the walls lest they fall down. In the four corners of a white sheet of paper I saw red monkeys."

This example is noteworthy for the early initiation to alcohol, the commission of an alcohol-related crime, family drunkenness (together with the wife) and mental disorder in the form of delirium tremens.

The initial period of delirium tremens may last a few days with an exacerbation of symptoms toward nighttime and clearing of consciousness during the day. The psychosis more often ends critically after prolonged sleep. The average duration of delirium tremens is three to five days. But the disease may also drag on for two weeks. Following severe forms of the disease and its abatement, marked asthenia with psychic weakness, irritability, headaches, intermittent hearing of voices, and some perception disorders may linger on for a few weeks or months.

After the psychotic state is over patients remember their experiences and may coherently describe them. Delirium tremens may occur repeatedly, sometimes taking a protracted course with periodic exacerbations, and other times transforming into chronic hallucinosis, "Korsakoff's psychosis." Some investigators distinguish several stages in the course of delirium tremens according to the changes or complications of the clinical picture.

There are mild abortive forms of psychosis, when the clinical manifestations abate without really developing, and severe forms, which are complicated by amential or oneiric changes of consciousness with occupational or muttering delirium (all in all, there are 14 different variants of the course the psychosis may take). In severe cases there is excitation, incoherent speech and still deeper changes of consciousness. An average of 1.7% of delirium tremens cases are lethal.

Case Illustration Patient: Male, age 37, driver. *Anamnesis*: His family background showed no history of alcoholism or mental illness and he grew up and developed normally. He completed seven years of schooling and drivers' courses, after which he worked as a driver. He married, but had no children. Systematic alcohol abuse began at the age of 26, and at 28, the hangover syndrome developed. Frequent amnesic forms of drunkenness occurred. Heavy drinking started, the bouts lasting three to four days, and eventually, up to one month. The last drinking bout lasted two weeks, with a three-day interval. When denied alcohol, anxiety appeared and he experienced fears and sleeplessness. "Saw" some bandits attacking him, heard threats, and felt bugs and flies crawl over his body. He was admitted to a mental hospital. On admission he correctly told his surname and first name, but did not know his whereabouts. He appeared anxious, restless and fearful, and kept "pulling" a nonexistent thread from the mouth, saying that he sees it. He heard "voices" of relatives, spoke to them and kept asking for vodka. Thinking he is in the garage, he talked shop, demanded the switching on of the ignition, and performed unnecessary movements. He shook off "insects," threw them to the floor, with his glances traced "mice" running about the room, and saw "horrible faces" in front of himself. He could not keep still though in bed, was constantly turning about, wanted to get up, and waved his arms as though going through the occupational motions of a driver.

Physical status: The patient showed general emaciation, sweating, and facial hyperemia. His tongue had a thick brown coat. There were tremors of the body, arms, eyelids and tongue. His tendon reflexes were uniformly elevated. *Mental status*: Consciousness cleared after six days of combined treatment and a normal sleep. Although he became capable of a critical attitude toward his drinking, symptoms of general asthenia persisted for about two months. Despite its severe course, this case of psychosis ended in recovery, albeit with a lasting asthenic syndrome. (Not infrequently such occupational deliria result in death.)

Alcoholic hallucinoses may be acute (eight variants have been described), subacute (four variants), and chronic (three variants). *Acute alcoholic hallucinosis* begins against a background of the abstinence syndrome, as if becoming its continuation, but is saturated, however, with psychopathologic products, i.e., acquires a new quality. Hallucinosis may occasionally develop during delirium tremens.

The main symptoms are auditory hallucinations. At first they appear as individual sounds, then voices from outside. They may be many or only one voice, male or female, adult's or children's, of different pitch and sound, loud, dull, or in whispers. They may run a commentary on the patient's actions, criticize and condemn, or praise. At times there is one voice branding the patient a "drunkard," "parasite," "rogue," and other unflattering epithets, while another voice softens down this criticism by saying, "There, there, old boy, you are not alone," "you will get well and you'll be okay," etc.

Visual hallucinations are few; tactile and olfactory seldom occur. Arising from the auditory hallucinations there rapidly forms a delusion of persecution and reference. It begins to seem to the patient that a gang is plotting around him intent on killing, quartering, and abusing him. The patients are glum, grim, and filled with anxiety and fear, and their behavior corresponds to those with delirium or hallucinations. They hide away, try to cover up and arm themselves with different objects for self-defense. Cases have been described when the patients attack first, fearing aggressiveness of people around them. Acute alcoholic hallucinosis lasts, as a rule, from two to three days to several weeks, though an abortive course of the psychosis is also possible.

Case Illustration Patient: Male, age 32, recently unemployed. *Anamnesis*: His family history was uncomplicated, and he grew up and developed normally. He finished seven years of schooling and then a technical school. He enrolled at the Physical Culture Institute but was dismissed for lack of progress and absenteeism. He began drinking alcoholic beverages at age 22, and started systematic alcohol abuse at 24, when psychic dependence appeared for the first time. At the age of 25, the hangover syndrome formed and amnesic forms of drunkenness appeared. Drinking binges lasted for periods of up to one month, and after drinking bouts he experienced giddiness, nausea, anorexia, and sweating. Before admission to the hospital he had been drinking for a week and a half. At the time of hangover he could not sleep at night, experienced fears, and became suspicious. He declared that the neighbors were constantly eavesdropping on him and that he "listened" to "voices" from above assuring him that his wife was unfaithful, and pointing out certain individuals who "had been with her." The voices belonged to the neighbors who openly ridiculed him because of his wife's unfaithfulness. He closed all cracks, ventilation vents and doors, and asked his wife to keep away from open windows since "everything can be seen through and listened through." He also maintained that bandits were trying to break into his room threatening to kill him. Convinced that a gang of bandits was plotting against him, he was extremely excited and carried about a hammer as a defense weapon. After "seeing" some shady individuals under his apartment's windows, he was brought to a mental hospital. On admission he was well oriented in his own personality, place and time. However, he experienced fear, looked around and anxiously listened in to some apparent plot. He heard the "voices" of bandits threatening to kill him, and spoke about a group of them pursuing him. On the fifth day hallucinations and delirial ideas passed away, and a critical attitude toward his disease appeared.

Summary: This case is typical: hallucinatory experiences are being transformed into delirial ideas.

Subacute alcoholic hallucinosis is a psychosis that drags on for several months and assumes a subacute course. In such cases the affect dulls and is dominated not by fear, but by anxiety and apprehension. The patients become sedentary and spend a lot of time in bed listening to voices. The delusion of persecution loses its dominance, giving place to delusions of reference and self-accusations. Such patients require close supervision and observation, since suicidal attempts are possible.

Chronic alcoholic hallucinosis is most frequently precipitated by acute mental diseases and disorders. At the initial stages there may be auditory hallucinations and delusions of persecution and reference. Very soon only auditory hallucinations remain, which trouble the patients all day long, and occasionally they continue to hear them at night. The voices vary—loud, soft, male, female. Some of them criticize thoughts and actions and are abusive; the others praise and exonerate. Not infrequently they argue among themselves. With time the patients get used to these voices, which can turn into habitual irritants. In these cases the patients only occasionally answer to the voices, being able even to perform some work the rest of the time. The mood is constantly glum, grim and low-keyed. Criticism of one's condition appears, then disappears. Chronic hallucinoses are extremely resistant to therapy.

Case Illustration Patient: Male, age 52. *Anamnesis*: The patient has been drinking for some time but in moderation. After the death of his wife he began drinking more and more. He married again, his new wife frequently having a drink with him. About two years previously, for the first time he thought he heard his name called in the street. He turned around but saw no one. Just my imagination, he thought. This happened several times. Then he began hearing voices of people seemingly coming from outside, very clearly, mostly male, but also occasionally female. All spoke at once, discoursing, arguing, most frequently about him, his behavior, criticizing or praising him. At first the patient was afraid of these voices but eventually got used to them. At the beginning he just listened, but then began joining in the conversation, answering questions and arguing. Sometimes during forced abstentions from alcohol, bright periods occurred during which he heard nothing. But no sooner would he start drinking and the voices would appear again. For a year nobody around him noticed this condition because he entered the conversation with the imagined voices when at home, with nobody around. Eventually he began whispering in the presence of other people. This drew attention, and he was regarded as somewhat odd. Then the voices multiplied, all the time commenting on his actions and behavior, interfering with his life and work. At work he was apt to ruin a component or incorrectly assemble an engine, since he was entirely absorbed in the conversation and arguments with the voices. Nor did he regard these voices as in any way associated with his morbid condition; he got accustomed to them. The patient underwent treatment, but without success.

Summary: The above example clearly demonstrates the chronic course of the psychosis and the failure of treatment.

Delirial psychoses are precipitated in alcoholics by massive intoxication, as a rule in difficult life situations, during travel, under strain, in unfamiliar locality, or in the presence of craniocerebral injury. A leading symptom of these psychoses is not hallucinations, but delirium. Most frequently these are ideas of persecution. The patient is under the delusion that people speak about him, giving signs to each other, plotting to kill him or inventing some subtle torture, that they want to ruin not only him, but also his children and all the family. Trying to escape his imagined persecutors, the patient himself may become a persecutor and be the first to attack out of fear, in apprehension of a dreaded misfortune. Some patients commit suicide. Most of them are in a depressive mood, gripped with fear. Anxiety and restlessness are constantly revealed in their behavior. They are suspicious, and because of that frequently reject medicines and food, fearing poisoning.

The patients are wholly in the power of their morbid experiences and therefore, for all practical purposes, are unable to perceive the surrounding reality.

Alcoholic delusion of jealousy occurs in 10% of all cases of alcoholic psychoses. The alcoholic delusion of jealousy is regarded as one of the syndromes of alcoholic paranoia, frequently concurrent with other experiences. As a rule the delirial suspicions are absurd; the reproaches of marital infidelity are groundless and naive. Often the wife and children condemn the drunkard's behavior and marital relations are soured, which serves to sustain the patient's delusion that the wife "has taken a lover."

The onset of impotence and sexual weakness may occur early in chronic alcoholics, which in turn stimulates delirial predispositions. Uncritical of themselves, they tend to blame their wives; ideas of jealousy eventually develop into a stable delusion. Occasionally these ideas occur during simple drunkenness, delirium tremens and hallucinosis, and eventually become fixed. At times suspiciousness and apprehension play a role, appearing in chronic alcoholics as a result of personality changes. It becomes impossible to convince the patients of being wrong, and this frequently leads to quarrels and family breakups, or sometimes, to more tragic consequences.

Case Illustration Patient: Male, age 43, employed as an electrician. *Anamnesis*: He showed a normal family history. After eight years of schooling, he was employed in different occupations. From 1941 to 1946 he worked in a mine and since then has been drinking alcoholic beverages. He drank on holidays and days off in the company of friends. He was married and had two children. Since 1970 he has been using alcohol systematically. Drinking bouts last two to three days occurring in intervals of two to three days. He drinks on "the morning after," and his tolerance is increased to 500 grams of vodka. When drunk he forgets what happened to him and with whom he had been. In addition, his personality traits have altered: he has become hot-tempered, irritable, quarrelsome and jealous, and accuses his wife of infidelity. Jealousy manifests itself in snooping on his wife, constantly checking up on her at work and dropping in, as if by accident, to see when she comes back from work. He inspects her underwear, charging that she frequently washed her underwear in secret. In recent years he has become intolerable, beating his wife when drunk and insisting she has a lover which he gathered from a conversation with his wife's colleagues. A number of clues made him guess that during his absence (away on commissions) his wife terminated pregnancy on two occasions. He expounded a system of proofs confirming her infidelity, and told his children of their mother's moral degradation. He also restricted his wife's budget, demanding complete accounting of her spending. From the beginning of 1976, after a four-day drinking bout he became particularly suspicious, complaining of pain through his insides because his wife had added some powder to his food. He "realized" that the wife wanted to do away with him in order to remain with her lover. When his wife returned from work, he beat her up trying to make her confess to "poisoning" him. The neighbors summoned an ambulance and the patient was taken to the hospital.

Physical status: On admission the patient's liver was enlarged and tender. He showed tremor of the fingers, eyelids, tongue, and whole body. His gait was unsteady in Romberg's posture. *Mental status*: The patient showed adequate orientation, and maintained verbal contact. He presented with verbosity, and overriding all objections, accused his wife of infidelity and intent to kill him with a slow-acting poison. He "saw" his wife adding something to the food, serving them from different dishes. After the meal he felt a burning in his stomach, heaviness in his head and weakness in his legs, which he "realized" was the effect of the poison. During the intake examination he is irascible, sexually uninhibited, and without a shade of self-consciousness discloses intimate details of his relations with his wife. He objects to hospitalization, blaming everything on his wife. He is emotionally labile, tending to outbursts of anger. He is convinced that his wife has been unfaithful. He is not amenable to treatment and criticism of his status is absent.

Summary: This case history demonstrates that the patient has a stable, intense delusion of jealousy and of being poisoned. Treatment merely resulted in removing the emotional intensity of the situation, but failed to fully restore his critical capacity.

The courses of alcoholic delirial (paranoid) psychoses may run according to several variants. Four of them belong to acute alcoholic delirial psychoses, and two to protracted, chronic ones.

Alcoholic encephalopathies are also divided into acute (3 forms) and chronic (ten forms). They develop in persons with a lasting history of using alcohol, mainly vodka, substitutes and strong wines. All the variants of encephalopathies occur against a background of chronic alcoholism marked by frequent alcohol drinking or drinking bouts. Most frequently these are stage III alcoholics with pronounced somatic and neurological disorders, the latter often dominating the clinical picture.

Alcoholic encephalopathies present a mixed clinical picture. Their pathogenesis is based on metabolic disorders, in particular, B-hypovitaminosis. Alcohol use precipitates vitamin B_1 deficiency, compounded by functional disorders of the liver, which in turn impairs carbohydrate metabolism, which is the main energy source for cerebral activity. Also present in encephalopathies is an imbalance of the vitamins B_6 and PP. Good results in the treatment of these conditions are obtained with high doses of the vitamins B_1, B_{12}, B_6, ascorbic and nicotinic acids, and rutin.

One of the acute alcoholic encephalopathies is Wernicke's disease. Wernicke's encephalopathy occupies a central place among acute conditions. This is a complex disease which combines somatic, neurological and psychiatric disorders, underlying which are degenerative and destructive processes. It is, in effect, hemorrhagic polioencephalitis.

Observed in the prodromal period (three to four months) are adynamia, dyspeptic vegetative disorders, poor sleep and also pronounced neurological symptoms, such as tremor, dysarthria, ataxic symptoms, oculomotor and bulbar disorders (blocking of the pharyngial, palatal, respiratory and sneezing reflexes).

Psychiatric disorders proceed in the form of a severe delirium (more frequently the muttering and occupational variants), with excitation when bedridden, and the condition may exacerbate and develop into amentia or stupor. The aggravation occurs with both somatic and neurological symptoms. Arterial pressure drops, the rate of respiration increases, and the liver is enlarged and becomes tender. There are frequent stools, muscular itching and hypertonia or hypotonia of the limbs, and complex hyperkinesias. There are constant neurological automatisms, pronounced ataxia, ocular symptoms, hypertonia, polyneurites, and pyramidal signs.

The health status may improve, then may worsen. Lethal outcomes are possible, more frequently from some intercurrent diseases. Evolution into the chronic stage of an encephalopathy of the Korsakoff's psychosis type is also possible. A disease with a "lightning course," accompanied by high temperature and terminating in death within three to five days, is also classified among the acute forms of the encephalopathies.

Case Illustration Patient: Male, age 43, employed as a gas and electric welder at a wine distillery. *Anamnesis*: The patient's heredity was uncomplicated. Married twice, he had been an alcohol abuser for many years. During the last five years he had been drinking heavily, and the abstinence syndrome was clearly pronounced. Before admission to the hospital he had been drinking for ten days. There was anxiety, sleeplessness, feeling of fear, visual and auditory hallucinations. He "saw" some people behind bushes, argued with them, laughed without cause, wept, and kept hiding from them. At home, he dismantled the sewing machine in search for a welding apparatus. On admission to the mental hospital he showed disorientation in place, time, and in his surroundings. He was fussy, and experienced fears and confusion. He "spoke" with imaginary drinking companions and "saw" unfamiliar people threatening to hurt or kill him and attempted to escape from them.

Toward the end of the first week of treatment the disturbances of thought processes abated, but disorders of memory became prominent, and he was unable to tell the date, time of day, or current year; he also could not say what he had eaten during the day. He showed signs of helplessness, could not find his ward, could not remember the name and surname of the attending physician, and related in detail events of early childhood, but was unable to remember any recent or current events. He filled in gaps in his memory with made-up events that actually never took place, or transferred past events into the present. He mistook people around him for other persons and showed no interest in his surroundings. Although he took life easy, attention was rapidly exhausted, particularly toward the end of the conversation. He got irritable, claiming tiredness whenever the physician pointed out mistakes in his recollection of recent events. The longer the conversation, the greater were the lapses of memory. The attitude toward his alcoholic status was uncritical.

Neurological status: Craniocerebral innervation without pathological changes was revealed. He showed weakening of tendon reflexes on leads from his right arm and tenderness along the brachial and median nerves. There was also reduced sensitivity in the area of the medial surface of the right upper arm. *Physical status*: The patient's heart sounded dulled, rhythmic. The pulse rate was 96 per minute, blood pressure 190/80 mmHg. The abdomen was soft, and his liver protruded 1-2 cm from under the costal arch.

Summary: Following intensive detoxification and general roborant therapy, including tonics, the patient's condition improved; however, the restoration of memory was far from complete. This case is typical for the acute alcoholic psychosis which gave place to a pronounced Korsakoff psychosis with deep and virtually irreversible impairment of memory.

Alcoholic depression as a separate disease seldom occurs. More frequently, depression lasts from several days to several weeks. Alcoholic depression is characterized by anguish, with delusions of accusation and irritability. Afflicted persons blame those around them, especially friends and relatives, of treating them without due consideration, while they themselves feel their inadequacy and guilt before their relatives. There are diurnal fluctuations of mood; there may be depressions with dysphoria and tearfulness. All investigators stress frequent and stable suicidal ideas and the patients' attempts to realize them. Therefore, close observation is required.

Dipsomania is a sudden compulsion to drink heavily. It is a state occurring in psychopathic personalities, individuals suffering from an endocrine-related psychosyndrome, in some cases epilepsy, or manic-depressive psychosis. The drinking bout lasts from a few days to two to three weeks, beginning suddenly, precipitated by lasting abstention from alcohol, and ending equally abruptly. At this point aversion to alcohol may appear. A bout is not infrequently preceded by poor sleep and various phenomena exhausting the organism. The quantity of alcohol consumed varies broadly from light to heavy intake, causing severe intoxication.

Antabuse psychoses. Antabuse (disulfiram) is a medicinal drug used since 1958 for the treatment of alcoholism. The average therapeutic dose is 0.5 gram. In a hospital setting a 1-gram dose may be used on the test day.

Psychoses appear to be one of the grave complications of antabuse treatment. High doses, or increased sensitivity to antabuse due to organic CNS deficiency caused by chronic alcohol intoxication or craniocerebral injury, may result in psychoses. Most frequently the psychoses may appear in the process of antabuse therapy during the ethanol-antabuse reaction, while supportive therapy is given.

Three stages of antabuse psychoses are distinguished. The prodromal stage lasts from two to three days to two weeks. There is headache, giddiness, drowsiness, torpidity, sleep disorders, unpleasant sensations in the area of the heart, hyperesthesia, depression, and suicidal ideas.

At the peak of the disease, several variants of its course are distinguished: a variant with confused consciousness (delirial-amential, delirial-oneiric), and disturbance of allopsychic orientation. The syndrome's structure includes visual and verbal hallucinations. In distinction from ordinary abuse and threats characteristic of alcoholic psychoses, the auditory hallucinations include mystic-prophetic elements. The affective background is hypomanic or depressive.

Then, there is a variant with hallucinatory-paranoid and paranoid disorders in the form of an acute syndrome of persecution, poisoning, acute delirium with dual orientation and false recognitions; it lasts from two to five days and is fully reversible—there is no amnesia and a critical attitude is eventually restored. Frequent replacement of syndromes is observed. The disturbed thought process is characterized by affective-delirial manic states.

The variant with the manic condition is neither striking nor pronounced, and the patients are characterized by their carefree attitude, and at times viciousness; they are importunate, pointlessly fussy, and incoherent. Motor excitation bears a shade of foolishness.

Manic states are often combined with delusions of reference. In some cases memory disorders loom large in the clinical picture. The inversion of the psychosis proceeds slowly, with exhaustion of all mental processes.

The psychosis ends with asthenic phenomena dominated by torpidity and weakness rather than emotive lability. Recall of the acute period is blurred and fragmentary. The psychosis lasts from a few days to one to two months.

Chapter 14

Combination of Alcoholism with Various Mental Disorders

Sometimes the onset of alcoholism may be caused by some form of mental disease, or it may be superimposed on this affliction as some concurrent illness.

ALCOHOLISM AND SCHIZOPHRENIA

Cases of alcohol abuse in youth are particularly suspicious in regard to the schizophrenic process. A characteristic is unmotivated solitary alcohol abuse and drinking, which at once assumes a periodic or systematic course without changes in quantity control. The abstinence syndrome forms very slowly and not in every case. Withdrawal, delusional suspicion, and difficulty in adaptation gradually increase. A particular feature of these symptoms is that with the passage of years they may smooth out, and these patients manifest a greater capacity to maintain the necessary contacts with reality than schizophrenics without alcoholization. Alcohol abuse in such patients may be unmotivated and end as unexpectedly as it began. A clinically pronounced psychotic seizure is more likely to develop two to three years after the beginning of alcohol abuse and without any connection with the abstinence syndrome, which may be absent.

The form of the psychosis is always atypical and, in contrast with acute alcoholic psychosis, is frequently protracted (up to two to three months). Verbal hallucinosis and symptoms belonging to the Kandinskii-Clerambault syndrome are nearly always present. A special feature in these conditions is that, though criticism is lacking, the patients are more accessible and usually seek aid themselves, their complaints resembling those of somatic patients. The end of the psychosis is virtually always characterized by residual delirial phenomena.

The first to elaborate the problem of the relationships between alcoholic psychoses and schizophrenia was Gretär, who observed alcohol-precipitated onsets of schizophrenia and noted the mild and benign character of its course when beginning in this variant. The main diagnostic difficulty lies in the fact that in alcoholic psychoses the clinical picture frequently presents scattered delusional ideas of persecution, reference and even action, while on the other hand, during the onset of acute schizophrenia there are delirial conditions in the form of visual hallucinations and illusory perception of the surroundings in combination with the affect of dread.

Conditionally, the psychopathologic picture at the onset of alcohol-related schizophrenia may be divided into two stages: during stage I the clinical manifestations approximate alcoholic psychosis; during stage II there is a buildup of schizophrenic symptoms. These stages evolve from one to the other either gradually, or with a lucid interval between them. This apparently depends on the nature of the course of schizophrenia, even without further alcohol abuse.

A special feature of the initial psychotic picture in schizophrenia complicated by alcoholism is the abortive nature of the delirium and its atypical manifestations, particularly the predominance of paranoid signs (delusions of persecution and reference) in the absence of pronounced disorders of consciousness.

Occasionally, even at an early period of the disease, there are characteristic disorders of thought, symptoms of psychic automatism or some withdrawal, which help to diagnose schizophrenia with a high degree of probability.

During stage II a clear set of schizophrenic symptoms develops with increasing changes of personality, which makes the diagnosis of schizophrenia unquestionable. Characteristic of such patients is the absence of personality changes typical of chronic alcoholism both before the beginning of the psychosis and after its cessation. Occurring in a majority of patients are diseases of the liver and a vascular pathology which may precipitate the development of a psychosis.

Case Illustration Patient: Male, age 63. *Anamnesis*: The patient's family had a history of schizophrenia, i.e., the patient's father and sister suffered from schizophrenia. His early development occurred without peculiarities. In childhood he had measles, scarlet fever, and colds. He finished ten-year schooling, then higher education. He had been unsociable and stubborn, and achieved his set goals. At the age of 29, he developed anxiety, irritability and undefined fears, experienced the "effects of some apparatus," and heard an "inner voice" commenting on his actions. His low-key mood was coupled with anxiety and anguish increasing toward evening. Periodically he displayed inappropriate behavior, gesticulatively speaking to himself. He was treated at a mental hospital, and after discharge, complete remission lasted 18 years. In subsequent years, he periodically went for treatment at a mental hospital. At the age of 45, he began to drink alcohol daily. The hangover syndrome developed and tolerance to alcohol diminished. Alcohol improved his mood and alleviated the anguish, but massive alcoholization led to the worsening of the patient's condition: he was excited, restless, experienced fears, did not know where he was. Ultimately, he was admitted to a hospital.

Mental status: The patient showed symptoms of restlessness, motor excitation, confusion, disorientation in time and in surroundings and failed to recognize members of the medical staff; he also "saw running mice and rabbits" and heard "voices" threatening to kill him. During treatment he became calmer, and his behavior become more orderly; yet, he continued to feel himself under the influence of an apparatus which transmitted his thoughts and heard "an inner voice" telling him he was "a great man, receiving high awards, and called upon to protect the world from invaders." Lasting therapy resulted in an improvement and the appearance of a formally critical attitude toward his disease.

Summary: Here the morbid state is remarkable in that the patient has been a schizophrenic for many years. The disease proceeds with lasting and stable remissions; then alcoholism is added to it. Alcohol provokes an exacerbation of the psychosis, whose clinical picture contains symptoms of both an alcoholic and a schizophrenic.

ALCOHOLISM AND MANIC-DEPRESSIVE PSYCHOSIS

Alcohol abuse in manic-depressive psychosis may be observed in the depressive as well as in the manic phase, but more frequently in the depressive. The following points are important for diagnosis. In the anamnesis of such patients one may detect periods of low-key moods accompanied by drinking; not infrequently the patients themselves associate drinking with changes in mood. Unexpected drunkenness stands out in contrast against the background of the patient's ordinary behavior, yet moodiness also persists during the drinking period. The compulsion to drink alcoholic beverages disappears only after the phase is over, when there is no need to drink "the morning after," and subsequent intake of alcoholic beverages is determined by desire.

Alcohol, even without the influence of any other additional factors, may precipitate spastic syndromes. The spastic syndrome occurs mainly after a long history of alcohol use and has its own peculiarities. Most frequently the convulsions occur during the abstinence syndrome, and disappear completely after prolonged and strict abstention from alcohol.

The spastic syndrome is characterized by the presence of paroxysms and the predominance of tonic convulsions. Frequently delirial conditions develop after the spastic syndrome. It is important to note that in these patients personality changes follow the epileptic pattern.

Case Illustration Patient: Male, age 40, was admitted to a mental hospital in a very grave condition. *Anamnesis*: The patient had been using alcoholic beverages for more than ten years. During the last two years, he had been drinking virtually daily, not only wine and vodka, but different substitutes as well. He had been unemployed for about a year, and before admission to the hospital had not slept for four nights in a row. He experienced constant anxiety and fear and kept shutting windows and doors. According to his wife, the patient had convulsive seizures several months previously, but did not go to the doctor. The day before admission to the hospital there were three convulsive seizures one after another. The neuropathologist found alcoholic polyneurites (multiple lesions of the peripheral nerves) and pneumonia and affected heart muscles in the internal organs. Despite vigorous treatment, the patient died in the hospital within 24 hours.

Summary: In this case the overall gravity of the patient's condition, with the presence of spastic seizures, was complicated by neurological symptoms, pneumonia and lesions of the muscles of the heart. All these resulted in death.

ALCOHOLISM AND EPILEPSY

Alcoholic epilepsy is characterized by two variants in its course: (1) progressive, when the seizures occur even despite lasting abstention from alcohol, and (2) regressive, when the seizures disappear, even without any treatment, upon the discontinuation of alcoholic intoxication.

The regression is due to functional disorders of the higher portions of the CNS and the progression to organic, local disorders, though some degree of compensation in these cases is possible.

Medium or grave alcoholic epilepsy develops in chronic alcoholics after a drinking history of six to ten years. In comparison with persons afflicted with chronic alcoholism without seizures, such patients have a notable predisposition to alcoholic psychoses.

Psychic changes are characteristic of chronic alcoholism, with the predominance of increased irritability, hot temper, falsity, a diminution of the will-to-work, depletion of memory, etc. No characterological changes inherent in general epilepsy are noted. The convulsive seizures occur most frequently during the abstinence period.

A characteristic of alcohol abusers with genuine epilepsy is the rather rapid appearance of the main syndromes of chronic alcoholism. Dysphoria is observed in the abstinence period. The patients become surly, fault-finding, express various hypochondriacal complaints, and experience an increased craving for alcohol. Along with the epileptic features there are psychic changes characteristic of chronic alcoholics. Drunkenness precipitates seizures, with the possible development of the epileptic status. Such patients often willfully interrupt the course of treatment, which leads to more frequent seizures.

Chronic alcoholic intoxication considerably aggravates the course of traumatic epilepsy. Such patients are distinguished by increased excitability, irritability and rudeness; they have a predilection for quarrels and immoral actions. Their critical attitude to their state is, as a rule, sharply reduced. Their mood is dysphoric, fatigability is increased, and their range of interests is narrowed. Strong headaches which seem to be "removed only by alcohol" frequently occur. The compulsion to use alcoholic beverages is so strong that even more frequent epileptic seizures are not always a deterrent.

In traumatic cerebral lesions, affective-volitional disorders caused by the injury (for example, the psychopathiclike variant of the psycho-organic syndrome or posttraumatic deterioration of the personality) are conducive to the appearance and fixation of a pathological craving for alcohol. Alcoholic changes of the personality in turn facilitate a weakening of moral-volitional restraints. Therefore, there appears a kind of vicious circle and, in such cases, it is frequently difficult to determine the respective weights of the personality's posttraumatic and alcoholic changes.

ALCOHOLISM AND CEREBRAL TRAUMA

Characteristic of persons who have experienced craniocerebral injuries is an increased sensitivity to alcohol. Under the effect of alcohol they easily develop increased affective excitability and motor discharges, which is frequently the cause of socially dangerous actions. The superimposition of alcoholism upon cerebral trauma may precipitate the progressive development of traumatic dementia.

The combination of alcoholism and cerebral atherosclerosis leads to a malignant course of both diseases and may result in serious mental disorders, even dementia at a comparatively young age. In all probability, a great role is played here by individual sensitivity of the metabolic processes and cerebral vessels to alcohol. It has been established that the cerebral-atherosclerotic process progresses rapidly when combined with alcoholism, and there is higher incidence and greater severity of cerebral vascular complications. When psychoses develop, their clinical picture is of a mixed nature, with symptoms characteristic of both alcoholism and cerebral atherosclerosis. Such psychoses frequently take a rapid course, and in short order lead to a stable mental defect.

Alcoholism and Psychopathy

Persons suffering from psychopathies frequently become chronic alcoholics. It is believed that from 10 to 40% of alcoholics are psychopaths. Most frequently alcoholism in psychopaths begins at an early age. They quickly lose quantitative and situational control, tolerance increases and drunkenness becomes unbridled. Given to frequent fluctuations of mood, psychopaths pass the first stage of alcoholism at a faster rate. Later it develops according to the general norm. Psychoses in psychopaths do not occur more often than in other alcoholics.

Rather frequently associated with drinking and chronic alcoholism is a psychopathic-like variant of so-called "simple schizophrenia." This variant of the schizophrenic process is also called hebetic (pertaining to youth), since its onset usually occurs at the age of puberty. As is known, simple schizophrenia is characterized mainly by the slowly building up of symptoms of dissociation (torpidity, apathy, lack of will-power, and a spontaneity based on a schizophrenically noncritical attitude to these disorders). Productive symptoms (e.g., delirium, hallucinations, affective and catatonic disorders) may occur in these cases only in reduced form. But in the psychopathic-like variant of simple schizophrenia, such disorders come to the fore as rudeness, severe irritability and negativism in regard to any advice and actions. All these unfold against a background of depleted higher emotional-volitional activity and a diminution of the energy potential. At the same time, there is a disinhibition of urges (sexual, aggressive, and anti-social, for example, toward vagrancy and the use of alcohol and narcotics).

Chronic alcoholism, which complicates all of these cases of the schizophrenic process, usually takes a rather mild course in the sense that pronounced abstinence disorders and symptoms of alcoholic deterioration of personality are absent for a long time. What is most depressing here, both for the afflicted person and for the people around him, is the unrestrained pathological craving for alcohol, marked by its impulsiveness.

Therapy first should be aimed at medication for alleviating pathologically strained urges, including the craving for alcohol (by administering small doses of periciazine, perphenazine, chlorpromazine, or thioproperazine). At the same time, lasting psychotherapeutic stimulation and correction is essential, utilizing a variety of approaches for the patient's emotional restitution (e.g., hobby therapy, interesting work or study, caring for pets, music therapy, creative activities, sports, etc.).

ALCOHOLISM AND NEUROSES

Alcoholism is frequently combined with neurosis. It is common knowledge that alcohol relieves feelings of anxiety and fear, and, at least initially, improves the mood. Apparently because of this persons suffering from neuroses readily begin to use alcohol. They often resort to it alone, taking it in small doses. At first alcohol abuse coincides with the exacerbation of the principal disease. Then the patient drinks even without such exacerbations. In a matter of a few years tolerance increases, and the abstinence syndrome slowly takes shape. However, the course of alcoholism itself is of a malignant character. Severe drinking binges with decompensation of the principal psychic disorder often occur together.

The treatment of symptomatic alcoholism always should be conducted with the principal disease in mind.

Chapter 15

Somatic and Neurological Disorders in Alcoholism

As alcoholism develops, complications occur in the patients' somatic and neurological status. These are most pronounced in stages II and III of alcoholism. Underlying their pathogenesis is the toxic effect of alcohol on the various portions of the nervous system, disorders in nervous regulation, and a resultant somatic and neurological pathology.

SOMATIC DISORDERS

Alcoholic beverages are absorbed from the stomach and the upper part of the intestine and carried with the blood throughout the body. Due to their different properties, the organs and tissues retain and accumulate alcohol differently. If blood alcohol concentration (BAC) is 100%, the BAC in the brain will be 175%, in the spinal fluid 150%, in the liver 148%, etc. (see Figure 2).[5]

Under the effect of alcohol the blood vessels dilate and the blood flows to the surface of the body producing a sensation of warmth. Soon a redistribution of blood takes place as it flows back to the internal organs. The area of body contact with the cold air is large,

[5] This figure is borrowed from the book: A. V. Voropai "Chtoby ne bylo bedy" ("Do Not Let Disaster Strike"), Moscow, 1972 (in Russian).

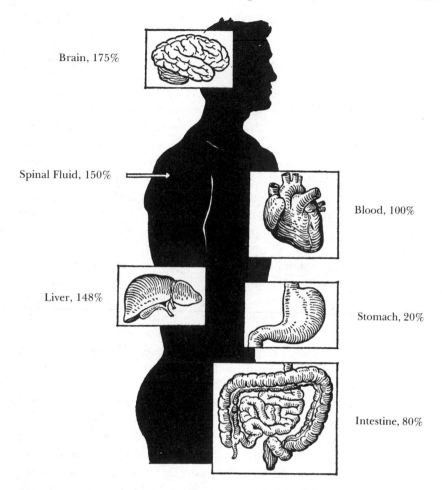

Brain, 175%

Spinal Fluid, 150%

Blood, 100%

Liver, 148%

Stomach, 20%

Intestine, 80%

Figure 2. Alcohol content in different organs and tissues of the human organism

causing an increased dissipation of heat. The processes of heat formation and heat emission are regulated by the nervous system. Yet, under the effect of alcohol these regulatory functions are disturbed, which results in the overcooling of the organism and may lead to frostbite and even death.

Many people believe it beneficial to drink one or two wine glasses of an alcoholic beverage before a meal, trusting it improves the appetite and digestion. The constant irritation of the mucous membranes soon leads to various diseases and dulls the appetite. In order to whet it one has to take more alcohol.

The amount of gastric juice also increases under the effect of alcohol, but it contains much hydrochloric acid and very little pepsin, the enzyme essential in food digestion. The gradually excreted acid in itself produces a searing effect on the mucosa which atrophies, upsetting the stomach's secretory and motor functions, with the onset and worsening of such gastrointestinal diseases as gastritis, gastric and duodenal ulcer. The gastric juice, altered under the effect of alcohol and of smoking, frequently precipitates the development of gastric cancer.

There are cases when physicians prescribe wine for improving the appetite. But, in such cases, very small quantities of fine wine or beer are recommended for a short period, a week or two, after which they are discontinued. Alcohol, by irritating the mucous membranes of the oral cavity and the stomach, causes the excretion of saliva and gastric juice, and this somewhat improves the appetite. But upon reaching this effect alcohol is discontinued and normal nutrition recommended.

The food of human beings consists of proteins, carbohydrates, fats and water. In the body all these food products undergo complex processes of digestion whereby energy is released and spent for the functioning of different organs, systems and muscles. One gram of carbohydrates and proteins produces up to 4.1 kilocalories of heat; when a gram of fat burns up it liberates 9.3 calories. One gram of alcohol liberates 7.1 calories, nearly twice the amount of the same quantity of carbohydrates and proteins. But apart from energy, the human organism also needs building materials for replacing the cells which gradually die off in the life process. For this the food must be diverse, producing the necessary energy and quantity of materials to be used even over large intervals after the intake of foodstuffs. Alcohol does not meet these needs of the body. It burns out quickly, liberating energy most of which is wasted by the organism.

Under the effect of alcohol, changes occur in the kidneys and the liver. The liver is an important organ where bile is formed for proper alimentation. Besides, it serves as a filter which retains toxic substances formed during the splitting of products. Alcohol blocks the liver, and worsens alimentation and bile secretion, which in turn affects food digestion.

Depending on the frequency of alcohol use, on the strength of alcoholic beverages, and the intake of alcohol substitutes, alcoholic dystrophy of the liver, alcoholic hepatitis, and cirrhosis of the liver may develop. Alcoholic hepatitis occurs in about 40% of persons who have been abusing alcohol for a long time, and in 25-36% of cases it develops into cirrhosis of the liver, a serious disease frequently leading to death. This is why the intake of even small doses of alcohol when a liver disease is present can be likened to little blows that may lead to a catastrophe. The main victims are males with long records of alcohol use. The exacerbation of the somatic condition coincides with alcohol abuse and heavy drinking. Somatic and laboratory examinations help in establishing the diagnosis.

Case Illustration Patient: Male, age 42. *Anamnesis*: The patient had been a heavy drinker for 11 years. The hangover syndrome was recorded during the last five years. The patient showed alcoholic type of personality changes. He would drink only wine or beer, 200-300 grams of wine or 4-6 glasses of beer to produce the effect of drunkenness. He has been admitted to a psychiatric hospital four times. He experienced alcoholic delirium. Treatment resulted in a remission lasting from one year to two years. During the last three years he had been feeling pain in the right epigastric area, of late complaining of general weakness, increased fatigability, and watery stools, and lost 16 pounds. At admission he had the same complaints, icteric sclera and enlarged liver (under pulpation the surface was dense and lumpy).

Examinations of the punctate and biochemical tests were carried out, with the diagnosis—cirrhosis of the liver.

While in the hospital the patient broke the rules and drank 200 grams of wine. Four hours later his status steeply worsened, with jaundice, tremor of the arms, and a drop in arterial pressure. All medical measures failed, and the patient died. An autopsy confirmed the diagnosis.

Summary: The example demonstrates that this patient had a rather aggravated anamnesis—stage III alcoholism, psychosis and a serious disease of the liver, cirrhosis. An intake of alcohol in violation of the rules resulted in death.

Reaching the muscles with the blood and taking part in the chemistry of muscular work, alcohol lowers the working capacity of the muscles; an intake of 100 grams of vodka reduces muscular strength by 17%.

When there is a high alcohol content in the blood, the alcohol permeates the tissues and organs, penetrating across the blood-brain barrier into the spinal fluid and with it into the brain. Alcohol circulates in the blood in the following way: during mild intoxication 100 ml of blood contains 0.15 ml of alcohol, in stronger intoxication, 0.25-0.3 ml, and when insensible, 0.4-0.5 ml.

The lethal dose has not been determined since it depends on individual tolerance. In some people the cells acquire the capacity to destroy alcohol and they develop an increased tolerance to alcoholic beverages. In others, on the contrary, even small doses make them drunk.

Alcoholism leads to disorders on the part of the cardiovascular system. The intake of small doses reduces the tone of peripheral vessels which dilate, and the blood flows to the surface of the body, to the face, after which a redistribution takes place, with its concentration in the internal organs. Such "pumping over" of the blood at times leads to collapse of cardiac activity.

Constant alcohol use upsets metabolism, which in turn causes changes in the walls of blood vessels: fatty substances and calcium salts begin to accumulate in them; the vessels lose elasticity, become fragile and brittle, and their lumen narrows. As a result, blood flows through them with difficulty, which upsets the nutrition of organs and tissues. In other words, alcohol speeds up the onset of early atherosclerosis and, not infrequently, precipitates myocardial infarctions and cerebral hemorrhages.

A large group of people with atherosclerosis in the age group from 25 to 50 years were screened, though according to age they should not have had pronounced symptoms of that disease. Moreover, none of the subjects had problematic histories. It was found that the majority of them (93%) began to abuse alcohol at an age below 25 years, when the formation of the organism was under way or nearing completion. It is believed, therefore, that the main cause of atherosclerosis in this group of people was early excessive use of alcohol. Changes in the heart muscle developed, from mild (functional) to severe (organic). All types of cardiac pathology developed: alcoholic hypertension, the postalcoholic somatovegetative syndrome, alcoholic cardiopathy, myocardial dystrophy, cardiosclerosis, myocardial infarction. Nearly all these conditions are diagnosed during examinations by the therapist and confirmed by ECG. Functional states are amenable to treatment, while organic ones can frequently lead to death.

Alcohol affects the muscular fibers of the heart, causing their fatty degeneration. The cross section of the heart becomes enlarged and the organ changes its position. Becoming weak, it no longer can adequately cope with its customary work. There appears pain in the region of the heart, dyspnea, and, in serious cases, edema. A French proverb says: "He who lives in wine dies in water" (see Figure 3).

Case Illustration Patient: Male, age 42. *Anamnesis*: The patient has a history of alcohol abuse of about 20 years' duration, with the hangover syndrome for 10-12 years. He showed pronounced alcoholic-type personality changes. He drank 300-400 grams of wine virtually daily or during drinking bouts. On admission he had the general aspect of a very aged person; his face was deeply wrinkled, he had many bruises, and tissue turgor was diminished. He looked 12-15 years older than his age and has long been experiencing pain in the area of the heart. Upon admission to the hospital after the last drinking bout, his pulse rate was 110 per minute, rhythmical, and AP 170/100 mmHg.Retrosternal pain had been troubling him for ten months, recently becoming more frequent and intensive. Several times he had to summon emergency aid, at which time pain was

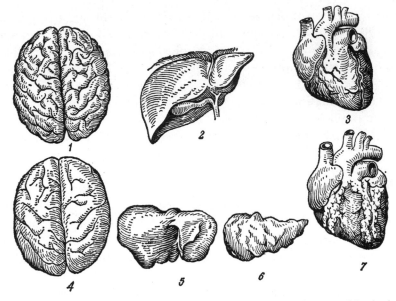

Figure 3. Healthy organs: 1—brain; 2—liver; 3—heart. Alcohol-affected organs: 4—brain; 5, 6—liver; 7—heart

relieved by injections of analgesics. His diagnosis was confirmed by ECG —myocardial infarction. Treatment by abstinence from alcohol resulted in improvement, and the patient was discharged in satisfactory condition.

Summary: In the above example, we see many years of systematic alcohol use which caused cardiovascular insufficiency and myocardial infarction.

Moderate doses of alcohol increase the respiration rate, with a greater volume of oxygen entering the lungs and enhancing the release of carbon dioxide, but this state is short-lived, as the exhaled air increasingly contains alcohol fumes given off at first through the lungs and then through the kidneys. During alcohol intoxication, paralysis of the respiratory center and arrest of respiration may occur.

Observations show that the resistance and activity of the alcoholic's organism become steeply reduced and he becomes more susceptible to infections. For example, ordinary influenza in alcoholics as a rule takes a severe course with high temperature, not infrequently accompanied by pneumonia and cardiovascular insufficiency.

Metabolic disorders and secondary avitaminoses are constant conditions in alcoholism. Not only complete expenditure of fats takes place, but carbohydrates are poorly utilized, mineral metabolism is upset and there are deep disorders in the protein metabolism and avitaminoses (deficiency of the B, PP, and C vitamin groups). The disruption of the protective function of the liver results in hypercholesterization. Changes occur in hydroelectric equilibrium, with a depletion of sodium, magnesium, potassium, chlorine, and calcium, and an increase of protein and fatty metabolism with azotemia, acidosis, ketonuria and loss of weight.

Alcoholism is frequently combined with tuberculosis. It is known that the incidence of tuberculosis among alcohol abusers is six times higher than in nonusers. This is due to many factors, including the physical state of the organism (reduced resistance, metabolic disorders, the state of respiratory organs), as well as environmental factors, the unsanitary surroundings of such patients, their unwillingness to accept treatment, and the low efficacy of medicinal drugs.

Alcoholism takes less time to form in tuberculosis patients than in healthy patients and its course is more malignant. At first, tolerance to alcohol rises in shorter periods only to quickly diminish afterward. The use of alcoholic beverages assumes the character of drinking bouts. Psychoses more frequently proceed as delirial-amential with a protracted course and pass off slowly. Among the alcoholics suffering from tuberculosis there are many who are severely incapacitated.

NEUROLOGICAL DISORDERS

Neurological disorders of different character occur in alcoholism rather frequently. They involve the brain (alcoholic encephalopathy) and the peripheral nervous system (alcoholic polyneuropathy), occurring most frequently in persons in the 35 to 50 years age bracket. In alcohol abuse (for 15-30 years) and stages II and III of alcoholism, there appear different types of alcoholic encephalopathy.

Psychic disorders in the Korsakoff psychosis are characterized mainly by loss of memory (amnesia), disorientation and confabulation (filling in gaps in memory with made-up tales). The entire psychic structure of an individual's personality undergoes change. The patients become childish and foolish, coherent thoughts difficult, and their minds are nourished only by old ideas, concepts and habits. Standing out against this background is the chief symptom of the disease, loss of memory. More specifically, patients stop remembering current events and gradually forget what happened to them before. Sometimes events that happened long ago are perceived as recent, or the patients begin to describe events that had actually never happened to them.

The disease begins gradually, with complaints of headache or giddiness, pain in the legs, sensation of creeping, poor sleep or nightmares. Occasionally, acute psychic disorders of a type similar to the above-described delirium tremens take place, followed by the development of symptoms of the Korsakoff psychosis. Psychic disorders are compounded by physical emaciation, whereby the patients move their feet with difficulty or cannot move at all and are completely bedridden. Timely treatment may considerably alleviate the patients' conditions, though without complete recovery. Repeated alcohol abuse may lead to a lethal outcome or the development of advanced dementia. Other forms of chronic encephalopathy seldom occur.

Alcoholic tremor appears in the upper limbs, the eyelids and the tongue. At first it is manifested at the time of hangover, but eventually becomes permanent. This symptom may develop chronically or acutely. It affects the gait, which becomes shaky, and the patients walk gingerly, especially if movements are not controlled by vision. Deep sensitivity is also involved with blocking of reflexes. Paresthesias with the sensation of small creeping insects are noted.

Case Illustration Patient: Male, age 32. *Anamnesis*: According to his wife, the patient had been drinking alcoholic beverages for about 20 years. In recent years, he has been drinking about a bottle of wine daily and using different substitutes. The hangover syndrome has been in evidence for about 8-10 years. During this period he has been treated twice in a psychiatric hospital and has had two years of compulsory treatment at a WTP. During the last two to two and a half months the patient had headaches, weakness in his legs, and loss of appetite. He lost 16 pounds. On admission and subsequently, he had an unsteady gait, was unable to stand on his feet, and lurched from side to side when walking. He showed reflex pathology and restricted movement of his eyeballs. There were also disorders of swallowing and dysarthria. Muscular tone increased, then reduced. Consciousness altered according to the stupefaction type. He also had several convulsive seizures. Treatment relieved some of the symptoms, yet the unsteady gait, pronounced tremor of the fingers and neurological symptoms persisted for another three months. At the time of discharge there was noticeable dementia with reduced criticism, considerable memory disorders and an affective plateau.

Summary: The above patient's clinical picture was grave with abounding neurological symptoms. After an improvement of the general status there was dementia with pronounced deterioration of memory.

One of the chronic alcoholic encephalopathies is the Korsakoff psychosis (alcoholic paralysis, polyneurotic psychosis, alcoholic pseudoparalysis, and alcoholic encephalopathies with beriberi, a vitamin B_1 deficiency), and pellagra (Vitamin PP deficiency). Some authors include alcoholic tremor, the ataxic syndrome, sleep disorders (alcoholic agrypnia), functional disorders of the pyramidal and vegetative nervous systems, and alcoholic deterioration of the personality. Sleep disorders occur very frequently in alcoholic encephalopathies. The patients have difficulty in falling asleep, have nightmares filled with ferocious animals and dreadful scenes, and experience fears of what they perceive as reality. They wake up often and fall asleep with difficulty.

Functional changes of the pyramidal system are manifested in increased tendon and abdominal reflexes. In cases of pathological changes of the vegetative nervous system, there is tachycardia, elevated arterial pressure, palpitations, a sensation of fever, and headaches.

When the peripheral nervous system is affected there are disorders caused by the destruction of tissue. The initial stages of polyneurites are characterized by cold hands, hyperesthesia or hypesthesia, and pain that spreads along the nerve trunk when pressure is applied. Subsequently, peripheral pareses may develop, predominantly of the legs. Muscular hypertonia, muscular atrophy and blocking of reflexes are also noted.

In other cases, disorders are expressed in pain in the arms and legs, sensations of chilliness, numbness, and cramps of the gastroc-nemius muscles. Occasionally there are sensations of heat, hot flushes, and irregularities of pain or temperature sensitivity. In addition, there may be an ataxic syndrome, i.e., an unstable, shaky gait.

Alcoholism frequently causes disorders of cerebral circulation. Alcoholic stroke may be precipitated by a drinking bout and is char-acterized by strong headaches, giddiness, weakness, nausea, and vom-iting. Dysarthria, facial asymmetry and hemipareses appear. There are changes of consciousness ranging in degree from mild to severe. Subarachnoidal hemorrhages occur in cases of head injury, even if mild, since the weak vascular walls cannot withstand even superficial concussions.

Chapter 16

Pathology of Higher Nervous Activity in Alcoholism

At the turn of the 20th century Danilevsky drew attention to the fact that the highest alcohol concentration is always found in the nerve cells of the brain. The first reaction to alcohol intake comes from the CNS. Initially affected is the cerebral cortex, then the subcortical areas, then the spinal cord, and lastly, the vital centers of the medulla oblongata.

Three stages are distinguished in the action of alcohol on the CNS. Stage 1: excitation, or mild drunkenness; stage 2: depression of the CNS; and stage 3: narcosis. In accordance with these stages of alcohol's action, drunkenness manifests itself in different variants and degrees. Its form, sequel and duration depend on the individual properties of the organism and of the higher nervous activity and on the ingested dose.

During the first stage the ingested dose of alcohol is small and its effect is that of a stimulant. Psychic manifestations usually include slackening of attention, excessive self-confidence and touchiness. Under the effect of alcohol peripheral vessels dilate and the skin reddens, producing a sensation of warmth and physical vigor; there is also motor excitation.

Alcohol affects the nerve cell (neuron) and interferes with its capacity to transmit impulses (excitation) from one neuron to another, a property which reveals itself before any changes in the organism's

165

metabolic processes. Numerous tests and investigations have confirmed that even with small alcohol doses (20-30 grams) the phase of intellectual and motor excitation is short: as the effect of alcohol takes hold the velocity of associations slows down, also diminishing the number of inherent logical associations, while associations of conformity, habitual conceptions and superficial connections begin to predominate. The quantity of such outside associations changes from 10% at the beginning of the tests to 40-45% at their conclusion. These parameters were also studied when performing physical work. It was found that after brief phases of excitation and seemingly increased stamina there comes a decline and marked exhaustion of the nervous system.

It is noteworthy that during the tests many subjects believed they were coping well with the assignments, that their psychic processes proceeded easily and rapidly, and showed surprise when the results turned out absolutely different from their subjective evaluation.

The state of slight excitation is succeeded, as a rule, by the stage of torpidity and somnolence. This is due to the fact that following alcohol's short-lived exciting effect on the nerve cells there is the inevitable period of inhibitory action. Strelchuk and Gavrilova studied the effect of alcohol on the bioelectric potentials of the brain. The results confirm other experimental data indicating that alcohol affects the brain's bioelectrical activity. A direct dependence was noted: the higher the dose of ingested alcohol, the greater the disorganization of the brain's bioelectrical potentials. This is one of the objective criteria characterizing the state of cortical processes.

What, then, are the basic pathophysiological mechanisms of alcoholic intoxication? Pavlov regarded the picture of alcoholic intoxication as a variant of central inhibition. In his article "A Physiologist's Tentative Excursion into the Realm of Psychiatry," he wrote: "Lastly, here, in the same group of all kinds of variations of central inhibition, we must place the symptom of playfulness particularly observed in hebephrenics, and also flare-ups of excitation with the character of aggressiveness, which occur among the above-mentioned symptoms in other schizophrenics. All these phenomena closely resemble the pictures of ordinary initial alcoholic intoxication. In these cases there is every ground for regarding the matter as a result of beginning general inhibition of the cerebral hemispheres, due to which the nearest subcortex is just liberated from permanent control, permanent inhibition on the part of the hemispheres in a wakeful state, and even on the basis of the positive induction mechanism it is brought, together with all its centers, into a chaotic, excited state. Hence in alcoholic narcosis we have now unmotivated and unusual playfulness and hilarity, now excessive maudlin sensitivity and tears, now anger."

Along with the development of alcoholic intoxication the dynamics of cortical processes, i.e., of excitation and inhibition, become disrupted, and proper interrelationships between the cortex and the subcortical areas are upset. When the disorders on the part of the cortex and subcortex become significant, marked alcoholic intoxication sets in. People become excessively lively, hilarious or, on the contrary, sad, apathetic, and losing the sense of tact and restraint in regard to others. Criticism of one's actions diminishes, just as does the sense of responsibility, and instincts are bared. All reactions to external stimulants acquire an affective coloring; insignificant factors may bring joy or fear, cast one into despair, or cause wrath and fury.

The concentration of attention and logical thought are also disrupted. An intoxicated person is unable to listen to others, strives to attract attention, at times becomes foolish, reveals a tendency to brag and to find fault with everything. In some cases he voices ideas of sinfulness and guilt. Suggestability is increased. In addition, motor reactions are upset so that the drunk person becomes excessively restless, displays aggressiveness in regard to other people and himself, or, on the contrary, becomes generous and magnanimous. Speech may slow down and become slurred, the perception of external impressions is distorted, and sensitivity to pain is reduced. The functioning of internal organs also undergoes changes: at the beginning of drunkenness the rate of respiration increases, then becomes slower and deeper, the heart rate increases, and arterial pressure rises.

With the deepening of the narcosis, inhibition involves cortical ganglia, draws the cerebellum and partially the spinal cord into the process, and upsets the vegetative-vascular functions, causing the appearance of such symptoms as salivation and vomiting. Walking and precision of movements are impaired. With the further increase of inhibition, the drunk falls into deep slumber.

A person's psychic reactions to alcohol intake largely depend on the type of nervous system and higher nervous activity, on such qualities as strength and level-headedness, and on the mobility of the excitatory and inhibitory processes and their correlation. Overfatigue, brain injury and other factors may increase the reactions to alcohol ingestion.

Very large doses of alcohol cause massive functional disorders of the CNS with rapid involvement of the spinal cord and the medulla oblongata. Here deep narcosis and loss of consciousness take place. Heat regulation, cardiac activity and respiration are upset. Reactions to external stimuli, for example, to a call or to a needle prick are depressed, and there is a weakening of muscular tone. Pupils are dilated and do not respond to light. In this state, death may occur.

Still deeper and more stable changes of higher nervous activity have been revealed in chronic alcoholics. Experiments conducted in animals and observations of humans demonstrated that, first of all, there is a reduction of the inhibitory process followed by inadequate excitability. Initially this is expressed in the upset mobility of these processes, then in pathological inertia and lability. Changes have also been revealed in the interactions between the primary and secondary signal systems, finding expression in inadequate responses to stimuli. It was found that vascular reactions to environmental changes in alcoholics are either reduced or absent altogether.

All of the above are very stable conditions. During abstention from alcohol for six months and longer they may return to normal in the most simple cases, but in most others they persist at a pathological level for a long time. The obtained data and their dynamics may be traced on an encephalogram, which indicates cortical exhaustion with inert processes of inhibition and excitation.

Chapter 17

Pathological Anatomy

Acute alcohol intoxication may be lethal. The higher the alcohol content of the beverage, the more dangerous it becomes. It is considered that 250-300 ml of alcohol (600-700 grams of vodka) may prove lethal for a nondrinking adult. But the doses may be even lower. This depends on the type of higher nervous activity, the presence of factors weakening the nervous system, on insomnia and even such trivial factors as preliminary fasting or taking alcohol on an empty stomach.

Age, too, is of great importance. For example, a baby may die from 20-30 ml of alcohol, while the ordinary adult "norm" of 100-150 grams of vodka might be lethal for a six to eight-year-old child. Alcohol intoxication in teenagers frequently results in a comatose state requiring resuscitation measures, and sometimes, in death.

Some medicinal drugs have a potentiating effect; their administration enhances the action of alcohol. The administration of nitroglycerin and alcohol may cause collapse, with loss of consciousness and possible death due to sharp vasodilation. For example, the simultaneous administration of sedatives, soporifics of the glutethimide type, or tranquilizers like diazepam, steeply enhance the effect of alcohol. Investigations into the causes of sudden death have revealed the presence of alcohol and medicinal drugs in the blood.

In all cases of acute alcohol intoxication the entire organism is affected. The pathoanatomical picture typical for these cases is characterized by increased permeability of the vascular walls, the involve-

169

ment of the endothelium, hemorrhages, destructive changes, cerebral edema, etc.

In chronic alcohol intoxication, irreversible changes and organic processes take place in various organs and tissues. The most pronounced are changes in the CNS (nerve cells and fibers). These include diffuse disorders affecting the entire cerebral tissue and focal lesions which may manifest themselves in the form of hemorrhages, glial cicatrices, etc. The nerve cells swell, and some of them undergo wrinkling, fatty degeneration and the proliferation of glial elements. Part of the nerve cells die; in some of them, the changes concentrate within the nuclei.

Most frequently affected are the cells of the cortical layers III-IV-V, of the subcortical ganglia, and of the cerebellum and spinal cord. Atrophy of the brain occurs in 80.2% of cases. As a rule significant changes are noted in the cerebral vessels and also in the vessels of the heart, lungs, liver and spleen. Multiple hemorrhages occur in the cerebral meninges. Turbidity and swelling of the meninges and, sometimes, cerebral edema, an increased quantity of fluid in the subarachnoid space, ventricular ectasis, isolated areas of atrophy in the frontal and occipital lobes and subcortical formations, and mixed cortical-subcortical atrophy with ventricular ectasis have been revealed macroscopically.

In far advanced cases of alcoholism and in the presence of pronounced symptoms of dementia, macroscopically one may observe atrophy of cerebral tissue with collapse and ectasis of the entire ventricular system. Particularly affected is the cerebellum, which reveals atrophic, necrobiotic and dystrophic changes. The same alterations are observed in the subcortical ganglia, in the thalamus, the medulla oblongata and other areas. These changes may be observed in living patients by means of pneumoencephalography. Atherosclerotic disorders also become visible.

Apart from general changes inherent in alcoholism, different investigators find specific disorders characteristic of different forms and stages of the disease. For example, the phenomenon of hemorrhagic encephalitis in the mesencephalic region and cell degeneration are regarded as routine findings in delirium.

Wernicke's acute alcoholic encephalopathy is the severest mani-
festation of chronic alcoholism. In this condition edema and swelling
of the brain and meninges are revealed macroscopically, as well as
plethoric congestion of cerebral matter and capillary dilation in all
parts of the brain and smoothed gyri. Punctate hemorrhages do not
necessarily occur. There is moderately pronounced cortical-subcortical atrophy, hydrocephalus, and chronic arachnoiditis. On the part
of the internal organs, one finds congestion pneumonia, fatty degeneration of the liver, chronic hepatitis developing into cirrhosis, alcoholic cardiosclerosis, and chronic gastritis. There is also loss of weight.
The grey matter around the third ventricle, the aqueduct of Sylvius
is severely affected, where strong proliferation of glial vessels is observed. There are no inflammatory infiltrates and diapedetic hemorrhages are possible (not always). There is pronounced gliofibrosis
beneath the appendima of the ventricles. Cortical nerve cells, particularly in the second-third layers of the frontal lobes, are atrophic,
overloaded with lipofuscin. Cell-free fields form in place of focal
collapse. The number of Purkinje's cells in the cerebellum is reduced.

Metabolic disorders, vitamin deficiency are reflected in pathological anatomy. For example, pellagra leads to the swelling of nerve cells
and changes in the nuclei. In far advanced cases, small punctate hemorrhages into the cortex and subcortical formations are revealed.

Serious changes take place in the internal organs. In stages II-III
of alcoholism the most frequent effects are atherosclerotic changes
in the vascular walls and possible disorders on the part of the heart
muscles: they are flabby, the heart itself is transversely enlarged, and
in beer abuse there may be a "beer" or extremely hypertrophied heart.
Fatty degeneration of cells is noted in all muscular layers, and the
cavities are dilated. As a rule the liver is affected. In 95% of the cases
there is fatty degeneration of the cells, atypical structure of liver lobes
and atrophy of part of the cells. Depending on the stage of the disease
there occur necrotic and dystrophic processes, indicating the different
degrees of liver cirrhosis. A frequent complication in alcoholism is
polyneuritis, more often of the upper and lower extremities. This is
a degenerative process with the dissolution of myelin, the destruction
of axial cylinders and the replacement of nerve tissue with connective
tissue.

It should be noted that some organic changes are gradually alleviated during abstention from alcohol and during treatment, a certain portion of which are not specific to alcoholism alone; therefore, when determining the pathoanatomical diagnosis, these data should be compared with the clinical picture of the disease itself.

Chapter 18

Narcomanias

Narcomanias have been known for a long time. Following the Second World War they became particularly widespread not only in Asian countries, but in Europe and America, too. The spread of narcomanias is due to a variety of factors. The use of narcotics is probably connected with the desire to escape, if only temporarily, the hardships of life. Some people see these substances as a means to derive thrilling experiences. In addition, habit formation may occur in sick people since a number of medicinal remedies used for therapeutic purposes to alleviate pain do cause a morbid craving for them in the process of treatment. In a certain segment of young people, an important role is also played by lack of discipline, character immaturity, weak self-control and increased interest in unfamiliar sensations.

Narcomanias evolve from habituation to a narcotic drug to the syndrome of narcotic addition per se. Initially, depending on the type of higher nervous activity, the narcotic drug, the dose, the method of administration into the body and the subject's mental disposition, a euphoric effect is produced. The recipient develops a preference for that narcotic drug, which he begins to take regularly.

Then there occurs a change in the reactivity of the organism; protective reactions disappear (for example, suppression of the vomiting reflex). The consumption of the narcotic assumes a systematic character and increases in tolerance occur. Drug addicts take doses from two to ten times greater than those used for medical purposes.

Gradually psychic dependence on the narcotic drug takes shape. Subsequently, physical dependence develops with an uncontrollable craving for narcotics and a pronounced abstinence syndrome, whose structure may include asthenodepressive, hypomanic and explosive elements. Thus, just as in alcoholism, in the formed state of narcotic addiction we observe changes of tolerance, the appearance of psychic and physical dependence, and a pronounced abstinence syndrome.

In the developmental dynamics of this syndrome one may conditionally distinguish three stages: first, adaptation (changes in the reactivity of the organism and the appearance of psychic dependence); second, appearance of physical dependence in the form of the abstinence syndrome; and third, the exhaustion of all systems (decrease of tolerance, protracted abstinence syndrome, and the appearance, in a number of cases, of addiction to several drugs simultaneously, i.e., polynarcomania). Changes in the psychic sphere proceed in parallel in the form of neurotic and psychopathic changes in the personality according to the hysterical, asthenic, explosive or apathetic types.

The pathogenesis of narcotic addiction is extremely complicated and, to this day, there is no consensus of opinion on this matter. However, it should be viewed according to the stages of the disease; neurotropic, humoral, endocrine, metabolic and other systems are involved in the process, and a change in one of them precipitates changes in the others.

There are several classes of narcotic substances—tranquilizers, opiates, barbiturates, hallucinogens, etc.—whose clinical manifestations differ.

HASHISH AND OTHER TRANQUILIZERS

This group of narcotics includes the derivatives of different varieties of hemp (tranquilizers or "fantasizers"), for example, anasha, marijuana, hashish, bang, etc. These plants originate from the countries of Asia, Africa and Latin America. The active component is the aromatic aldehyde cannabinol contained in hemp extract, whose concentration is of great importance in the developmental pattern of the intoxication. Anasha is used in different ways; it is chewed, smoked, or taken in drinks. In the USSR anasha is smoked. A small grain of the drug is put into the tobacco of a cigarette and smoked. The effect is felt within 15-30 minutes. Not infrequently the first episodes, far from causing pleasant sensations, cause nausea, a burning sensation in the mouth, salivation, and a slight giddiness. Despite this the smokers keep smoking and the unpleasant sensations pass away. As a rule, the effect of hashish begins with some physical manifestations, such as thirst, hunger, and slight dryness of the mucous membranes. Then there appears a sensation of warmth which spreads throughout the body. A state of lightness and weightlessness evolves. There appears the wish to jump, dance, or assume bizarre postures. There is a lot of uncontrollable giggling, and the slightest movement or posture of another elicits repeated uncontrollable fits of laughter. Attention is easily distracted, and different associations appear without getting fixed for any length on a single object or phenomenon. The rate of thinking is accelerated, with thoughts crowding one another, rapidly replacing each other or overlapping. There is excessive verbosity, sentences are frequently without ending, and words fail to express thoughts clearly. The smoker loses contact with the people around him and finds it strange that they do not share his hilarity, which irritates and angers him. There are abrupt emotional shifts, first anger and wrath, then excessive cheerfulness and hilarity, reaching exaltation. Appearing against this background are runaway fantasies and illusions. The surrounding world is seen in bright colors, and sounds become loud and resounding, sometimes booming out like an echo.

These states are characteristic of the first phase of hashish intoxication, the stage of excitation. It is followed by the second stage, depression. Some smokers say the transition from one stage to another is sudden; others, on the contrary, note a gradual change of the surrounding world, with colors turning dull. Illusions disappear, fantasies are extinguished, and cerebration is steeply inhibited. This is followed by fears, delusions of persecution, and deep despondency. The state is accompanied by vegetative crises.

Symptoms of hashish intoxication depend on the quantity used, the frequency of administration, and the individual characteristics of higher nervous activity of the user. In mild intoxication we observe a state of mild euphoria; medium severity is characterized by more pronounced symptoms with fantasies, illusions and a state of light motor excitation, and acute hashish intoxication lasts from one to three hours and ends in deep slumber or weakness and apathy.

With further hashish abuse the intoxication picture undergoes additional changes. In some subjects there develop disorders of the emotional-volitional sphere, leading to psychopathization of the personality, or even to schizophrenic symptoms. Less frequently, in some subjects psychoses develop with pronounced disorders of consciousness, visual and auditory hallucinations, delusions of persecution and reference, and sometimes, acute motor excitation. Systematic use of hashish for two to six months leads to the appearance of psychic asthenia and deterioration of memory. Eventually, the addict loses his friends. As time goes on, emotional dullness and apathy set in, there is total dissociation from people, with increased delusions of reference and persecution.

Case Illustration Patient: Male, age 27. *Anamnesis*: This patient, a second-course student of polytechnical institute, was a sociable person who had many friends. Once, when still at school in the 9th grade, he was invited to a party in the company of age-mates, and an older boy who was present suggested a smoke of hashish. Although the patient had already learned to smoke cigarettes, at first he rejected the proposal. Afterwards however, upon seeing the merriment of his friends who already had a smoke, he ventured to try it himself. He felt an unpleasant sensation in his mouth and, after a few drags, experienced giddiness and nausea. Upon throwing away the cigarette, he braved the ridicule of those present and did not smoke any more on that occasion. He soon found himself in the same company and started smoking again. He remembered that at first everything around him became illusory; he saw people as if through a haze, and at times, everything became brightly colored and sounds were very loud. His friends made "faces" at him and he giggled uncontrollably for about two to three hours. He also recalled the subsequent very unpleasant feeling in his mouth, began to fear he would go crazy and ran out-doors, but his friends dragged him back into the room. At one moment it seemed to him that his heart had stopped and he shouted out. Then everything passed away and he fell asleep.

There were no more episodes of hashish smoking before he en-rolled at the institute. During the first course at the institute he boasted about having smoked hashish and began smoking again. Thereafter he smoked frequently and spoke mostly of positive reactions. He began to long for the pleasurable state caused by the hashish cigarette and in an attempt to substitute alcohol for the not always available hashish, began to drink.

His parents and the patient himself recall that he tried to leave home, became irritable, rude and pugnacious. Poor progress at the institute led to his expulsion. He lost all interest in books, films or television, sought to be alone, and tried to get the narcotic or a drink by any means available. He fell in with a company of tramps, became untidy, and at times had a feeling of being pursued by someone. At first he tried not to pay attention but then he began hiding from imagined pursuers. Once he sought the protection of the police, but his words were not taken seriously. After that depression and anxiety increased. His parents drew attention to their son's plight and he was forcibly placed in a psychiatric hospital, where a marked depressive-delirial syndrome was diagnosed.

Withdrawal from the narcotic caused no distress, though he made several attempts to obtain it from outside. He was discharged following a four-month intensive course of detoxification and general strength-ening treatment, as well as psychotherapy and work therapy.

Summary: The above example demonstrates how gradually habit-uation to the narcotic drug developed, and how the subject's character began changing and psychic disorders appeared.

MORPHINE AND OTHER OPIATES

This group of narcotics includes opium and its preparations (pan-topon, omnopon, laudonone, pectol), some 20 alkaloids and derivatives of opium (morphine, codeine, thebaine, heroin, ethylmorphine hydrochloride, papaverine, noscapine, laudanine and others), and synthetic preparations with a morphine-like effect (methadone, trimeperidine hydrochloride, etc.). The latter, i.e., the morphine-like effect, is common to all these substances.

Morphine-type addiction occurs in localities where opium grows and is cultivated. Not infrequently it appears as a consequence of incorrect utilization of these preparations by physicians for medical purposes.

Habit formation to morphine preparations takes place comparatively quickly. Opium is used by oral, subcutaneous, and intravenous administration, or it is smoked. Codeine is administered orally, morphine and trimeperidine, subcutaneously and intravenously. In the absence of the substance in pure form various opium-containing medicinal drugs are used, e.g., stomach drops. The narcotic is frequently administered by means of a nonsterile syringe, diluted in tap water, and injected in all accessible parts of the body. The lethal dose of the pure substance is 0.3-0.5 grams. Addicts quickly acquire the tendency to increase the dose because of developing tolerance to the drug. This is why cases occur in which patients use doses ten times greater than those mentioned above.

Acute intoxication is characterized by euphoria which reaches the stage of pronounced excitation. At the same time there appears dryness in the mouth, sensations of heat, great weakness, tinnitus, headache, and sweating. There are increased urinary, cardiovascular and respiratory disorders. Consciousness is changed. During an unfavorable course there is an onset of cyanosis, bloody stools, and convulsions caused by paralysis of the respiratory center. Sometimes there are skin symptoms such as itching and all kinds of rashes, and the face becomes dark red; there is also somnolence and deep sleep. Chronic use of the narcotic produces euphoria, a feeling of bliss and, occasionally, illusions. Soon after taking several drags the opium addict enters into a world of dreams and fantastic experiences and boundless pleasure. After 30-40 minutes the euphoric phase is replaced by somnolence, drowsiness and a pleasant languor.

In morphine addiction, abstinence occurs several hours after the intake of the last dose of the narcotic and lasts for five to seven days. Various somatovegetative and psychoneurological symptoms occur: yawning, sweating, lacrimation, nose-running, tremor, fever, dilation of the pupils, nausea, vomiting, flushes, increased temperature and respiratory rate, spasm of abdominal muscles and other groups of muscles, muscular pain, dehydration of the organism and loss of weight. Mentally, there is anxiety, worry and, from time to time, unfounded fear of death. They also show poor sleep with frequent nightmares. There are also fluctuating moods: now mild euphoria with overestimation of one's own personality and potentials, then low-key mood with depression, or irritability and anger with apathy and aggression.

Short-lived psychoses with an altered state of consciousness occasionally occur. The Korsakoff amnesic syndrome and spastic seizures may also occur.

Case Illustration Patient: Male, age 27. *Anamnesis*: This patient fell in with elder boys when he was in the 8th grade. During that period he tasted hashish, liked it and quickly developed the habit; a week later he was smoking in earnest. Progress at school became poor; he shirked from doing lessons, quarreled with teachers and finished eight classes with difficulty. Soon he began smoking three times a day. Thoughts crowded his head, he fantasized frequently and at the beginning laughed a lot; then laughter and hilarity disappeared. In 1968 for the first time he injected 0.5 ml of opium, which he liked. Soon the initial dose no longer satisfied him. Gradually he brought it up to 2 ml twice a day. Then the average dose settled at 1 gram a day of dry opium. Character changes set in. He became hot-tempered, and involvement in fights and theft led to a criminal indictment. Then in 1970 he was drafted for army service. Before departure he bought a portion of dry opium which he took with him. He never stopped taking it, and when the stock ran out he badly suffered from abstinence. He felt weakness all over his body, and his boots seemed very heavy. After meals he experienced pain in his stomach, heartburn, and pain in the region of the liver. Eventually he was sent to a mental hospital. On admission, he experienced pain all over his body and in his muscles, weakness, diarrhea, poor sleep, and tearfulness. He quickly tired from conversations. With tears in his eyes he begged for help. His status was somewhat improved on the third day, and symptoms of abstinence disappeared on the seventh day. However, asthenia, general weakness, tearfulness and increased tiredness persisted for a long time.

Summary: In the above case the patient systematically took increased doses of the narcotic. As a result there were changes in his character, and he committed criminal offenses. States of abstinence were particularly severe, and because of them, he was afraid to give up narcotics.

BARBITURATES AND OTHER SOPORIFICS

This group of substances possessing a hypnotic effect consists of two subgroups: (a) derivatives of barbituric acid, and (b) substances of the nonbarbituric series but producing a soporific effect. These two groups of drugs are united by the same clinical picture arising as a result of constant or periodically resumed intake. These drugs are characterized by the fact that the doses of the medicines taken, as a rule, exceed therapeutic ones.

Addiction to these substances proceeds along several paths: careless and lasting treatment of insomnia, carried out at first under medical control and then by self-medication; intake of medicines without medical advice and control; and the use of these substances as narcotics.

Acute intoxications are possible during suicidal attempts. In these cases deep sleep occurs which at times may be interrupted, but diffused cortical inhibition may persist; this is why hypnotic phases are noted in the patients. Such states may last for days or weeks.

In some cases the intake of doses considerably in excess of therapeutic ones may have the effect of severe symptoms of motor uncoordination, muscular weakening, diminution or disappearance of reflexes, particularly abdominal, and dysarthria. Multiple vegetative symptoms (drop of arterial pressure, elevated temperature, slow

pulse, acrocyanosis) can be observed simultaneously. Changes of consciousness in the form of stupefaction may be added to this picture.

Chronic use of soporifics gradually builds up the need or strong
desire to continue their intake and to increase the dose of the narcotic.
Many addicts begin taking narcotics several times a day, upon which
psychic dependence, associated with the subjective evaluation of the
drug's effect, increases.

Changes of personality become increasingly prominent. Predominant at first are irritability, explosiveness, egotism to the point of
egocentrism, and malice. Then memory disorders appear, which may
develop into the Korsakoff syndrome, possibly in the pseudoparalytic
form. The rate of cerebration slows down until it becomes torpid.
Often one observes spastic seizures of the epileptiform type.

Physical symptoms of chronic intoxication, such as anemia, agran-
ulocytosis, and polyneuritic symptoms, become pronounced. Skin
rashes on the arms, legs, and oral mucosa are also possible. Neurological symptoms include ataxia, with elements of movement uncoordination and reflex disorders. All these symptoms are characteristic
of this kind of addiction and, together with anamnestic data, help in
making the diagnosis.

The abstinence syndrome is clearly pronounced and characteristic
of this kind of addiction. It is revealed as early as 20-24 hours after
discontinuing the narcotic and reaches its peak intensity within three
to four days, after which the symptoms begin to abate. At the time
of the abstinence syndrome a wide range of vegetative-vascular, neurological and psychotic symptoms are observed. There is anxiety, poor
sleep, weakness, giddiness, nausea, vomiting, collaptoid conditions,
and a steep drop in arterial pressure. Distortions of visual perception
are possible. Involuntary movements and tremor to the extent of
muscular tic markedly increase. In many patients there appear epileptiform seizures. They become irritable, angry and malicious. Such
dysphoric conditions become stable. Short-lived and, at times, lasting
delirial states and hallucinoses are also possible.

COCAINE ADDICTION

This group of narcotics mainly includes cocaine. In recent years
its use in medical practice has been virtually discontinued. Yet, cocaine
intoxication may be acute and chronic.

Acute intoxication is characterized by pallor of the face, dilation of the pupils, general weakness, giddiness, palpitation, irregular pulse, and dyspnea. This is followed by severe circulatory and respiratory functional disorders. Death may be caused by paralysis of the respiratory center. The psychic status is marked by changes in the state of consciousness and psychomotor excitation.

Chronic intoxication evolves gradually as a result of continuous use of the drug. The first cocaine doses are followed by the appearance of slight giddiness and a mild headache, soon replaced by heightened intellectual vigor and a pleasant sensation of wellbeing. Graphomania may also develop; chronic users write many letters and statements of endless discourse and repetition. Excitation lasts two hours, after which there is tiredness, apathy, and depression. Some patients experience a sensation of weightlessness. Illusions and hallucinations also appear, mostly of an optical and auditory nature, not infrequently accompanied by fear.

Habituation to cocaine develops rather quickly. Work begins to be a nuisance, and memory gradually diminishes. Cocaine addicts become callous and egotistic, touchy and suspicious. Some physical symptoms are noted: the pupils dilate, pupillary reaction to light is diminished, the eyes acquire a peculiar glitter, and there is dryness in the mouth, noise in the ears, and palpitation. Patients lose their appetite. The skin is pale and muscles become flaccid. Some patients imagine that there are crystals of cocaine under the skin, where worms or bugs are crawling.

Cocaine psychosis, or cocaine delirium, is characterized by the sudden appearance of hallucinations, which may be optical, auditory, or tactile, etc. Delusions of persecution and jealousy occur. It seems to such persons that someone reads their thoughts, or affects them by electricity or hypnosis. They commit aggressive offenses and attack imaginary adversaries. In cocaine dependence, the drug's harmful effects tell, first of all, on the addict himself. The exhaustion of the organism and diminution of reactivity lead to increased susceptibility to infectious diseases. There are furunculoses; if present, chronic diseases like tuberculosis become exacerbated. Harm to society stems from the fact that cocaine abusers gradually drop out of work and begin to lead parasitic modes of life. They eventually may even become capable of committing crimes against society.

CNS Stimulants

A narcotic effect can also be produced by preparations from the group of CNS stimulants, for example, phenamine, benzedrine, and others. These drugs may be prescribed for reducing sensations of fatigue, improving the mood, giving a sensation of strength and cheerfulness, increasing working ability, and reducing the need for sleep. However, erroneous or excessive administration of these drugs may result in the development of narcomanias. Addiction occurs quickly followed by tolerance to the drug and a desire to increase the dose in order to produce euphoria or overcome depression and fatigue. The effect is expressed in the development of euphoria with symptoms of cheerfulness, in an urge for work and activity, and is accompanied by acceleration of thought functions.

LSD and Other Hallucinogens

The next group of narcotics consists of lysergic acid diethylamide, LSD, a semisynthetic derivative of the ergonovine psilocybine, contained in some mushrooms. LSD preparations have become rather widespread in some countries of Western Europe and the United States, especially among a segment of mentally unstable and socially unsettled people, who are unable to adapt to the way of life prevalent in those societies. The symptoms of acute intoxication include nausea, vomiting, salivation, a drop of arterial pressure, excitation, sometimes ataxia, spastic paralysis, and even death due to respiratory paralysis.

Symptoms of mental disorders appear 15-30 minutes after ingestion and resemble the state of mild alcoholic intoxication. Then there is general weakness: it is difficult to move arms and legs. The eyes are closed and pictures of the past follow as in a movie before one's inner gaze. Sounds seem louder, objects become remote and hazy, and there are symptoms of depersonalization. Visual hallucinations are bright and kaleidoscopic, but not pleasurable to the recipient. Subsequently, there also are elements of depression, delusions of perception, and eventually suicidal thoughts.

Along with visual hallucinations are illusions, and tactile-olfactory- and pseudo-hallucinations. Auditory hallucinations seldom occur. Thought processes are disordered, first accelerating, then slowing down. There may appear feelings of dread, suspicion, delusions of reference and persecution.

The psychic characteristics of intoxication depend on individual traits and typological peculiarities of the subject's higher nervous activity. They may manifest themselves in hallucinatory-illusory, hallucinatory-paranoid or schizophrenic-like syndromes.

Chapter 19

Toxicomanias

As has been mentioned above, those substances listed as causing tox-icomanias are chemical, biological, vegetable or medicinal substances which cause symptoms of habituation, but are not recognized as nar-cotics by current legislation. In the event of change of their legal status, namely, upon recognizing them as "narcotic" substances, per-sons using these drugs would be considered narcotic addicts and their addictions classified as "narcomanias."

A predominant place among substances causing toxicomanias goes to psychotropic substances, some hypnotics and stimulants. Habit-uation (addiction dependence) may be of two kinds: persons using these substances seek (1) to enjoy the effect of euphoria and comfort, or (2) to escape distress and discomfort. However, in both variants, in order to achieve the desired state one has to repeat the intake of substances.

Toxicomanias develop as a consequence of several factors. One of the main causes is excessive or incorrect drug therapy by physicians. Frequent intake of medicines during insomnia and for various un-favorable life situations, or their use by hypochondriacs constantly seeking treatment are also of importance. Not infrequently psycho-pathic individuals also fall victim to addiction. The clinical picture and course in toxicomanias just as in narcomanias, depends on the prop-erties of the substance or medicinal drug used.

Table 5 lists the groups of psychotropic and other preparations likely to cause toxicomanias.

TABLE 5
Psychotropic and Other Substances Likely to Cause Toxicomanias[a]

Group	Subgroup	Drugs
Psycholeptics	1. Tranquilizers	Diazepam, chlordiazepoxide, oxazepam, nitrazepam, phenazepam, trioxazin, meprobamate
	2. Soporifics	Most of the barbituric acid derivatives, including: amobarbital sodium, barbital, pentobarbital, phenobarbital, etc. Bromural, carbromal
Psychoanaleptics	1. CNS stimulants	Mesocarb, sydnophen, centrophinoxine
	2. Other stimulants	Caffeine alkaloids (tea, coffee) Analgesics (metapyrine aminopyrine)
Other	1. Anti-parkinsonians	Benzhexol (trihexyphenidyl hydrochloride, artane hydrochloride), norakin, ridinol.
	2. Antihistamines	Diphenylhydramine hydrochloride, promethazine hydrochloride

[a] Given at the end of the Textbook is the official List of Narcotic Substances and Narcotic Medicinal Drugs authorized by the USSR Ministry of Health (see Supplement 3).

There is no final opinion so far about the structure of the developing dependence in cases of psychopharmacological drug abuse. However, a majority of authors believe that the so-called mild neuroleptics reveal a predominantly physical dependence. This is expressed in fever, tachycardia, headaches, giddiness, insomnia, nausea, vomiting, and collapse-like states. On rare occasions there may be tremor and other symptoms. Increased tolerance does not occur, just as there are no epileptic manifestations and psychoses.

Tranquilizers (meprobamate, diazepam, chlordiazepoxide, trioxazin, nitrazepam) are addictive; in the process of ingestion of these medicines tolerance increases, and abstinence psychoses and epileptiform manifestations are possible. The syndrome of physical dependence is manifested in anxiety, fears, insomnia, sweating, tremor, and muscular tics.

When antidepressant treatment is discontinued there may be physical dependence in the form of vegetative symptoms. There are no symptoms of psychic addiction, nor is there any increased tolerance.

Individual cases of caffeine-induced toxicomanias also occur. After the ingestion of heavy doses of caffeine (in chifir or coffee) euphoria or excitation appears, lasting several hours. Chronic use of these substances may cause toxicomania with giddiness, headaches, insomnia, and even, nightmares. There may be spastic seizures, tic of the calf muscles, tremor of the tongue, lips and fingers. Irregularities in the function of the heart are accompanied by anxiety and fear. Thought processes become torpid and stagnant. Males experience a diminution of potency. The abstinence syndrome is distinct but very mild.

Of special interest is chifir, a highly concentrated concoction of tea (variety of tea addiction), in which the acting principle are alkaloids of caffeine. Pronounced symptoms of "drunkenness" occur 30-40 minutes after an intake of an average dose of chifir, characterized by euphoria, and easy and accelerated thought processes accompanied by excitation. There is increased working capacity, absence of fatigue, easy sequel of associations and images, and thoughts usually of a pleasant content. Depression is seldom observed.

In chronic use of chifir, the clinical picture is characterized by psychomotor and intellectual excitation. The effect lasts four to five hours and, as a rule, produces sleeplessness. Addiction to chifir is individual and subjective. The abstinence syndrome is practically absent. Chifir addicts may gradually develop changes of personality, with notable fluctuations of mood and lability of affect, narrowing of interests and a slipping down the social ladder.

Among the CNS correctives (antiparkinsonians) are benzhexol, artane, trihexyphenidyl hydrochloride, and narcopan, preparations that have found broad application in neuropathology and psychiatry for arresting extrapyramidal disorders. Owing to its euphorizing, intoxicating and hallucinogenic properties, benzhexol addiction has been spreading in recent years. Acute benzhexol intoxication has four stages: (1) euphoric, (2) diminished consciousness, (3) hallucinatory, and (4) recovery.

Actually benzhexol is used for the sake of the first and third phases: the hallucinations are of an acutely sensual character with everything seen as if in an enjoyable animated cartoon, with pleasant associations. During the phase of diminished consciousness sensations of flight are experienced.

Benzhexol is usually taken after being initiated to other substances, such as hashish, barbiturates, or alcohol. The initial phase, as a rule, develops after the ingestion of a dose equal to two to three normal therapeutic doses, i.e., four to eight tablets. Addiction develops quickly, within one to one and a half months. After the same period of time an affective defect is observed. Very quickly, during stage one, notable changes of the CNS, the formation of the abstinence syndrome and dynamic changes in the organism's reactivity or tolerance are revealed. The intake of benzhexol may build up to 30-40 tablets a day.

The syndrome of psychic dependence forms quickly. Untreated abstinence lasts 7-12 days and is a rather distressing experience. At the beginning there is tremor of the hands, then of the body muscles. Psychic and physical discomfort are accompanied by intensive affect, irritability, and maliciousness. Overdosage may lead to psychoses.[6]

---

[6] For details about benzhexol, see Methodological Recommendations, in "Tsiklodolovaya Intoksikatsiya" (Benzhexol Intoxication), USSR Ministry of Health, 1978 (in Russian).

Another variety of toxicomania is tobacco smoking. It was Christopher Columbus who brought tobacco to Europe and, at first, smoking was considered to be good for the health; this is why, one may presume, the first tobacco plantation was established by a physician, Francesco Hernandes. Some seeds of the tobacco plant (New Latin Herba Nicotiana, "herb of Nicot," after Jean Nicot) were sent in 1560 to the French Queen Catherine de Medicis by the French Ambassador at Lisbon, Jean Nicot. His name was eventually incorporated in that of the alkaloid nicotine, the chief active ingredient of tobacco. Believing tobacco to be healthful, physicians of the age described it as a medicinal remedy and promoted its dissemination. However, although people rather quickly got disappointed in tobacco's medicinal properties, tobacco smoking kept spreading.

It is interesting to note that at the beginning of the 17th century in Russia tobacco smoking was not only proscribed, but even punished with 120 strokes of the stick, 60 upon the head and 60 on the soles of the feet. A person caught smoking again was deprived of his nose, which was cut off. Tobacco peddlers had their nostrils and noses torn off. Yet Peter I, himself a smoker, introduced smoking among his entourage. Since then it began rapidly spreading in Russia, too.

With the passage of years smoking for many people has turned into a toxicomania, with millions using tobacco constantly and in fairly high doses. For example, there are some 70 million smokers in the United States. Tobacco is cultivated by 600,000 farmers and the tobacco industry employs 125,000 factory and 66,000 office workers, and more than 5 million people are engaged in tobacco sales.

Conscious of the harm to human health and to the economy, tobacco smoking control has begun in recent years. Thus, cigarette packages in the United States bear a label warning of tobacco's harmfulness. Since 1970 the advertisement of tobacco products has been proscribed in the press, over the radio and on television; 30 states have passed legislation prohibiting smoking in public places; in theaters, museums, subways, and elevators, violators are subject to heavy fines and even prison terms. Anti-tobacco smoking societies are springing up. These measures have already yielded fruit.

A plan drawn up in Sweden is aimed at ridding the country of tobacco smoking within 25 years. In Poland, even when hiring people for work, preference is given to nonsmokers, and smoking is prohibited in many public places. In France, legislation has been passed recommending Frenchmen to smoke less in public places, particularly in places frequented by persons under the age of 16. A smoker may be heavily fined. Britain, too, is enacting measures to restrict the output of tobacco; its advertisement as well as smoking per se in public places have been prohibited. Similar measures are being carried out in a number of other capitalist countries.

Comparable work is being carried out in this country, where it is assigned to medical workers. Health education conducted by health education centers called the "Znaniye" (Knowledge) Society concentrates efforts on explaining the hazards of tobacco and the consequences of systematic smoking. Smoking has been prohibited in public places and in medical institutions; entire businesses and institutions, even cities (for example, the city of Sochi), are working vigorously to eliminate the problem.

Tobacco goods are made of dried tobacco leaves. They contain cellulose, enzymes, carbohydrates, proteins, mineral salts, and fatty acids, more than 30 different ingredients in all, most of them harmfully affecting the organism. The harm comes chiefly from the alkaloid nicotine, a substance belonging to the isocrenoids group.

Nicotine gets into the organism together with the inhaled air and tobacco smoke, which comprises various irritants. These include carcinogenic ones, benzpyrene and dibenzpyrene, which stimulate the growth of malignant tumors, as well as carbon monoxide and carbon dioxide, the amount of which (9.5%) exceeds its content in the air (0.046%). Although the atmosphere is virtually clear of carbon monoxide, the inhaled smoke contains about 5%. Dry distilled tobacco also contains substances possessing carcinogenic properties (benzpyrene).

Low doses of nicotine excite the cells of the CNS, which results in higher pulse rate and respiration, disorders of cardiac contractions, and sometimes, in nausea and vomiting. High doses of nicotine act as a nerve poison and may cause paralysis of the CNS. The amount of nicotine contained in 25 cigarettes is lethal. Death does not occur only because the individual gets used to tobacco and increases the number of cigarettes smoked.

Nicotine renders a negative effect on endocrine glands, particularly the adrenal glands, which excrete the hormone epinephrine. The latter causes vascular spasm and increases arterial pressure.

Upon entering the organism, carbon monoxide contained in tobacco (tobacco smoke) combines with the hemoglobin of the blood, displacing oxygen, leading to the phenomena accompanying oxygen deficiency. Initiation to tobacco smoking frequently causes unpleasant sensations, including tickling in the throat, nausea and vomiting; however, when the individual continues to smoke the unpleasant sensations gradually abate and the habit develops.

What gradually develops in smokers is the so-called "nicotinic syndrome." It has much in common with the alcoholic or narcomania syndrome. The beginning of the nicotinic syndrome is the period when one no longer feels the unpleasant sensations caused by smoking.

The dynamics of the nicotinic syndrome may be conditionally divided into three stages, as follows:

Stage One. Psychic addiction is manifested as an obsessive desire, with diminution of control over the quantity of nicotine used.

1. There is no physical addiction.

2. Tolerance to nicotine increases.

3. There are no signs of somatic or psychic changes.

4. The individual feels the desire to smoke and uses more and more cigarettes. There is a sense that smoking increases working capacity and improves the feeling of wellbeing.

5. This stage lasts from one to five years.

Stage Two. Psychic addiction is obsessive, periodically resulting in a sense of comfort, and sometimes, in the need to keep smoking. Smoking is of the character of an obsessive desire, whose purpose at times is to obtain outward comfort, accompanied by the wish to show off before one's young peers or other persons.

1. There is no physical craving.

2. Tolerance is high, with an established norm of nicotine use. The first somatic symptoms appear, and mild neurotic-like symptoms reveal themselves. The organism's reactivity is high, tolerance increasing until it reaches the peak and remains high (an average of one to two packs, i.e., 20-40 cigarettes a day).

3. The first symptoms of physical ill health are manifested as bronchites, the initial symptoms occurring on the part of the stomach (heartburn, unpleasant sensations, and occasionally, pain), rare and short-lived unpleasant sensations in the region of the heart, fluctuations of pulse, and arterial pressure.

4. The neurotic-like symptoms are mild, quickly passing away, given smoking in moderation or abstaining altogether. They consist of an unpleasant sensation of a "heavy head," insomnia, increased irritability, and a slight reduction in working capacity.

5. The duration of the stage varies individually, lasting on the average from 5 to 15-20 years.

Stage Three. Psychic addiction diminishes, without any states of comfort. Smoking becomes automatic. Physical craving is manifested in the form of a shallow abstinence syndrome. Tolerance to nicotine drops; high nicotine doses cause discomfort.

1. The psychic craving gradually diminishes. The comfort induced by the use of tobacco during the first and second stages is less and less pronounced as the years go by, eventually to disappear altogether, replaced by an automatic habit to smoke (keep on "dragging" a cigarette). The desire to have a smoke on an empty stomach appears. This desire is due to the need to remove unpleasant sensations usual in the morning, particularly in case of coughing ("smokers' morning cough"). There is also insomnia; at times the smoker wakes up at night in order to have a smoke.

2. The organism's reactivity to tobacco changes considerably, which finds expression in lower tolerance. At this stage smoking causes unpleasant sensations in the region of the heart, palpitation, rise of arterial pressure, and a dry, wracking cough.

3. Somatic changes on the part of the internal organs and systems (organs of respiration, the gastrointestinal tract, the cardiovascular system) may manifest themselves in complications in the form of precancer or cancer diseases.

4. Some smokers develop pronounced neurasthenic conditions. Patients complain of systematic headaches or a "foggy head," lower working capacity, moodiness, impairment of memory, increased irritability, and depression.

5. It is hardly possible to establish the duration of this stage.

The stages of the nicotinic syndrome develop quite individually and depend on many factors: the duration of cigarette smoking, and the age, sex, and physical status of the individual. The rate of development of the syndrome also depends on the type of higher nervous activity and the presence of other harmful habits (alcohol abuse).

The majority of smokers attempt to give up nicotine use on their own. The duration of lucid intervals varies the breakdown of remissions occurring most frequently because of assorted extraneous events, worries, emotional instability, etc. It seldom happens because of the appearance of the abstinence syndrome or so-called "cigarette dreams."

It should be noted that the majority of smokers do not regard smoking as a problem; rather, their attitude to the possible harmful consequences of nicotine use is one of lack of concern. Moreover, they believe that they are being intimidated, while regarding smoking as harmless.

Smoking as a result of which tobacco pitch settles on the walls of the bronchi leads, as a rule, to chronic inflammatory processes, such as bronchites, accompanied by alteration of the voice, which becomes wheezy. A dry, choking cough accompanies these conditions. Bronchiectasis, emphysema, or pulmonary heart are possible. Susceptibility to tuberculosis increases steeply. It is believed that out of 200 people in whom tuberculosis develops, 95 had been smokers.

Nicotine and other noxious substances lead to the narrowing of the vessels, particularly those of the heart and brain, which results in increased arterial pressure. It is difficult for the heart to cope with its workload and it functions under strain, which leads to increased pulse rate. Thus, the heart rate of nonsmokers after running a 100 mile race will be 120-130 beats per minute and in smokers, 150-160 beats. According to statistics the death rate caused by myocardial infarction is five times higher among smokers than nonsmokers, while the incidence of cerebral hemorrhage is three to four times higher. Smoking is the frequent cause of stable narrowing of the vessels of the legs, which leads to such a grave condition as obliterating endarteritis, which in turn may necessitate the amputation of the limbs.

It is known that each cigarette smoked destroys as much vitamin C as is contained in an orange. Dissolving in the saliva, nicotine and other noxious substances irritate the walls of the esophagus and, particularly, of the stomach, which excretes considerable gastric juices; this may cause nausea and vomiting, and eventually, the development of peptic ulcer. Nicotine may harmfully affect the oral cavity, badly impairing the teeth. Not infrequently, the gums begin to bleed, a dirty gray coating appears on the tongue, and there are traces of irritation. Cases of complete blindness caused by heavy smoking have been reported.

Increasing material has been accumulated recently which indicates that the incidence of cancer and precancer conditions is much (20 times) higher among smokers than among the rest of the population. In recent years the percentage of deaths caused by malignant neoplasms of the respiratory organs in smokers increased throughout the world (in the Soviet Union, it doubled). In people who had been using nicotine for many years, cancer of the lip, esophagus, larynx and stomach are not infrequent. Smoking is particularly harmful to children and teenagers. As a result of smoking they lag behind their agemates in physical development and are more nervous and undisciplined. Smoking is extremely harmful to pregnant and breastfeeding women, who may poison the fetus or inadequately suckle the newborn.

Smokers are quite a menace to nonsmokers, for the smoldering of tobacco releases nicotine and other noxious substances into the air. Thus, after staying for one and a half hours in a smoke-filled room the concentration of nicotine in the body of a nonsmoker increases eightfold. A smoker, therefore, is a hazard not only to himself but to other people as well. Thus, it was not fortuitous that the 45th session of the Executive Committee of the World Health Organization passed a resolution in January 1970 urging all national health organizations not to remain aloof from the organization of tobacco smoking control.

Chapter 20

Polytoxicomanias, Polynarcomanias, Aggravated Narcomanias and Toxicomanias. Transformations of Different Kinds of Narcomanias and Toxicomanias

In determining the correct diagnosis and treatment strategy for those afflicted with narcomanias, toxicomanias, polynarcomanias or poly-toxicomanias, the terms by which these conditions are designated must be accurately defined. *Polynarcomania* means the intake of two or more narcotic drugs. A polynarcomaniac is a person who either takes a combination of two or more narcotic drugs simultaneously, or takes different narcotics according to a definite pattern by alternating their combinations. The simultaneous intake of a narcotic drug in combination with other substances, alcohol or medicinal preparations not listed as narcotic, constitutes *complicated narcomania*. The simultaneous intake of a combination of drugs or substances not listed as narcotics, or the combination of such substances and medicinal drugs taken in a certain combination or sequel constitutes *polytoxicomania*.

Cases of alcoholism, when the alcoholic takes some narcotic drugs at the same time, should be diagnosed as complicated narcomanias, meaning narcomanias complicated by alcoholism. Similarly, when a person takes medicinal drugs or substances not listed as narcotics, combined with the consumption of alcoholic beverages, the diagnosis would be *complicated toxicomania*. Narcomanias and toxicomanias complicated by alcoholism determine the physician's strategy, because hospitalization measures in these cases should meet all the demands to departments and units for the treatment of narcomaniac and toxicomaniac patients—strict isolation from the outside world in order to prevent the smuggling in of narcotics or other substances that are objects of abuse.

As a rule, toxicomanias develop in regard to a single narcotic drug. For different reasons, such as failure to obtain the habitual narcotic or a striving to increase (potentiate) the effect of the substance taken, narcotic addicts gravitate to the use of several narcotic drugs. Their use may be in sequel or in parallel and, whenever possible, the user tries to take substances producing a similar effect. In polynarcomanias the nature of the craving may become compulsive, the abstinence syndrome becomes more severe, and personality changes set in sooner and go deeper.

In complicated toxicomanias, alcohol is most frequently combined with soporifics which increase its effect. Acute intoxication by these substances may lead to severe barbiturism, alcoholic intoxication, or a comatose state. During stages I-II of alcoholism, complicated toxicomanias develop slowly (six to eight months); during stage III of alcoholism the process proceeds faster, with symptoms of barbiturism gradually displacing those of alcoholism. Episodes of drunkenness acquire features more and more similar to barbituric intoxication, and conditions of amnesia occur more frequently and become deeper. Groundless changes of mood occur, particularly depression, which may lead to suicide. The abstinence syndrome becomes more pronounced and severe, and features of barbiturism predominate. This lingers for four to five weeks. On the 7th-8th day epileptic-type seizures may occur and dyspeptic symptoms are frequent. In addition to dysphorias one of the early symptoms is a marked impairment of memory. The process of memorizing suffers most of all, leading to a narrowing of interests with lapses of memory and a diminution of intellect.

In barbiturate-alcoholic-complicated toxicomania, severe psychoses appear early with a protracted course proceeding according to the delirial type or acute delirial states. Severe asthenia and pronounced amnesia linger on for a long time after recovery from the psychosis.

Complicated narcomania via the combined use of alcohol and Indian hemp preparations (hashish) occurs comparatively seldom. More frequently there may be episodic smoking of hashish when drunk, while chronic use of alcohol and a narcotic drug is rare. In the nonsystematic use of both substances there occurs giggling on the slightest pretext and there is a hypertrophied perception of external stimulants, e.g., ordinary words and sounds seem very loud. All experiences and emotions are intensified. Memory changes are shallow. Comparatively quick (two to three hours) euphoria gives place to anxiety and fear. There are illusions and unusual sensations in the internal organs and the entire body. This state undergoes changes, alternately improving and worsening. Lastly, somatovegetative disorders and sleep occur.

Long-term combined intake of alcohol and hashish occasionally occurs and may lead to acute (delirial type) or chronic psychosis (most characteristic is a schizophrenia-like picture). The abstinence syndrome is mild. Long-term alcohol-hashish-complicated narcomania leads to somatic and intellectual changes. Sometimes chronic alcohol abuse occurs together with the use of chifir or caffeine (which can be diagnosed as complicated alcoholism or polytoxicomania). Their effect is enhanced stimulation of the cerebral cortex.

Complicated narcomanias occur in which opium preparations are added to alcohol use. In some cases opium preparations are intended to alleviate abstinence symptoms; in others, they suppress a pathological craving for alcohol. In both cases the course of the narcomanias becomes more severe. The abstinence syndrome proceeds according to the opium type and is manifested in a morbid craving for the narcotic, low-key mood, pronounced physical weakness, symptoms of asthenia with irritation, and vegetative crises. Unpleasant sensations and pain are felt in the muscles and bones. Some patients constantly move and pace about the ward, groaning and shouting. There is sleeplessness, anxiety, fear, and suicidal ideas. The gait becomes shaky. At the peak of the abstinence syndrome there may be delirial disorders of consciousness and epileptic-type seizures. After the abstinence syndrome is alleviated, asthenia lingers for up to four to eight weeks. Transformations of narcomanias are also possible when the abuse of hashish is replaced by opiates and other narcotics.

Case Illustration Patient: Male, age 26, currently unemployed. *Anamnesis*: The patient showed normal heredity and early development without peculiarities. He was sociable and quiet. He started school at age seven and finished nine grades. At the age of 12 he underwent a character change, becoming rude, irritable, and pugnacious. Progress at school diminished until he dropped out and associated with a company of street children. Since then he began to use alcoholic beverages and to smoke. In 1968, in anticipation of a "good time," he was initiated to hashish smoking in the company of friends.

When in the state of narcotic intoxication, he had the pleasant sensation of lightness, carelessness, aloofness and flight. In 1970, after a year of abstinence, he began to use hashish again. Hashish-smoking became systematic, and intervals caused unpleasant sensations in the form of chills, weakness, sweatiness, pain in the muscles, restlessness and watery stools. In 1972 he underwent compulsory treatments for narcomania. Upon discharge a remission lasted for about a year, according to the patient. Then he again began using hashish. Eventually he changed to intravenous daily injections of up to 6 ml of raw opium and gave up alcohol use. He was brought to the ward by policemen, having been taken there on suspicion of using and trafficking in narcotics.

Physical status: On admission his skin was hyperemic, dry, and scaling off, and his tongue showed a dirty coating. His heart sounds were rhythmical; his pulse, 62 beats per minute. Blood pressure 110/70 mmHg. He had tremor of the fingers and eyelids, and his gait unsteady in Romberg's posture. *Mental status*: He showed complete orientation. However, he was restless and anxious, and complained that before falling asleep he "sees" horrible beasts. His mood was low-key and his movement torpid and slow. His gaze was absent. He answered questions with single words, after a pause. He was indifferent to his surroundings and his fate. He did not conceal the use of narcotics, and explained the forced interval by inability to get opium for two days. His volitional processes were diminished, but he showed a formal critical attitude to his state.

Opium narcomania may undergo transformation into barbiturate series soporific toxicomania or glutethimide narcomania (glutethimide is listed as a narcotic drug). More often opium is primary. The soporific (barbiturates, glutethimide) may gradually displace a certain amount of the opiate preparation even with its complete replacement. Addiction occurs quickly (one and a half to two months). Addicts note a "purer" euphoria and a positive motor effect (better movement coordination) when soporifics are added to opiates. Acute intoxication and chronically combined intake of opium and soporifics may occur. This produces increased hilarity, verbosity and a number of somatic disorders. The addicts appearances change, the faces constantly being pale and sallow. Gradually personality changes occur, the afflicted persons become irritable, angry, and inclined to aggression. There is also impairment and loss of memory. Opium-barbiturate abstinence is severe. The addicts experience excruciating pain in the joints and back. They may have severe convulsive seizures, dyspeptic disorders, or vegetative crises. The abstinence syndrome lasts one and a half to two months. At the peak, acute psychoses are possible.

Case Illustration Patient: Male, age 28, worked as a technical school instructor. *Anamnesis*: The history showed normal heredity and early development without peculiar features. An only child, he was lively, sociable, yet hot-tempered and stubborn, demanding the fulfillment of every wish. He started school at age eight and finished 11 grades. He enrolled at a medical institute but dropped out. He then enrolled at the economic faculty of the University, graduating in 1970. He had always been the center of attention of his peers, regarded as the "live-wire," and was active in sports. After graduating from the University he worked as a teacher, planning to enroll for postgraduate training. He married in 1970, and had one child.

Under the influence of friends the patient began using narcotics in 1966 "for the sake of idle curiosity." He injected omnopon, then gave it up and resumed in 1969 in order to "distract himself." Since 1971 he took opium, then transferred to glutethimide, taking up to 20 tablets daily. Ingestion was followed by pleasant sensations that he described as follows: "It gets dark and everything swims before the eyes, a lightness and groundless hilarity appears, with the wish to move, act, do something."

Physical status: Upon admission the patient's skin was hyperemic, his heart sounds rhythmical, his pulse rate 60 per minute, and blood pressure 90/60 mmHg. His tongue had a grayish coating. He used sweeping, coarse, fussy movements. There was tremor of the fingers and eyelids, and unsteadiness in Romberg's posture. *Mental status*: His place orientation was intact and his mood cheerful. His speech was verbose, abounding in sayings and proverbs. Somewhat affected, he smiled benevolently during examination. His attention wandered, subjects and actions constantly changed, and he showed no sense of distance. Apparently lying, he tried to belittle his involvement in narcotics abuse. Although his volitional processes appeared weakened, he was formally critical of his affliction.

Summary: As seen in the above patient, the transformation to polynarcomania results in a qualitatively new state when the separate symptoms of mononarcomania not merely add up, but acquire new characteristics.

EXERCISES FOR REVIEW

1. Give a pharmacological description of alcohol (ethanol).

2. Describe acute alcoholic intoxication and pathological forms of drunkenness.

3. Describe and cite examples of stages I, II, and III alcoholism. Describe the dynamics of symptoms in psychological and physical addiction and tolerance; somatoneurological and psychic disorders in the developmental dynamics of alcoholism.

4. Describe the basic trends in the etiology and pathogenesis of alcoholism.

5. Describe the main psychic disorders: deliria, acute and chronic

hallucinoses, delirial psychoses and delusions of jealousy, encephalopathies: Korsakoff's disease, Wernicke's disease, alcoholic depressions, dipsomanias, and antabuse-related psychoses.

6. Describe sex and age characteristics in the onset and development of alcoholism; the pathology of the individual organs (liver, heart, lungs, etc.) and systems of the human organism (cardiovascular, gastrointestinal) occurring under the effect of acute and chronic alcoholic intoxication.

7. Describe the course of alcoholism complicated by other diseases, mental included, such as schizophrenia, epilepsy, atherosclerosis, psychopathies, and neuroses.

8. Describe the basic processes supporting man's higher nervous activity and their alcohol-related pathologies; detect pathoanatomical changes in the brain and internal organs of persons who had died of alcoholism or had been afflicted by stages II, III of alcoholism in life.

9. Describe the basic symptoms of the narcotics addiction syndrome and the varieties of narcomanias; demonstrate the formative process of polynarcomanias complicated by narcomanias and toxicomanias, the transformation of different types of narcomanias and toxicomanias and their distinction from mononarcomanias; describe the main polynarcomanias.

10. Offer some clinical examples of toxicomanias; describe the symptoms of tobacco smoking as a toxicomania.

CHAPTERS 9-20 QUESTIONS

1. A drunk person has been brought to the reception ward of a drug treatment center. What symptoms will help to distinguish between ordinary, aggravated and pathological intoxication?

2. A person comes to see a doctor, who must determine whether the affliction is habitual drinking or alcoholism. What are the differential-diagnostic criteria of habitual (ordinary) drinking and alcoholism—stage I, stage II and stage III?

3. A patient says he takes a drink on the "morning after" to chase away unpleasant somatovegetative disorders. What stage of alcoholism is this? How does it differ from the preceding stage?

4. The anamnesis of a patient who is seeing the doctor after another drinking bout includes a past psychosis. What will be the diagnosis, and on the grounds of which symptoms?

5. Alcoholism is not pronounced in the anamnesis, but during the visit one can clearly see alcoholism-type personality changes. What stage of alcoholism is present?

6. A patient makes somatoneurological complaints against the background of alcohol abuse. What stage of alcoholism is present?

7. A patient experiences fears, hallucinations, delirium, and anxiety. Which psychosis does this suggest?

8. The patient is reserved and reticent. According to his wife, though outwardly calm, the patient had for many days previously been constantly listening in to something, and muttering. How would you assess this state?

9. A patient, known as a heavy drinker, has been brought from the resuscitation ward after his second suicidal attempt. What does this suggest?

10. There is no patient in the consulting room. Instead, his wife came to see the doctor. She says that of late her husband has been persecuting her, seeing her off to work and meeting back home, and inspecting her underwear. What diagnosis is suggested?

11. The patient is a 16-year-old youth. He shows symptoms of the hangover syndrome, amnesic forms of intoxication, and pronounced psychopathic behavior. Can the diagnosis "alcoholism" be pronounced? If the answer is yes, what stage?

12. A woman is brought in for the third time to a medical alcoholism unit. She offers a confusing anamnesis, trying to exonerate herself. Is it possible to arrive at the preliminary diagnosis of "alcoholism"? What should be done to confirm it?

13. A patient is complaining to his physician (internist) of physical illness. Would the physician be justified in suspecting an alcohol-related etiology of these afflictions? If so, what are the signs? What ought to be done?

14. The psychiatrist is alarmed by the worsening state of a schizophrenic patient after alcohol use. What ought to be done?

15. An alcoholic is complaining of the appearance of epileptic

seizures. What does this suggest? What disease must be kept in mind while carrying out differential diagnosis?

16. A patient who had never been treated for alcoholism, nor been diagnosed as such in the past, died of cardiovascular insufficiency. Is it possible to diagnose "alcoholism" on the basis of macro- and micro-preparations during an autopsy? If so, what are the signs?

17. A person is describing his abuse of narcotics. What are the symptoms pointing to the diagnosis of narcomania? How can the stage be determined?

18. A citizen has been sent for hospital examination on suspicion of narcotics abuse. What are the symptoms necessary for a possible diagnosis? Is it possible to indicate the type of narcomania?

19. While recording the anamnesis it is revealed that a patient is using different kinds of narcotic drugs. Is it possible to establish the type of his affliction: polynarcomania or complicated narcomania?

20. A patient has been abusing medicinal drugs. How can one decide whether his affliction is narcomania or toxicomania?

PART FOUR

THERAPY

Chapter 21

Basic Principles of Therapy for Alcoholism, Narcomanias and Toxicomanias

The majority of people use alcoholic beverages to a greater or lesser degree. Due to a number of reasons—the individual's genetic development, personality, type of higher nervous activity—only 3-6% of the total number of drinkers succumb to alcoholism.

Typically the disease develops slowly and latently, so that neither relatives nor friends nor the subject himself, realize the approaching illness. Eventually others begin to feel the gravity of the situation, but not the afflicted ones themselves, since their critical capacity diminishes and personality changes set in. Indeed, those around him also drink and he views himself as drinking "just a little, like everyone else," so why should he go for treatment and especially, why should he be the one to start?

Today the armamentarium of alcoholism remedies is broad and varied. However, therapeutic theory and practice indicate that success in the treatment of alcoholism and drug addiction depends upon the motivation of the afflicted person to recover health. Without such a psychological attitude the effectiveness of treatment is much lower, at times without any positive results at all. This becomes even more obvious if we take into account that one of the main factors in the development of alcoholism is the social milieu. This is why the chief principle of alcoholism treatment is voluntary, active, personal striving toward recovery.

Therapeutic effectiveness is ensured by the duration and continuity of treatment. As has been noted earlier, relevant Orders of the USSR Ministry of Health prescribe the terms and sequence of therapeutic measures for alcoholism and drug addiction. These Orders combine aspects of both treatment and prevention; thus their observance maximizes the prospects of alcoholism therapy efficacy. More specifically, these Orders recommend minimum but obligatory courses of special alcoholism therapy either in the hospital or in the outpatient network.

The choice of inpatient or outpatient treatment and the intensity of the care given lies with the physician, who proceeds from the principle of an individualized approach to the selection of the modalities and techniques of therapy. For example, treatment may start in the hospital for the duration of at least 45 or 60 days when dealing with narcomanias. This time is necessary for carrying out the detoxification, general roborant and other active alcoholism therapies. In other cases, treatment may begin on an outpatient basis, and some authors believe that under certain circumstances this kind of treatment is even more effective than hospitalization. Outpatient treatment at different stages is indicated for all patients without exception, including those not requiring hospitalization, those discharged from drug or psychiatric hospitals, and those who have already undergone a therapy course in a WTP.

Psychotherapy should be given priority in the overall treatment plan. In fact, it already has begun during the person's preparation for consciously undertaking an alcoholism treatment regime and ought to be available at every stage of inpatient or outpatient treatment. The course of psychotherapy must be vigorous, purposeful, and consistent. The particular kind of psychotherapy should be prescribed individually by the attending physician. Moreover, when there are contraindications to conditioned-reflex and disulfiram treatment, psychotherapy remains the basic method of alcoholism treatment.

In addition to psychotherapy, work therapy must begin, if possible, from the first days of the patient's stay in the hospital and continue after discharge. Work therapy is an educative, corrective, as well as potent medical factor.

In all cases of inpatient or outpatient treatment it is necessary to distinguish individual stages. The first stage consists of detoxification of the organism, improving general fitness, and stimulation. This stage lasts, on the average, two to three weeks, depending on the state of the patient, and in cases of narcomanias, up to three to four weeks. The second stage consists of active alcoholism treatment in combination with different remedies aimed at developing an aversion to alcohol. The third stage of treatment is essentially for stabilizing therapeutic results, i.e., addressed to the prevention of relapses and remission breakdowns. To achieve this the Orders prescribe outpatient treatment and the administration of special therapeutic courses over a five-year period, given that the remission holds. Here, during the first three years the patient is under active observation, receiving courses of supportive therapy according to specific requirements. For the last two years the patient is transferred to the passive registration file, so that treatment is not discontinued. Dynamic and therapeutic registration is maintained accordingly. In cases of remission breakdown, treatment shall start again or be repeated, according to special instructions.

Along with the different types of treatment, there should also be health education and intervention aimed at the microsocial environment. Such programs should be implemented at every stage of alcoholism treatment, for treatment effectiveness drops steeply when the patient's home or work environment renders a negative effect. Health education and inculcation of a hygienic understanding of the problem among the population is one of the ways to prevent the spread of alcoholism and narcomanias.

Persons suffering from alcoholism or drug addiction do not always agree to undergo treatment voluntarily. In such cases compulsory treatment should be prescribed. Compulsory treatment is generally carried out at the WTP, or at psychiatric or narcological institutions, for persons who must not be sent to a WTP because of age or somatic contraindications.

During the stay in a WTP or narcological institution the patient must receive the full range of medication, his outlook on life must be changed, and temperance attitudes reinforced. At the same time he should also undergo work therapy at the WTP and in industry, and experience the psychological and moral impact of his environment in reorienting him toward leading a proper life. After discharge from the WTP the patient is again placed on the dynamic observation register in the narcological institution of the public health network.

When the behavior of a person suffering from alcoholism or drug addiction is considered socially dangerous, this constitutes an absolute indication for immediate hospitalization. Subsequent inpatient treatment is also required for acute alcoholic psychosis (delirium tremens, hallucinosis, etc.), chronic psychosis (chronic hallucinosis, delusions of jealousy), tendencies toward aggressive actions against other people or the subject himself (injury), pronounced and unreasonable fluctuations of mood (stagnant, torpid, affect, deep depression with suicidal thoughts and intent), and some states of the abstinence syndrome with gross somatovegetative and psychoneurological disorders (vegetative crises, cardiovascular disorders, ataxia, depressions, suicidal ideas). In addition, the patient's strict isolation is obligatory in the treatment of narcomanias and toxicomanias, since addicts, particularly in the abstinence period, always seek to obtain the narcotics they crave and often will not even stop at committing a crime.

Chapter 22

Detoxification, General Roborant and Stimulating Therapy

A person who has long abused alcohol is always debilitated. His organism's metabolic processes are upset; there is vitamin deficiency, an imbalance of carbohydrates, proteins and fats, and a considerable quantity of intermediate products of ethanol decomposition. At this stage a person is usually physically weak, since drinkers eat little, if at all, during alcohol abuse and drinking bouts. Psychic asthenia is also present since the brain is literally poisoned by a considerable quantity of alcohol. For all these reasons, alcoholism treatment must begin with detoxification and general strengthening of the organism as preparation for active alcoholism therapy. It goes without saying that when drawing up a treatment plan one should take into account the individual features of the organism in assessing the clinical picture of the disease.

Depending on the general status of the organism, the average duration of the first therapeutic stage is from five to ten days to two to three weeks. During this time all the necessary laboratory examinations are carried out although, irrespective of this, treatment is started at once. Provided there are no contraindications to the cardiovascular system, a liberal intake of fluids is prescribed (tea, milk, mineral water, but *no* fruit water, because it contains alcohol). Ten to 20 ml of a 40% glucose solution with 5 ml of a 5% ascorbate sodium solution is given intravenously. From 10 to 15 injections are made.

It is also recommended that a three- to four-day course of analeptics (caffeine, cordiamine), spasmolytics and coronarolytics (papaverine, aminophylline, corvalol, and others) be given. In addition, an antitoxic remedy, such as unithiol, is administered in a two- to three-week course (6-10 injections). These injections are painful and sometimes cause side effects, like nausea, pallor, giddiness, or tachycardia. In cases of intolerance they should be discontinued.

For purposes of detoxification, 5 to 30 ml of a 30% sterile solution of sodium thiosulfate are recommended, from 8 to 10 injections for a course of treatment. Methionine is prescribed in 0.5-1 gram doses three times a day, to be taken 30 minutes before meals for 15-30 days. This preparation participates in the synthesis of vitamins and enzymes, is good for the removal of excessive fats from the liver, and is an active antitoxic remedy. It is also advisable to administer pirocetam to these patients, which speeds up the detoxification process and disappearance of abstinence manifestations. This drug may be administered orally, intramuscularly or intravenously. The method of administration and dosage depends on the state of the patient. Pirocetam is prescribed orally in 400 mg capsules, two to three capsules three times a day; or 5-15 ml of a 20% solution one to three times a day is administered intravenously.

The administration of a vitamin complex is obligatory. One powder is given twice a day for a month; then the course of treatment is repeated from five to six times. The powder, in addition to 0.5 gram of glucose, includes 0.05 gram of nicotinic acid, 0.2 gram of ascorbic acid, 0.05 gram of vitamin P, 0.02 gram of pyridoxine hydrochloride, 0.02 gram of thiamine bromide and 0.005 gram of riboflavin.

A positive effect is rendered by vitamin B_{15} (calcium pangamate). On the one hand, it somewhat reduces the pathological craving for alcohol, and on the other, it is indicated in lesions of the liver and the cardiovascular system. Courses last for 20 days with intervals of two to three months between them. All in all, four to five courses are given. Vitamin B_{15} is prescribed in 50-75 mg doses twice a day. For impotence, vitamin E is indicated, prescribed in one ml doses of a 5–30% solution intramuscularly. Glutaminic acid is prescribed in 0.5-1 gram doses two to three times a day before meals for three to six months. Courses of treatment may be repeated. This preparation improves memory and levels out the mood.

For normalizing inhibition and excitation processes throughout all the stages of treatment, particularly initially, it is recommended that sedatives be used. Among these are Pavlov tablets, one tablet to be taken three times a day, or Pavlov mixture, one tablespoonful three times a day, and Bekhterev's coated pills, one pill three times a day, or Bekhterev's mixture, one tablespoonful three times a day. Though preparations of barbituric acid (amobarbital, phenobarbital, pentobarbital and others) produce a calming and soporific effect, they must be prescribed very cautiously and for short periods (three to four days) since addiction to them appears quickly, particularly in persons afflicted with alcoholism.

Psychotropic substances are also very important in the treatment of alcoholism. They help to improve the mood, relieve anxiety and tension, improve sleep, bring about general sedation quickly and in some cases, alleviate the state of abstinence. These are the so-called "tranquilizers." In symptoms of asthenia, states of anxiety and general nervousness, benactyzine is indicated, 0.001-0.002 gram doses twice a day for 15-20 days. Conditions of inner unrest, fears, anxieties, dysphorias and shallow dysthymias are alleviated by chlordiazepoxide (Librium), which is prescribed in 5-10 mg doses two to three times a day for 10-15 days. Diazepam (Valium) is prescribed for anxiety, low-key mood, and insomnia in 5 mg daily doses for seven to ten days. When required the daily dose may be increased to 20-30 mg. In cases of poor sleep, nitrazepam is prescribed in 5–10 mg doses at bedtime for no longer than 10-15 days.

Meprobamate, a relaxant that removes symptoms of depression and increased irritability, is effective in arresting abstinence symptoms. However, the most pronounced positive effect in arresting abstinence conditions is produced by pyrroxan. This is administered orally in 0.015-0.03 gram doses, two to three times a day in tablets; and parenterally, 1-3 ml of a 1% solution is injected one to three times a day. A course of treatment lasts from 5 to 10-15 days.

Among other drugs with a positive influence on abnormal excitation, anxiety and inner turmoil, the most effective is phenazepam, prescribed in 0.005-0.001 gram doses two to four times a day. This drug has also a pronounced soporific effect. Another is trioxazin, given in 0.3-0.9 gram doses two to three times a day. All of the enumerated tranquilizers may potentiate the effect of alcohol, and addiction to them may quickly appear. This is why their continuous administration in alcoholics should not exceed two to four weeks. Therapy must be conducted under strict control.

Benzoclidin hydrochloride, in addition to a tranquilizing effect, has also a spasmolytic action; it is indicated when alcoholism is combined with atherosclerosis and hypertonic disease. The drug is given orally (in 0.02-0.04 gram doses two to four times a day), subcutaneously (1-2 ml of a 2% or 5% solution), or intramuscularly.

Another group of psychotropic substances is made up of neuroleptics. These are used chiefly for the treatment of alcoholic psychoses (and will be described in detail in Chapter 28), but some of them may be used for other conditions as well. For example, chlorpromazine effectively arrests the beginning of psychosis, persistent insomnia and excitation. It is used intramuscularly in 0.5-1.5 ml doses of a 2.5% solution. Perphenazine (trilafon) suppresses the pathologic craving for alcohol, and its tranquilizing effect is five times and antiemetic effect ten times stronger than that of chlorpromazine. Chronic alcoholics with a strong craving for alcoholic beverages are prescribed perphenazine in 0.005 gram doses one to two times a day together with 0.02 gram doses of benzhexol. A total of four to five courses of 20-day duration are given over two to three-month intervals.

Trifluoperazine (stelazine) is used for the treatment of neurotic-like, psychopathic-like and hallucinatory-delirial disorders in alcoholics, and in combination with antidepressants, for coping with early depressive-delirial and depressive-hallucinatory conditions. It is prescribed in 1-2 mg doses intramuscularly every four to six hours (approximately 6 mg daily). A 1-5 mg single oral dose given at the beginning of treatment is brought up to 10-30 mg in the period of intensive care (daily dose reaching 20-80 mg). In addition, haloperidol frequently proves effective in patients resistant to other neuroleptics, particularly for arresting excitation during manic conditions and acute delirium. It is used for the treatment of alcoholic psychoses. Doses of

2-5 mg are injected two to three times a day, intramuscularly. The initial oral dose is 1.5-3 mg daily, to be increased to 10-15 mg three times daily.

Another group of drugs used in the treatment of alcoholics is antidepressants. Dizaphen, prescribed in depressive states, reduces anxiety, restlessness, irritability and, due to its sedative effect, improves sleep. The drug is used also in combination with neuroleptics for the treatment of alcoholic psychoses with depressive-delirial symptoms. It is well tolerated by patients with somatic complications. The initial daily dose is 50 mg, the optimal daily dose 150-200 mg (taken two or three times). Pyrazidol is used for the treatment of asthenodepressive and anxiety-depressive states in the abstinence period. It has a dominant thymoanaleptic effect (improving mood) while its stimulating and sedative action is less pronounced; it is well tolerated and combines well with tranquilizers and neuroleptics. The initial daily dose is 25-50 mg, to be increased to 150-200 mg (taken twice daily). Imipramine hydrochloride (tofranil) is used for the treatment of alcoholic depressions, apathetic-depressive and apathetic-abulic states. The drug is prescribed in daily doses from 75-100 mg (initial dose) increasing it to 200 mg to be taken twice a day (second administration not later than 4 p.m.). When given for anxiety, particularly in the state of acute anxiety, it should be taken in combination with tranquilizers and neuroleptics. If side effects of neuroleptics appear, they should be removed by corrective drugs, e.g., benzhexol.

In the totality of alcoholism treatment a positive effect is derived from general roborant and tonic remedies, for example, an extract of Manchurian aralia (15 drops three times a day for a month), ginseng root tablets (0.15 grams one to two times a day for 15-20 days), and pantocrine (one ml subcutaneously or orally two to three times a day for 15-20 days). Thyme extract has also been used in recent years. This is a perennial herbaceous plant which helps to eliminate quickly the alcohol habit by suppressing the craving for it. Because of its properties thyme is used for alleviating binge-drinking states and is particularly advisable on an outpatient basis. It is prescribed in oral doses of 50 ml twice a day for two to four weeks.

For general symptoms of asthenia, 0.001 grams of strychnine pills or strychnine in injections of 1-2 ml of a 0.1% solution daily for 20 days is indicated. Iron and arsenic preparations—ferrohematogen (0.5 gram three to four times a day), feramide (combination of iron with nicotinamide), or Blaud's tablets containing arsenic—are also given, in 15 to 30-day courses, together with preparations of phosphorus. Of the phosphorous preparations, phytin is given in 0.5 gram doses three times a day, phosphrene, 0.5 gram doses, lipocerebrin, 0.5 gram doses, and calcium glycerophosphate, 0.5 gram doses, with treatment continued for 20-30 days.

Biogenic stimulants of an aloe extract type are also used, one teaspoonful given orally three times a day, or 1 ml injected subcutaneously for 20-25 days. Others include 1 ml phytobiogenic stimulant administered subcutaneously, 1 ml vitreous body, or ATP (adenosine triphosphate) given as a 1% solution injected in 1-2 ml doses intravenously with 5 ml of a 40% glucose solution for 20-30 days. ATP alleviates the craving for alcohol, favorably affects the functions of higher nervous activity, and normalizes sleep. Bogomolets' antireticular cytotoxic serum (ACS) together with other drugs as CNS stimulants is also used, but its administration requires special caution.

In severe forms of alcoholism with symptoms of physical exhaustion, a course of treatment with small doses of insulin is recommended. Before beginning such treatment it is necessary to examine the patient and carry out the glucose tolerance test. Treatment should begin with injections of two to four units of insulin, adding daily two to four units to reach a dose of 20-26 units. The course of treatment lasts 25-30 days. Insulin influences the metabolic processes, improves the appetite, and removes anxiety and fear.

Sulfadiazine treatment is used for the same purposes. Sulfadiazine (0.5-1% sterile solution in peach oil) is injected into the upper outward quadrant of the gluteus, beginning with 0.5-2 ml and gradually increasing the dose to 3-5 ml. This treatment is given twice a week, five to six injections in all. After 8-12 hours the patient experiences a rise of temperature to 38-39°C, which persists for 24-36 hours. The therapeutic effect of sulfadiazine includes hyperthermia, detoxification and stimulation of the metabolic processes.

Autohemotherapy is also recommended. With this method of

treatment (therapy "with one's own blood") the patient is intramuscularly injected with 5 ml of his own blood. Every two to three days,
by adding 2-5 ml, the doses are brought up to 20-25 ml. A course of
treatment consists of 10-12 injections. The products of blood protein
decomposition irritate the higher portions of the CNS; such stimulation intensifies the defensive reaction of the organism and improves
the therapeutic effect of other remedies. Lastly, oxygen therapy consists of subcutaneous administration of oxygen into the subscapular
region or the thigh. A course of treatment includes 10-15 insufflations
of 300-500 ml of oxygen each. The oxygen is utilized as a means of
detoxification.

Apart from the above enumerated methods of therapy, various
types of physiotherapy—baths, showers, electrophoresis, diather-
mia—can be used at all stages of outpatient treatment. Therapeutic
sleep may also be used in different forms—medication, electric or
hypnotic. In medication sleep the patient is given a soporific mixture
of 0.1 gram amobarbital and 0.3 gram barbital sodium. The aim is
to prolong natural sleep to 12-18 hours, which is why the mixture is
administered after the usual sleep. Treatment lasts five to ten days
and must be conducted under the observation of the attending physician in a hospital setting. Electric sleep may be administered on an
outpatient basis, lasting two to three hours daily for 20-30 days. Hypnotic sleep treatment can be conducted daily, prolonging natural sleep
by one and a half to two hours every day or every other day; the
course lasts 15-20 sessions. In all cases sleep renders a favorable effect
on the major nerve processes and increases the effect of other alcoholism treatments.

As a means of suppressing conditioned-reflex bonds and facilitating the excretion of intermediate metabolic products, a reducing
diet may be applied. It is indicated when alcoholism is combined with
hypertonic disease and fat metabolic disorders. Regulated fasting,
according to Nikolayev is conducted for a period of 5 to 20 days under
medical supervision and the strictest observance of the regimen. More
generally, since the majority of alcoholics suffer from metabolic disorders and are easily exhausted, normal nutrition is one of the elements of treatment. A daily schedule of regular high-calorie meals

four to five times a day should be drawn up, with food rich in vitamins and carbohydrates, and with ample milk and vegetables. The use of fats should be avoided as much as possible. It is recommended that breakfast be of particularly high caloric value in order to preclude early morning craving for alcohol. The caloric value of the diet should be somewhat higher than usual in order to supplement the deficit in food value that appears in the process of alcoholization.

Chapter 23

Active Alcoholism Therapy

Active alcoholism therapy is one of the most important elements in the overall schedule of treatment. Depending on the state of the organism and the clinical picture of the disease, it is initiated, on the average, 5-15 days after detoxification, general roborant and stimulating therapy.

CONDITIONED-REFLEX THERAPY

The question of treating alcoholism with emetics in order to develop a negative reaction to alcohol is not new. Folk medicine was used for this purpose, with a tincture of thyme, copper sulfate, and other remedies. In 1910 Professor Minor recommended a tincture made up of different emetics. The idea of developing a negative-defensive reflex to alcohol was repeatedly voiced by V. M. Bekhterev, while Professor N. V. Kontorovich attempted to evoke such a reflex by combining alcoholic beverages with electric current stimulation. In 1933 I. F. Sluchevsky and A. A. Friken were the first to use apomorphine for conditioned-reflex therapy. They administered from 3 to 10 mg of apomorphine in vodka, and if vomiting did not appear, they injected apomorphine subcutaneously. Subsequently, apomorphine began to be used quite widely and in different modifications for treating alcoholism. Aversion to alcohol in the process of treatment

219

with emetics appears as a result of a complex of factors: the development of a conditioned reflex based on an unconditioned stimulant (apomorphine), suggestion during treatment sessions, and the emergence of a psychotherapeutic effect in a wide sense, with social reorientation of the personality.

Amorphine Treatment

Apomorphine, which belongs to the group of emetics and expectorants, is obtained synthetically from morphine by heating it with hydrochloric acid. It appears as a white or slightly yellowish powder, turns green in the air and under light, and only slightly soluble in water. Since it rapidly decomposes in the light, only a freshly prepared 0.5-1% solution is used. The apomorphine dose is strictly selected individually beginning from 0.1-0.2 ml of a 1% solution. In the absence of the expected reaction, 0.1-0.2 ml portions are increased up to 0.4-0.5 ml of a 1% solution for subcutaneous injection. The preparation selectively excites the vomiting center. At present the following technique (after Strelchuk) is adopted for treatment. A "drinking setting" is created, i.e., tables are laid with sandwiches, beverages are placed on the tables, and sometimes a bar with a counter is set up, its cupboards displaying bottles with alcoholic beverage labels. Sessions are held simultaneously for groups of patients.

This method facilitates induction, i.e., the influence of one patient on another, and the speediest development of the vomiting reflex and its stabilization. A patient is given sandwiches to eat and two cups of warm tea to drink. An initially determined dose of apomorphine is injected subcutaneously while the patient is given a glass with his "favorite beverage" (30 ml) to hold. The patient then smells the drink, rinses his mouth, and about 5-20 minutes before the onset of vomiting drinks half of the beverage. After the injection the vomiting reaction usually lasts 2-30 minutes. Within this time the patient drinks up the remaining portion of the alcoholic beverage. Vomiting brings relief, possibly sleep, which may be prolonged by drugs or hypnotic suggestion. If vomiting has been induced by large doses of the drug, then

10-15 minutes after the intake of apomorphine, cordiamine or caffeine should be administered. In order to enhance the vomiting reaction the injection of apomorphine may be followed by the administration of a mixture of emetics, as suggested by I. V. Strelchuk:

Rp.: 01. jecoris Aselli
      01. ricini aa 60.0
      Natrii sulfurici 30.0
      Cupri sulfurici 0.6
      Aq. destill 100.0

MDS. 50-100 ml per intake, washed down with 30-50 ml of vodka.
     Shake before use.

The course of treatment includes 15-20 daily sessions. After the administration of apomorphine the patients show the following symptoms: hypersalivation, reddening or paling of the face, sensations of heat or cold, giddiness, sweatiness, acceleration and then slowing down of the pulse rate, nausea, and vomiting. Arterial pressure usually drops. A vegetative reaction which ends in fainting or collapse is regarded as a complication. Such complications also may occur occasionally as seizures or gastric hemorrhage. If apomorphine causes intoxication rather than vomiting and nausea, it should be discontinued.

Contraindications of apomorphine are as follows: peptic ulcer, grave forms of pulmonary tuberculosis, preinfarction, postinfarction states, grave forms of the hypertonic disease, cardiosclerosis, stenocardia, hypotonia, bronchial asthma, age over 60, or following grave cerebrocranial injury. In some cases the use of small doses of apomorphine is possible (Rozhnov).

Emetine Treatment

Emetine, the principal alkaloid of the ipecacuanha root, is a white or slightly yellowish crystalline powder that is odorless, bitter to the taste, and readily soluble in water and alcohol. It possesses, apart from an emetic action, a specific chemotherapeutic effect with regard to amoebic dysentery. It may be used orally, subcutaneously, or intramuscularly in 1-2% solutions. The oral dose is 0.02-0.05 ml (maximum daily dose 0.1 ml). Emetic doses are selected individually. After taking the powder the patient is given one to two liters of water or warm tea to drink, and upon the onset of nausea and vomiting is made to smell and drink an alcoholic beverage. The vomiting reaction sets in 10-30 minutes after administration, sometimes later. A laxative effect may occur. Vegetative reactions are milder than during apomorphine treatment. In order to enhance apomorphine's reflex effect, 15-20 drops of a 10-20% emetine solution may be added to the vodka. Unaware of this, the patient supposes that it is the vodka alone which causes nausea or vomiting. It is also possible to alternate apomorphine with emetine. This is a specific reflex, only to a definite alcoholic beverage, and it easily fades away. A course of treatment consists of 20-30 sessions.

The course of treatment is as follows: A table with alcoholic beverages is brightly lit in a darkened room. The patient sits down at the table and is injected with 0.03-0.07 gram of emetine, and at the same time, given caffeine. During the latent period the patient drinks alcohol in the usual doses but regulated so that the euphoria coincides with nausea. The session is repeated until vomiting or nausea appears from one kind of alcoholic beverage. Complications in emetine treatment are rare. Its contraindications are the same as to apomorphine.

In cases when apomorphine or emetine do not produce the desired effect, emetic cocktails may be used. They consist of 200 ml of diluted distilled water containing 15 grams each of sodium chloride and sodium sulfate, 0.5-1 gram of ipecacuanha root powder, 30 grams of castor oil, and 50 grams of cod liver oil. The patient takes a sip of the alcoholic beverage and drinks a tablespoonful of the cocktail. Most frequently the reaction occurs at once, but it may be preceded by lasting nausea, and only later will copious vomiting occur. From 8 to 10 sessions suffice for developing a negative reaction.

In every case of conditioned-reflex therapy, verbal persuasion should be used. But the method of suggestion either in the waking state or in hypnotic sleep may be used independently.

Club Moss Treatment

Treatment with a tincture of club moss (lycopodium) was suggested by Strelchuk (1952). Club moss is an evergreen herbaceous plant. From 70 to 150 ml of club moss extract is used for the treatment of alcoholism. Taken orally, it causes a state of wretchedness whereby the patient feels sick all over, with headaches, giddiness, weakness, hypersalivation, sweatiness, nausea, repeated vomiting for a period from 30 minutes to 6 hours (up to 8-30 times), tremor of the arms and legs, and sometimes, watery stools. This condition develops 10-20 minutes after taking the medicine. The patient is given his habitual alcoholic beverage in small doses before each urge to be sick. Sometimes aversion develops within a single session, but it is better to take three to five alcohol-lycopodium tests.

Complications of club moss treatment include spasms, drop in arterial pressure and cardiac fibrillation. Relief is gotten from the administration of drugs improving the functioning of the cardiovascular system, and in case of severe dehydration, from drinking or intravenous administration of a 10% solution of sodium chloride. During repeated sessions the dose is increased or diminished, and vodka is given half an hour later to allow for absorption.

Contraindications of this treatment are diseases of the cardiovascular system, peptic ulcer, chronic gastritis, bronchial asthma, tuberculosis in its active form, craniocerebral injury, diseases of the liver and kidneys, and age over 50. Treatment with small doses of club moss produces practically no complications and therefore may be used fairly widely. A 5% solution of the mixture in 10-15 ml doses is administered during the first half of the day (daily dose 30-40 ml). The patient drinks a portion of club moss extract and sips his alcoholic beverage. Then he is present during sessions of apomorphine therapy given to other patients. For most of the patients this proves sufficient to cause nausea and even the vomiting reaction. In others there appears a pronounced vegetative reaction of sweating and salivation. Gradually, after 10-15 of such sessions, a negative reaction to alcoholic beverages develops.

When the use of club moss ends in failure due to diminished

sensitivity of the alcoholic's vomiting centers, it is recommended that massive doses of emetics be administered. However, treatment by this method requires caution and a thorough somatic examination. The mixture is prepared immediately before a therapeutic session. It is composed of 50 ml of a solution of heavy metal salts, 50 ml of a tincture of the herb thermopsis and 60 ml of a mixture of cod liver oil with castor oil. For making the smell less repellent 100 ml of cahors wine or mint tincture may be added.

Groups consisting of 5 to 20 persons are formed for treatment. Before starting treatment a psychotherapeutic talk is conducted with them and breakfast is served at a common table. Ample drink (up to one liter) must be given. After 20-30 minutes the vomiting mixture is taken and then 50-100 ml of an alcoholic beverage. Nausea and vomiting begin about ten minutes later, but the patient must be compelled to take additional portions of alcohol, which in turn causes repeated painful retching spasms. Cardiacs may be administered in order to prevent complications on the part of the cardiovascular system. Then in order to potentiate the action of the emetic mixture the patients are injected with 0.4-0.6 ml of a 1% apomorphine solution, freshly prepared. A new attack of nausea and vomiting will start.

In the course of four to five sessions such therapy will result in aversion to alcohol. It should be remembered, however, that each session may end in pronounced, and at times severe, states of cardiovascular insufficiency, occasionally even reaching the state of collapse. Hemorrhage from the esophagus and stomach due to the rupture of small vessels and epileptic seizures are also possible. Therefore, a first-aid kit should be fitted with all the essential drugs and kept at hand. In case of severe complications, particularly ones that recur, treatment by this method should be discontinued.

Sulfadiazine and Nicotinic Acid Treatments

Sulfadiazine, already mentioned above, may also be used to cause aversion to alcohol. For this purpose small doses of alcoholic beverages are given at the peak of hyperthermia. In a certain group of patients this combination causes aversion to alcoholic beverages.

Another treatment, nicotinic acid, may be used in two variants. For a period of 7 to 10 days, 0.1-0.2 gram doses of nicotinic acid are administered three times a day before meals. (It is known that this preparation causes reddening of the skin, sensations of heat, dyspnea, and other vegetative reactions.) On the 10th day the patient is given some alcohol to drink. In order to enhance the reaction, 1–2 ml of a 1% nicotinic acid solution may be injected intramuscularly. Sessions are held daily (15-25 in all), and after a few sessions an aversion to alcohol appears, and subsequently, a nausea-vomiting reaction.

Combining the administration of increasing doses of nicotinic acid (from 0.1-0.2 to 1-2 grams) with the intravenous injection of 15-20 ml doses of a 30% sodium thiosulfate solution produces still stronger nausea-vomiting reactions. Therapy should be conducted in groups, in which some patients may receive apomorphine therapy. A total of 15-20 sessions are held. Contraindications and complications are individual and are similar to those in apomorphine treatment. When adequate reactions are lacking after four to five sessions, this method of treatment should be changed.

Disulfiram Treatment

Disulfiram and similar remedies are substances which create increased sensitivity to alcoholic beverages, thus precluding their use. Such substances are numerous, but the effect of their application is distinguished by brevity. Disulfiram (antabuse, thiuram) proved to be a drug that causes a rather stable reaction. However, it should be borne in mind that disulfiram possesses a rather high toxicity, and at times the reactions of the organism to it are severe. In some patients disulfiram may precipitate pathological processes, and occasionally, even without conducting disulfiram-ethanol tests, antabuse-induced psychoses and epileptiform seizures occur. Myocardial infarctions, strokes and other complications are possible during treatment. Continued use of alcohol after disulfiram treatment is particularly dangerous. For these reasons, disulfiram treatment should always be conducted under medical supervision. Therapy is given in the form of ethanol-disulfiram tests and, as supportive therapy, without them, by lasting administration of small doses, creating so-called "chemical isolation."

Disulfiram is issued in tablets containing 0.1, 0.15 and 0.25 grams of active principle. It possesses the capacity to block some enzymatic systems and retard alcohol oxidation at the stage when acetaldehyde enters the blood from the liver and causes hyperemia of the skin of the face and upper half of the trunk, sensations of heat, dyspnea, headache, nausea, vomiting, a drop in arterial pressure, convulsions and collapse. Disulfiram is eliminated from the organism within 75 hours. Daily introduction of 0.5 gram doses for five to seven days builds up a concentration which ensures a disulfiram-ethanol reaction. The optimal daily dose is 0.25-0.5 grams.

Daily administration of the individually selected dose is well tolerated by patients and does not produce complications, even during lasting treatment. Daily doses of disulfiram below 0.15 grams, as a rule, do not cause sensitization since it is eliminated from the organism rapidly.

The first test is conducted seven to ten days from the beginning of treatment. After the morning administration of a 0.5-0.75 gram disulfiram dose the patient drinks 20-30 ml of an alcoholic beverage, most frequently 40% vodka. Subsequent tests are held in the hospital over one to two-day intervals, and on an outpatient basis over intervals of three to five days. When the reaction is inadequate the portion of the alcoholic beverage is increased by 10-20 ml. The maximum quantity of vodka is 100-120 ml. At the onset of a severe reaction the test should be discontinued. An indication of this is the reaction of strong headaches with sensations of pressure and pulsation, sharp difficulty in breathing, a drop in arterial pressure below 50-40 mmHg, dimming of consciousness, psychomotor excitation, and convulsions 1–1½ hours from the intake of the alcoholic beverage.

These complications can be arrested with methylene blue, 15-20 ml of a 1% aqueous solution administered intravenously. Then a subcutaneous injection is given of cordiamine, corasole or camphor, and intramuscularly, cytitone or lobeline. Ephedrine, strychnine, or oxygen inhalation is also given. Validol, valocordin, or nitroglycerin are indicated for pain in the heart. If the arterial pressure remains low, phenylephrine hydrochloride or epinephrine is administered after 15-30 minutes. In severe cases when cardiac activity steeply diminishes, 0.25-0.5 ml of a 0.05% strophanthine solution in 20 ml of an isotonic solution of sodium chloride is given intravenously. The intramuscular administration of 10 ml of a 25% magnesium sulfate solution is indicated for convulsions. For severe nausea and vomiting an intravenous injection of 10 ml of a 10% calcium chloride or calcium gluconate solution is given intravenously, 0.015 grams of belladonna extract is given orally, and 0.5 ml of an 0.1% atropine solution is injected subcutaneously. The intravenous administration of sodium metabisulfite in a dose of 5 mg per kg body weight is also recommended. It is believed that this is much more effective than the above-mentioned remedies.

Collapse, one of the various complications that may occur when conducting the tests, is arrested by the above-mentioned remedies. Convulsive seizures are effectively removed by methylene blue or magnesium sulfate, and strong psychomotor excitation is arrested by an intramuscular injection of a 1-2 ml dose of 2.5% chlorpromazine solution with 2 ml of cordiamine. Persistent convulsive states are relieved with chloral hydrate (15-20 ml of a 6% aqueous-starch solution in an enema) or with amobarbital (0.3-0.5 grams of amobarbital per 25 ml of water in an enema, or 3-4 ml of a 5% solution intramuscularly). Coronary spasm is treated with the above remedies, besides nitroglycerine, validol, aminophylline, drotaverine, etc. Acute disorders of coronary or cerebral circulation (infarction and stroke) are arrested by complete rest and repeated administrations of methylene blue. In case of stroke, 10 ml of a 2.4% solution of aminophylline is given intravenously in 10 ml of a 40% glucose solution.

It must be stressed that lasting use of the preparation at times results in various complications, particularly if the patient had been taking increased doses of the drug. The complications may occur on the part of the cardiovascular system, the peripheral nervous system, the gastrointestinal tract and the liver. Also possible is an exacerbation of earlier contracted diseases, such as gastritis, gastric or duodenal ulcer, thrombophlebites, etc. In all these cases disulfiram must be immediately dropped, careful examination of the patient carried out and the necessary treatment prescribed. In marked overdosage of the drug or increased sensitivity to it, disulfiram psychoses may occur. Disulfiram treatment can be resumed only three to four months later, but with great caution.

In order to create a deposit of the drug in the organism the preparation Radoter ("Esperal") is prescribed. This consists of ten 0.1 gram tablets of disulfiram prepared under sterile conditions and sealed in a special glass ampule. The tablets are implanted into the subcutaneous fatty layer of the thigh, buttock, or area of the back. Subsequently, a gradual absorption of the preparation takes place, which maintains a definite disulfiram concentration in the patient's blood. The intake of alcoholic beverages causes a vegetative-vascular reaction typical of disulfiram. Because of its dangers this therapy requires a special psychotherapeutic approach, and consent for the treatment must be obtained in writing from the patient himself and his relatives, with a warning about the possible complications of therapy, including death.

In conclusion, contraindications to the administration of all kinds of disulfiram treatments include ailments of the cardiovascular system, gastrointestinal tract, respiratory and urinary systems, organic lesions of the CNS, pregnancy, surgical (particularly suppurative) diseases, endocrine insufficiency, and age over 60 years, although the latter issue is decided individually.

The difficult decision to prescribe disulfiram therapy is made by the attending physician, since the same disease in a state of decompensation may prove an absolute contraindication, whereas in the stage of compensation, the drug may be prescribed with caution. Besides, this kind of treatment may be used in different modifications, with tests and without them, or with the implantation of Radoter ("Esperal").

As a modification of the method of active alcoholism treatment, Gulyamov suggested a combination of conditioned-reflex and disulfiram therapy, the disulfiram-apomorphine-ethanol reaction (DAER). For six days the patient receives 0.5 gram of disulfiram, morning and evening. On the morning of the 7th day he takes 1 gram of disulfiram and after breakfast is injected with 0.3-1 ml of a 1% apomorphine solution. Upon the appearance of mild nausea an alcoholic beverage is given.

This method produces a long and excruciating stage of unaccountable fear and the nausea-vomiting reaction, which persists for a long time, occasionally for the whole day. Repeated tests are conducted over seven-day intervals. When the reactions are well pronounced two to three tests prove sufficient.

For sensitizing therapy the preparation cyamid is used. The patient receives 0.5-0.1 gram doses of cyamid for five to six days. On the morning of the test day a 0.1 gram dose is given. Four hours later he is given 20-40 ml of an alcoholic beverage to drink. The reaction is similar to that produced by disulfiram, but milder.

In 1959 a method of active alcoholism treatment with metronidazole (flagyl) was suggested. It is prescribed for three to four days in 0.5-0.75 gram doses after a meal. When the patient is in good physical condition the daily dose can be increased to 1.5 grams, and the preparation can be continued for up to ten days. Then the dosage should be reduced back to the initial values, with which treatment is continued for 20-25 days. Metronidazole-ethanol tests may be conducted in combination with hypnotherapy.

Chapter 24

Psychotherapy

In ancient times it was said that people could be treated by means of "herbs, the knife and the word." Thus, the medicinal effect of one man's words on another has been known for a long time. However, only recently has it become a method of treatment that is theoretically substantiated and augmented with elaborate psychotherapeutic techniques.

Alcoholism is a disease for which influencing the patient's personality is crucial. Such influence may be rendered by means of various psychotherapeutic methods. Psychotherapy for alcoholism should be comprehensive and diverse, since it is used in an attempt, on the one hand, to breach the vicious pathological circle of a morbid state (i.e., addiction to alcoholic beverages), and on the other, to establish new social links between the patient and his environment. Thus, in the first case psychotherapy is a potent medical remedy, in the second, a special kind of social influence.

Psychotherapy ought to be used at every stage of alcoholism treatment, of course, with account of the patient's personality, stage of the disease, type of higher nervous activity, and social factors; in other words, it must be highly individualized. And, it is with the physician that the choice of the therapeutic method lies.

Special methods of psychotherapy in the treatment of alcoholism include rational, indirect psychotherapy, hypnotherapy, suggestion in the state of wakefulness, and forms of relaxation, like autotraining. Treatment may be conducted both individually and in groups.

Before starting therapy the physician must get well acquainted with each patient, gather the anamnesis, determine the patient's type of nervous system, decide how motivated the patient is to recover, and establish positive, trustworthy but objective relations with the patient. Without such preparatory work further treatment will be unsuccessful since the basic principle of psychotherapy is the effect of the physician's word on the object of psychotherapy influence, the patient. After carrying out the enumerated preliminary measures the method of psychotherapy can be chosen and the therapy itself started.

In the Soviet Union a collective approach like group psychotherapy is in keeping with the spirit of socialist relationships. Man lives in a social milieu and is brought up and educated by the collective. During an illness relationships between the patient and those around him get disrupted, and new pathological relationships take shape which facilitate the deepening of the morbid condition. Therefore group, rather than individual psychotherapy of alcoholism, yields a great effect. Treatment is immediately conducted with large groups. When working with a group it is possible to single out persons who may provide positive leadership or favorably influence the others, thus helping the physician.

Group psychotherapy is conducted in the following way. Groups from 5 to 10 or 20 persons are selected. The relatives of the patients—wives, parents, adult children—are invited to attend the sessions. A few patients with typical alcoholism and life histories are asked to speak of themselves. Then those present may ask questions and discuss with the patient what had led him to alcoholism. Relatives add to the patient's story, and the thoughts of those present involuntarily turn to their own lives. The physician skillfully directs the entire therapeutic session, offering remarks that emphasize the inadmissibility of drinking alcohol.

Thereafter, the talks assume the character of health education, with the physician explaining the social and medical aspects of alcoholism. First of all the patients must be convinced that there is nothing supernatural in hypnosis; that it is a method of therapy based on the physiological characteristics of man's nervous system, and there is nothing to be afraid of. Then, they must be told that not everybody falls asleep during sessions, but even the state of drowsiness has the same favorable effect as sleep. Making use of the latest scientific data, special emphasis is placed on the harm that alcohol inflicts on the human organism, the nervous system and internal organs.

Further, still in the state of wakefulness, thoughts of aversion to alcohol are suggested to the patients, who are told that the organism will not be able to ingest any kind of alcoholic beverages. The patients' desire to get well is reinforced and encouraged, as is their will to resist the addiction. At all times attention is placed on complete abstinence from alcohol and an exemplary mode of life.

In order to stabilize treatment effects some patients are prescribed active alcoholism medication, while others continue attending group therapy sessions or are given individual hypnotherapy. A classical method of group hypnotherapy has been suggested by V. N. Bekhterev. It includes three stages: preliminary psychotherapeutic talks, hypnotherapy, and self-suggestion training.

Hypnotherapy is best carried out in specially equipped rooms furnished with comfortable chairs or sofas, with subdued lighting and a restful, quiet atmosphere. Soft, pleasant music can be played. The session of hypnotherapy begins with inducing sleep. The next stage, suggestion, may be carried out more individually. Here the characteristics of certain patients are taken into account. The suggestions must be presented in clear simple language. For example: "The use of alcoholic beverages is bad for you. It undermines your health. You are absolutely indifferent to alcoholic beverages." The character of the suggestion must suppress the craving for alcohol as well as reinforce the patient's determination to get well.

In the process of hypnotherapy, conditioned-reflex therapy for cultivating aversion to the smell and taste of alcohol may be conducted. For this, suggestion is accompanied by actually smelling vodka or tasting a cottonwool wad moistened in it. Before awakening, the suggestion formula is fixed once again and the patient is told that he will feel cheerful, healthy, full of strength, and be rid of the craving for alcohol.

For one and a half to two months sessions are held twice a week, then twice a week for another two months, and once every two weeks for the next six months. If the therapeutic effect is good the patient remains on the register for five years, periodically visiting the doctor for supportive treatment.

By now many varieties of group psychotherapy have been suggested. Each of these methods has its own merits, and the physician, on the basis of the characteristics of the selected groups, chooses one of them. The method of group emotional-stress hypnotherapy for alcoholism, suggested by V. E. Rozhnov, is very popular. Rozhnov believes that ". . . hypnotherapy sessions are just one element in the overall system of psychotherapeutic measures in conjunction with drug and work therapy." In this kind of treatment great importance is attached to the emotional factor in the relationship between patient and physician. Here the latter must appear not as a lecturer or teacher, but as a kind, strong-willed, caring and truthful person, who profoundly believes in the success of the treatment. And the patient must realize this not only by his intellect; he must feel it "by the heart" and respond with trust and eager cooperation.

Before forming a group the case history of each patient is carefully studied. A single group includes from 10 to 20 persons. Before starting a course of treatment a psychotherapeutic talk is held, during which therapeutic procedures and the essence of hypnosis are explained. Though some patients do not fall asleep, in most of them the vomiting reflex to alcohol is worked out all the same. When the patients are put to hypnotic sleep, a talk is conducted in which the harmful effects of alcoholic beverages on the organism is stressed, with the unhappy effects on the family and the microenvironment. The physician specially utilizes the emotive impact of such suggestions.

The next stage involves developing a vomiting reflex to alcoholic beverages, reinforced with pure 96% alcohol. The session ends with accounts made by the patients themselves. The reflex may be considered sufficiently well developed if the mere word "vodka" evokes a pronounced vegetative reaction with nausea-vomiting symptoms in the members of the group. A course of treatment consists of 10-12 sessions, followed by supportive therapy given one to two times a month for the duration of a year.

For stabilizing the therapeutic effect the patients should be trained in methods of self-suggestion and relaxation. The purpose of such training is to teach the patient self-control. For this several tests are conducted and the patient is recommended a ready-made suggestion formula which he must repeat daily in the course of four to six months before falling asleep. This formula may contain the following suggestion: "I feel an ever-diminishing attraction to alcoholic beverages. I will not take them anymore, in spite of any persuasion and offers. I am healthy and the guarantee of my health is absolute abstention from alcohol."

The method of relaxation—autotraining—requires that after several training sessions the patient learns to relax the muscles of the face, the neck, the trunk, the back, the limbs, in fact, the whole body. Then the patient, having completely relaxed, learns to evoke a sensation of warmth in different parts of the body, and during the third stage starts self-suggestion. The formula should be brief and aimed at developing aversion to alcoholic beverages and the reinforcement of this reflex if it had already been developed. It is also aimed at instilling belief in complete recovery. A course of autotraining lasts for up to three months and may be repeated. The patient is taught both these methods by the physician, and they should be used in combination with other methods of treatment.

Chapter 25

The Production-Work Stage
in the System of Comprehensive
Rehabilitation Treatment

Work occupies a dominant position in the life of man. Learning from early childhood, vocational training and job placement create that working-life stereotype that is essential to everyone, for it makes life meaningful and gives joy and satisfaction from the fruits of one's labor.

However, alcoholism destroys working-life attitudes. In some this process drags out for a long time; in others it builds up quickly; but in all cases it proceeds steadily. The person descends the social ladder, since every member of society is appreciated, first of all, by his contribution to the social fabric in which he lives.

Some people believe that the intake of alcoholic beverages increases their mental and physical strength. The intake of small doses for a time lifts the mood and creates the illusion of increased working capacity, but the concentration of attention weakens and the alcohol drinker begins to make mistakes and blunders. As a consequence, there is sloppy work, failure to fulfill the production plan, and not infrequently, accidents. It has been established that when performing work in a state of drunkenness or hangover labor productivity drops by 15-30%. By sloppy work the alcoholic inflicts direct losses to industry, and by enticing other people into his company, this loss increases several times.

We live in an epoch of scientific and technical revolution. Individual jobs have become a thing of the past; single workers have lost their importance. High-precision machines, tools and mechanisms, higher speeds, close interdependence of different jobs, a single production line, all create conditions whereby the performance of one worker is closely linked with the work of another. Mistakes made by one immediately implicates the work of others. Thus, failure of an alcohol user who reports for work in a state of drunkenness to fulfill his output quota immediately affects the labor productivity of his workmates, and ultimately, the fulfillment of the plan by the entire workforce. The condition of a person the following morning after drinking alcoholic beverages also affects his work. Many arrive still sleepy, torpid, feeling weak, and needing to lie down at least for a few minutes. Because they are constantly distracted and cannot get into the usual working rhythm, they can cause injuries and accidents.

First of all, alcohol affects man's higher nervous system, the brain, and the main processes taking place in it, excitation and inhibition. If a person has ingested alcohol in the morning before starting work, or a mug of beer during a break, it is enough to upset the dynamic equilibrium in the brain so that excitation subdues inhibition. Outwardly it looks like this: the worker's attention wanders; he is frequently distracted; the working process seems to take place independently of his will. He is likely to overlook something, which often results in a mistake or accident. Not only is there a direct connection between the use of alcoholic beverages and the incidence of accidents, but since the reactivity and resistance of the organism is lowered, alcoholics succumb more frequently than others to different somatic diseases and account for a greater number of days on sick leave (which in turn burdens the budget).

Those who constantly use alcoholic beverages also experience a peculiar and drastic change of mental status. They may report for work strictly on time, even fulfill their production quotas, but are absolutely indifferent to the interests of production and have no wish to improve their work.

In short, under the effect of chronic alcoholic intoxication there develops, even during the initial stages of the disease, toxic encephalopathy, i.e., a decrease in the activity of the nerve cells of the brain, which manifests itself in diminishing working capacity. The bulk of the ingested alcohol undergoes oxidation, i.e., it is destroyed in the organism within 36-38 hours; yet part of it is retained for a longer time, particularly in the brain. Labeled atoms helped to prove that some part of the ethanol is present even after 18-21 days. Therefore, if one drinks only twice a month, this will be enough for the organism, particularly the brain, to be kept under the constant effect of ethanol. Specifically, observations over many years have led to the conclusion that the working capacity in any category of transport workers under the effect of alcohol is reduced by 20%.

Tests have proved that a glass of vodka alters auditory and visual perception. This is especially perilous for drivers. The depth of vision is impaired and orientation to the location of an object is lost, which may result in collisions. Orientation to signals and discernment of fluctuations in light intensity are steeply reduced, which is extremely dangerous since traffic in city streets is regulated by lights. Ten to 15 grams of alcohol or 20-25 grams of vodka suffice for changes in color perception to occur: dark colors, including green, are perceived as gray. The perception of red also changes. Thereby, clear traffic-light signals become blurred—gray. What we have described refers to a single intake of an alcoholic beverage. What, then, can be said of the auditory and visual capacities of chronic drinkers?

Scientists have reported the following findings. Two groups of people were studied, chronic alcoholics and healthy individuals. All the subjects at the moment of observation were in a state of mild drunkenness when the blood alcohol concentration was not high. The results indicated that with low illumination, adaptation in the control group of healthy individuals took 15-20 minutes on the average, while among the alcoholics it took 25-30 minutes. An examination of the eyes showed that chronic ethanol intoxication results in disturbances of the nerve fibers of the alcoholic's retina. Changes also take place in the auditory nerve endings, which lead to diminution of hearing acuity. Some sounds appear dull, weak, or even fail to be perceived. We need not elaborate the grave consequences which such a situation may lead to. Great danger is presented by the loss of capacity to respond quickly to new, unexpected situations. A driver who has taken a drink usually displays a devil-may-care attitude and when suddenly confronted with even a simple problem is unable to deal with it.

Thus, it initially would seem like a minor matter—the individual took a drink, was late for work, did not report for work, committed some error. Then there occurs a warning, reprimand, denial of a bonus, another reprimand, demotion, dismissal, and further degradation. At best, one is still tolerated at work; at first the attitude is that of condescension, then, scorn and contempt. Persons afflicted with alcoholism lose their critical attitude of themselves and their behavior, believe they are faulted over trifles, and that they are misunderstood or unappreciated. This leads to suspicion and malice and to the gradual withdrawal and banding together with other alcoholics like themselves. Meanwhile symptoms of dementia build up, and the degradation of the personality becomes ever more pronounced and noticeable to people around them. Unfortunately, the one who fails to realize this is the afflicted person himself.

It has been proved, though, that active alcoholism treatment and subsequent abstention from alcohol result in the restoration of psychic functions. The degree of this process depends on the depth of the deterioration. The deeper it is, the slower and shallower the restoration. In shallow initial disorders of the intellect one may count on adequate restoration of the lost abilities. Much also depends on the manner in which treatment is organized. In distinction from drug therapy, an important stage of rehabilitation treatment is aimed at the restoration or development of new working skills and social bonds. This is the production-work stage in the system of rehabilitation treatment, in which, just as in all kinds of treatment, psychotherapy is given one of the principal roles. The production-work stage of rehabilitation treatment comprises the following elements:

1. *Work therapy of inpatients and outpatients.* It is geared to those in the stage of pronounced deterioration of personality, who have lost working skills. Work may be conducted within hospital wards, providing services to institutions, at WTWs, and consists of the simplest jobs, which may be carefully graduated and combined with medication. Patients must be involved in self-servicing, in cultural and ed-

ucational work, and take part in social organizations of the drug and psychiatric institutions.

2. *Fulfillment of high-skilled jobs.* This element is implemented with a view to training for further job placement. It requires maximum involvement in cultural and educational programs and combines active alcoholism treatment with improvement of the microsocial environment.

3. *Job placement in production.* This is the final goal and demands the most from the patient. Here medical personnel are expected to give a great deal of assistance.

There are cases when the management of businesses and institutions themselves are reluctant to take back workers dismissed for systematic drunkenness and absenteeism. In other cases, before giving a rehabilitant a responsible job, there is the added burden that he must be trained in a new specialty. In addition, the old environment (workmates) may be unreliable in their attitude toward alcohol, and the rehabilitant must be kept away from them. Therefore, it is the duty of the medical worker to examine all of these situations beforehand and prepare the ground for the rehabilitant's successful employment. Nor should the rehabilitant's family be forgotten, the physical environment, as well as social support in ensuring that the alcoholism treatment be sustained.

It is somewhat easier to resolve these problems when drug departments at industrial institutions are part of the structure of addiction and psychiatric centers. In such cases the stages of job placement and adaptation to work take less time and proceed more directly and easily from the very beginning. Nevertheless, certain difficulties are encountered in the job placement of rehabilitants because of their somatic condition. Here, apart from the main alcoholic or other addictive disease, one has to take into account the rehabilitant's specific physical ailments, and therefore select the possible kind of employment with particular care. There are also special considerations when treating women, young people and persons discharged from a WTP. Especially in the case of young people, one should recommend raising the educational level. Such trust hopefully generates a desire for social advancement, increases motivation and further facilitates recovery.

Chapter 26

Supportive Therapy, Prevention and Treatment of Relapses

The supply of medicinal drugs for suppressing the pathological craving for alcoholic beverages and developing the aversion reflex to alcohol is large and varied. In skillful combination with psychotherapy, these medicinal drugs and methods yield a positive therapeutic effect in 60 to 70% of cases. Therefore, one can assume that in a number of instances failure is due to the incorrect selection of medicines and insufficiently thought-out therapeutic procedures.

The difficulty of treating alcoholism relates to the issue of the qualitative stabilization of its results. Unfortunately, a number of factors renders alcoholism a special disease. What, then, are its peculiarities? The first is that the majority of people believe the use of alcohol an ordinary phenomenon, never giving serious thought to the possible development of alcohol-related diseases. Their train of thought is usually this: "I drink a little, just like everyone else; Millions drink and never get ill, why should I be so unlucky? I can't keep temperate all my life when so many around me are drinking." Another peculiarity of alcoholism is that the treatment given is mainly pathogenetical, not etiological, i.e., we are attempting to disrupt the pathogenetical chain in the development of the disease, without eliminating the cause itself. In this connection many scientists believe that a person afflicted with alcoholism never recovers from it, but only enters a state of remission or improvement.

That this point of view may be incorrect can be seen from numerous examples in which early treatment arrests the development of the disease and completely restores the patient's good health and status in society. Besides, such an attitude causes a kind of pessimism in the patient himself and his relatives, undermining confidence in the success of treatment. As a result of these factors we have found it necessary in the present state of alcoholism treatment to carry on lasting supportive therapy for a period of five years; without it one can hardly hope for success.

The previously quoted Order "On the Establishment of Obligatory Minimum Courses of Treatment for Chronic Alcoholics" says in part: "Patients who had undergone an outpatient course of active alcoholism therapy, discharged from narcological (psychiatric) hospitals, and those who completed treatment in work therapy preventoriums, are subject to supportive outpatient treatment." Thus, supportive therapy is a general requirement in the treatment of alcoholism. And, just as with previous stages of treatment, psychotherapy in its various forms occupies one of the principal places in the structure of supportive therapy.

Periodically, depending on the general status of the organism, general roborant, invigorating or calming therapy is recommended. The latter kind of treatment primarily includes the utilization of various psychotropic drugs. Trioxazin, chlordiazepoxide, etc., are recommended for the alleviation of neurotic or psychopathic-like conditions. When it is necessary to reduce or suppress a growing craving for alcoholic beverages, neulepthyl, carbidine, perphenazine, etc., should be prescribed.

When using psychotropic substances one should not forget that alcoholics and alcohol abusers tend toward rapid addiction to psychotropic and narcotic drugs; therefore, they should be prescribed for a short time only and, better still, in combination with other remedies.

"Chemical isolation" from alcohol, which immediately follows the active phase of treatment after discharge from a WTP, is very important for some patients. In such cases supportive daily doses of disulfiram (0.15-0.25 grams), metronidazole (0.5-0.75 grams) and nicotinic acid (0.1 grams) may be prescribed. Then throughout the first year of remission these drugs are prescribed systematically in one to three-month courses of daily administration, with two-month intervals between them; in the second year of remission, daily for one to two months with intervals between the courses lasting up to three months; in the third year of remission, daily for one to one and a half months over four to six-month intervals; and during the fourth and fifth years of remission, treatment is given daily for one to one and a half months with five to six-month intervals between the courses. Depending on the patient's condition, especially for those with an increasing craving for alcohol and the extinction of the negative reflex to alcohol, it is recommended that disulfiram-ethanol and metronidazole-ethanol tests be carried out. Some patients should be invited to attend these simply for the benefit of their psychotherapeutic effect.

Conditioned-reflex therapy must be conducted depending on the duration of remission. In the first year, conditioned-reflex therapy is prescribed three times, once in the form of a course of active alcoholism treatment, then over an interval of three to six months; in the second year it is conducted twice; in the third year, once; and in the fourth to fifth years, according to indications. When necessary, patients may be periodically admitted to the hospital for a course of conditioned-reflex therapy. If the examinations are staged on an outpatient basis, then the patient should be given leave from work on the test day. Conditioned-reflex therapy with apomorphine, emetine, emetic cocktails comprise on an average five to seven sessions, and with a tincture of lycopodium, one to two sessions.

The question of the time when therapy should be given and the combination of different medications and their intensity are decided upon by the attending physician; however, all the drugs used for treatment must be administered strictly according to official Instructions authorized by the Board for the Introduction of New Medicinal Remedies and Medical Technology, USSR Ministry of Health.

For maintaining stable remissions it is recommended that patients should abstain from visiting restaurants and cafes, and, during the first and second year of remission, should even avoid formal parties. It is useful to lead a measured mode of life, keeping to a certain stereotype of working activity, recreation, and having regular meals. It is desirable that the food be rich in vitamins, primarily fruits and vegetables, with meat slightly restricted.

In some patients the state of remission may break down and a relapse of the disease occur. The chief causes of this are the following:

1. Alcoholics are susceptible to a variety of beliefs or rationalizations, such as "I have recovered, and now can begin again, little by little, to drink"; "I should not drink much, but I would like to put the results of my treatment to the test"; "Friends and relatives are drinking, urging me just to touch the glass to the lips, it would not do to refuse"; "The doctor said that I shouldn't drink for two years; now that this time is up, I can try and live as everyone else." These and similar utterings are called "autopsychological" causes of relapse.

2. Increased emotionality, inability to restrain affect, inadequate will power, minor misfortunes, or psychologically traumatic situations at home and work are frequently a pretext for the breakdown of remissions. We designate these causes as "emotional-situational."

3. Some patients, as a result of the weakening negative reflex to alcohol and growing craving for it, increased anxiety, inner discomfort and poor health, may at times experience the desire to take a drink that results in the breakdown of a remission. Special concern should be given to groundless moodiness and a craving for alcohol that appears without its recent use. We refer to such conditions as "endogenous-somatic," in that they depend on the former habituation to alcoholic beverages.

Remission breakdowns consisting of the periodic use of alcoholic drinks, but not leading to renewed abuse are distinguished. Here, a pathological (psychic and physical) craving for alcoholic beverages has had no time to develop, but frequent breakdowns may eventually induce it. We regard as relapses those states in which systematic use of alcoholic beverages is resumed, not infrequently of the drinking-binge type, which leads to the recurrence of all forms of pathology the patient had suffered before treatment.

Anticipating the possible breakdown of remission or alcoholic relapse, the patient, his relatives and close friends should be psychotherapeutically prepared for the event. This ensures that at the appearance of warning symptoms, the onset of breakdown, drinking bouts or relapses, they can immediately seek the aid of professionals. It is also important to resume psychotherapeutic contact with the patient, at first daily, then two to three times a week. Sessions of rational psychotherapy are recommended, suggesting to the patient the need to work out in himself a sincere wish to give up drinking. The patient should be warned that unless he does so he can expect nothing but compulsory treatment.

Therapeutic measures for remission breakdowns and relapses may be conditionally divided into several stages. The first is detoxification, when the patient has sought medical aid in a state of alcoholic intoxication or drinking binge. These procedures should be conducted at the medical sobering-up station. When possible they should not be done at a medical institution, so that patients are discouraged from relying on this kind of aid at such institutions.

The second stage is the arrest of the craving for alcoholic beverages, for which various means are used. Drugs with a pyrogenic action have well-proven effects. According to certain data, hyperthermia arrests drinking bouts and hangover conditions in 96-98% of cases; sulfadiazine and pyrogenal are used for this purpose. Intramuscular injections of 5-7 ml of a 0.37% sulfadiazine solution are injected into the upper outer quadrant of the gluteus muscle. Pyrogenal is also injected intramuscularly in increasing doses of 500, 750, 1,000, 1,250 and 1,500 minimal pyrogenic doses. Hyperthermia during sulfadiazine treatment sets in four to six hours later, and when treating with pyrogenal, two to three hours later, reaching 38-39°C and then dropping over the next 24 hours. Therefore, treatment can be conducted daily or every other day, with a total of three to five injections. In order to preclude the patient's striving to take alcohol before the rise of temperature, it is recommended to cause vomiting by administering 0.1-0.2 grams of nicotinic acid or 50 ml of a 1% copper sulfate solution orally. Pyrogenic therapy is contraindicated during pregnancy, in cardiovascular insufficiency, during exacerbations of kidney diseases, in tuberculosis and in feverish states. For arresting remission breakdowns and alcoholic relapses, 0.5-1 gram daily doses of disulfiram, and 1.5-2 grams doses of metronidazole administered three times over one hour intervals are given. Nausea, vomiting and the restoration of aversion to alcohol is caused by thiol preparations (unithiol, dimercaprol, sodium thiosulfate).

For the speedy alleviation of the abstinence syndrome symptomatic treatment should be started at once in order to check asthenia, neurotic symptoms, or disorders of sleep and appetite. The remedies prescribed for this are glucose, vitamins, oxygen insufflation, strychnine injections, small doses of insulin, soporifics and electric sleep. For removing hangover symptoms, normalizing sleep, and alleviating affective disorders and delusions of perception, tranquilizers, antidepressants, and neuroleptics are used in brief courses and in small doses. The prescription of these drugs and their combinations are selected by the attending physician.

During the third stage of treatment, once again active alcoholism therapy is combined with intensive psychotherapy. Alternating methods of treatment are recommended: whereas formerly the patient received conditioned-reflex therapy, it is advisable to prescribe DER or to carry out DAER. In some cases hospitalization is indicated, particularly if the patient has never been treated on an inpatient basis. Outpatient treatment of remission breakdowns and relapses also offers the advantages of not isolating the patient from work and family, adding confidence in the success of treatment.

In conclusion, successful treatment of remission breakdowns, drinking bouts and alcoholic relapses is only possible with comprehensive psychotherapy, as well as the use of pyrogenic, soporific drugs, psychotropic remedies and active methods of treatment.

Chapter 27

Specific Alcoholism Treatments

TREATMENT OF ALCOHOLIC WOMEN

Women seldom appeal for medical aid on their own. When they do, it is more often at the insistence of their relatives, while the patients themselves have little hope of recovery and during the first stages of treatment are rather uncooperative.

The choice of inpatient or outpatient treatment lies with the physician, who makes his decision after carefully studying the case, and talking to relatives and the patient herself. During drinking bouts, psychoses, or pregnancy, inpatient treatment is indicated. It is advisable to conduct outpatient treatment of women separately from men.

Whatever the circumstances, treatment must begin with rational psychotherapy of the patient and explanatory talks with relatives and colleagues, in other words, with health education. Later on, psychotherapeutic influence on the patient should be continued in the form of individual or group hypnotherapy and autotraining.

It should be borne in mind that in women a great role in the aggravation of their state is played by emotional situations and conditions which afford free access to alcoholic beverages (work in shops, restaurants, etc.). Therefore, all possible measures should be promptly taken to exclude these factors.

Women are subject to moodiness, with a predominance of depressive and hysterical reactions. In the menstrual and climacteric periods and during pregnancy, affective fluctuations are particularly noticeable. They should be carefully detected and, when possible, promptly alleviated, since not infrequently they may cause alcohol abuse. The administration of sedatives, antidepressants, neuroleptics and tranquilizers is indicated in these cases. Treatment courses should be short, with replacement of drugs so as to preclude habituation.

The principles of alcoholism treatment in women are similar to the general ones: the stages of detoxification, overall strengthening and stimulation of the organism, and active alcoholism treatment followed by five years of supportive therapy. Before beginning treatment, a careful physical examination should be carried out with special attention to the state of the cardiovascular system, the reproductive organs, and possible pregnancy.

It is recommended to start treatment by prescribing sulfadiazine and pyrogenal. In addition to detoxification and stimulation, these drugs effectively suppress in women an increased craving for alcohol; a similar effect is produced by carbidin. Measures should be taken to regulate sleep and improve their mood. The prescription of different vitamins, and for middle-aged women, hormonal preparations, is essential. Then, active conditioned-reflex or sensitizing alcoholism therapy is prescribed. Sensitizing therapy should be conducted with certain precautions, since in some patients it causes grave collaptoid states with a sharp drop in arterial pressure.

During periods of alcohol abuse women seldom conceive, and if this happens, they generally agree of their own will to termination of the pregnancy. In such situations, especially if the husband is also an alcoholic, this measure should be recommended. However, in cases when the woman wishes to bear the child, she should not be prevented from doing so. Vigorous measures must be taken to render the woman's organism healthy, with absolute abstention from alcohol; therefore, treatment at drug, psychiatric or medical hospitals (for example, in the gynecological ward) is advised and hospitalizations may be repeated several times.

During the period of breastfeeding the use of alcoholic beverages is absolutely contraindicated, and only upon its termination can active alcoholism treatment be given. Throughout the periods of pregnancy and breastfeeding the woman should be under the constant supervision of her gynecologist as well as the physician and psychiatrist treating her addiction. If observation shows that the woman is likely to continue alcohol abuse after childbirth, the question of depriving her of parental privileges under Article 19 of the "Fundamentals of Legislation on Marriage and the Family of the USSR and the Union Republics" should be considered.

TREATMENT OF YOUNG ALCOHOLICS

Alcoholism treatment for youths does not differ in principle from the treatment of adult males, though it has some specific features. It should begin in an outpatient setting; only in neglected cases and as an exception is inpatient treatment indicated. When schoolchildren are involved, it is necessary to begin from a study of the closest environment of relatives and friends. Health education should be combined with psychotherapeutic influence on the youth, both aimed at reorientation of his values, drawing him away from bad habits and company, and attracting him into social activities, persuading him to take up sports, etc. Often service in the army puts an end to the beginning affliction.

In cases when the formation of alcoholism is involved, detoxification, general roborant, and stimulating therapy combined with active alcoholism treatment are indicated in view of the possible rapid buildup of such symptoms as psychic and physical craving for alcohol, loss of control, amnesic forms of intoxication, and the hangover syndrome.

Youths afflicted with initial forms of alcoholism must be under constant medical supervision, since in them the disease frequently takes a pernicious course. Active alcoholism therapy should be conducted by all available means. Conditioned-reflex therapy followed by supportive disulfiram treatment is particularly indicated. Due to the low hypnotizability of young patients the effect of this therapy for youth alcoholism is negligent, and it is better to use other kinds of psychotherapeutic influence and autosuggestion. It is also recommended that youths not be sent to WTPs, since such centers are intended for severely ill alcoholics with pronounced personality changes and antisocial behavior, and the negative influence may have a deleterious effect on an unstable young person.

TREATMENT OF ELDERLY ALCOHOLICS

As a rule, by the time people grow old they are afflicted with different somatic ailments, many with signs of cerebral sclerosis. The age of 60 and older is a contraindication to compulsory treatment at a WTP. Therefore, when considering the choice of alcoholism therapy, preference should be given to admission to drug or psychiatric hospitals or to special wards of general medical institutions, particularly when a patient is seeking aid for the first time. In order to plan a therapeutic strategy, one must determine from the patient's history the time when alcoholization began, whether in youth or old age, and carry out careful physical, neurological and psychological examinations. Only then can treatment begin.

Symptomatic treatment, when necessary, must include in addition to detoxification, general roborant and stimulating therapy, hormonal drugs, and special antisclerotic medicines. Antidepressants, neuroleptics, or tranquilizers may be prescribed in small doses for short treatment courses, sometimes only once. This stage of premedication should be completed within three to four weeks.

Active alcoholism treatment in the absence of contraindications can be conducted in the form of conditioned-reflex therapy, given good tolerance to small doses of apomorphine. A course of treatment comprises five to seven sessions. Disulfiram (cyamide) treatment of 60-year-old and older people is inadmissible. It is sometimes not possible to use these drugs in minimal doses (0.15-0.1 gram of disulfiram, 0.25 gram of cyamide) and only as supportive therapy.

Unlike younger persons, the elderly are more susceptible to hypnotic suggestion and, generally, to psychotherapy. Therefore, in a number of cases it is possible to carry out 30-40 hypnotic sleep suggestions or attain lasting isolation from alcohol by using other kinds of psychotherapeutic intervention. In all cases involving elderly people, lasting treatment and observation of the somatic condition, improvement of the microsocial environment, giving assistance in accommodation, and job placement or arranging retirement on a pension are indicated.

TREATMENT OF ALCOHOLISM AGGRAVATED BY DISEASES OF THE INTERNAL ORGANS

When alcoholism is concurrent with diseases of the internal organs, as a rule it complicates treatment. In these cases it is recommended to start treatment in a hospital setting: this provides opportunities, depending on the severity of the somatic ailments, to select an appropriate, sparing kind of therapy to arrest a drinking bout or alleviate an abstinence condition. Then, upon careful examination of the patient's physical status, the question of further therapy can be decided. Conditions are often encountered when the gravity of the somatic or neurological affliction precludes active alcoholism treatment; in such cases the patient should be transferred to a hospital that directly treats the medical condition.

When it is necessary to start treating the somatic disease, detoxification and general roborant, and occasionally stimulating therapy, may be prescribed in parallel. One should remember that in the state of decompensation, active alcoholism therapies cannot be applied, while in the compensated state some of them can be used for the same disease. In every case a first-aid kit with cardiovascular, hemostatic and other remedies, should always be at hand. Eventually the patients may be transferred to outpatient supportive therapy, more often with the utilization of the entire armamentarium of alcoholism treatment.

In gastric or duodenal ulcer, conditioned-reflex therapy is contraindicated, and in diseases of the pancreas sensitizing therapy should not be prescribed because of its toxicity. In diseases of the respiratory tract all kinds of therapy are admissible, yet in the active phase of tuberculosis alcoholism treatment is contraindicated. Conditioned-reflex apomorphine-antabuse therapy must not be prescribed in a pre- or postinfarction state or following a stroke. After a certain period of time in the stage of compensation such treatment may be cautiously administered. A latent form of diabetes mellitus often occurs in alcoholics. In order to exclude the possibility of diabetic coma, the blood and urine should be examined for sugar content. When necessary treatment should be given for diabetes, and after the blood sugar content is brought down to normal, various kinds of alcoholism therapy can be prescribed.

TREATMENT OF ALCOHOLISM COMBINED WITH MENTAL DISORDERS

Certain difficulties arise when treating alcoholism which is concurrent with mental diseases—schizophrenia, epilepsy, traumatic lesion of the brain, atherosclerosis, etc. The treatment strategy in these cases is worked out depending on the severity of the principal mental process and the degree of dementia present, with the understanding that patients with such disorders may underestimate their condition, have little will to recover, and may be unable to control their actions in the period of medication.

In all cases therapy should take place in a psychiatric hospital and start with arresting alcoholic intoxication and the drinking bout. Then detoxification, and general roborant and stimulating therapy is conducted. Treatment of the principal mental disorder is conducted in parallel. The treatment plan of alcoholism therapy is drawn up individually, bearing in mind the recommendations presented in the Methodological Letter of the USSR Ministry of Health's "Methods of Conducting Alcoholism Therapy of Mental Patients, Aggravated by Chronic Alcoholism."

Chapter 28

Treatment of Alcoholic Psychoses

The hospitalization of patients with acute alcoholic psychoses is obligatory. This measure is dictated by the fact that under the influence of hallucinations, delirium or excitation such patients may commit socially dangerous acts harmful to other people or to themselves. This danger is not removed even in the hospital until symptoms of scute psychosis have been alleviated. This is why upon admission such patients must be maintained in the observation ward under close supervision of the medical personnel.

In all cases of alcohol-related mental disorders, the water-electrolyte and vitamin balance in the organism is upset, with hypoxia of the brain and tissues. In some patients the psychoses develop against the background of the hangover syndrome, when underoxidized intermediate products of ethanol decomposition have not been removed from the organism, which experiences an acute shortage of additional portions of alcohol. All these make it imperative to quickly but carefully study the patient, to gather, when possible, the anamnesis (most frequently from relatives and neighbors, since the patient is unable to provide adequate information about himself) and start treatment. The therapy for alcoholic psychoses should be comprehensive, continuous and strictly individualized. The task boils down to the arrest of psychic disorders, including excitation and insomnia. Somatic treatment is aimed at detoxification and dehydration of the organism while maintaining the functioning of the cardiovascular and respiratory systems, the correction of metabolic disorders and hypovitaminoses, and at averting symptoms of cerebral hypoxia and edema.

For alleviating psychotic disorders neuroleptics are employed, usually a 2.5% chlorpromazine solution given in 2-3 ml doses two to three times a day; other options are haloperidol or diazepam. Amobarbytal sodium can be given before bedtime either in an enema or intramuscularly. This treatment is recommended for a period from 2-5 to 10-15 days depending on the patient's condition.

According to our observations, a good therapeutic effect is produced by carbamazepin preparations. They are administered immediately upon the patient's admission to hospital in 200 mg doses three to four times a day, and on the next day the doses may be increased to 1,200-1,400 mg; the average daily dose is 600-800 mg. In contrast with neuroleptics, there are practically no contraindications to these preparations. They remove psychomotor excitation within approximately 36-48 hours leading to a reduction of psychopathological symptoms, are of low toxicity, and possess an anticonvulsive action. Intensive detoxification, dehydration and vitamin therapy are indicated with the use of symptomatic remedies aimed at removing excitation, hallucinations and delirium.

Delirium tremens is treated according to the stage of the disease. During stages I and II detoxification therapy is basic, and during stage III, dehydration. The dehydration of the organism should be compensated by copious drinking, and intravenous drip administration of a standard solution containing glucose, calcium chloride, calcium gluconate, insulin, cordiamine, a battery of vitamins B_1, B_6, C, PP, diazepam, and aminophylline with a sodium chloride isotonic solution.

A good effect is produced by the administration of a 15% mannitol solution and, if this is unavailable, a solution of urea, or urugluk. The two latter preparations can be used provided the patient has good renal function. From the first day of treatment vitamins in large doses should be given. Gradually, after 4-5 days, the doses of the drugs may be reduced and brought down to normal, but vitamin therapy should be continued for another 3-4 weeks. Up to 1,000 mg daily doses of vitamin B_1 are administered, partially intravenously (3 ml of a 6%

solution), intramuscularly (3 mg two to three times a day) and in tablets (two to three times a day). The organism is also enriched with vitamins B_6, B_{12}, B_{15}, C, and nicotinic acid. In case of a rising fever and suspicion of pneumonia, antibiotics are prescribed.

Symptoms pointing to possible cerebral edema call for intensive dehydration therapy; spinal puncture may be necessary. For preventing complications on the part of the cardiovascular system, it is recommended that cordiamine and corasole in 2 ml doses be administered to cardiacs 3-4 times a day. Besides this, the patients need a milk-vegetable diet, meticulous care, and attention given to their physiological functions.

The treatment of acute alcoholic hallucinosis is basically the same as for delirium tremens, though detoxification therapy may be briefer. Antipsychotic drugs used in these cases (diazepam in a detoxificating solution, or separately, chlorpromazine) often rather quickly arrest auditory hallucinosis. Good results are produced by carbamazepin in the above indicated doses; stazepine does not produce the same effect. Psychomotor excitation is relieved with chlorpromazine, levomepromazine hydrochloride and oxazepam.

Acute alcoholic paranoids are treated with detoxificating mixtures (by drip infusion with the addition of diazepam, 2-3 ml of a 0.5% solution). The use of other psychotropic drugs is possible, such as levomepromazine hydrochloride, haloperidol, and oxazepam. A 2 ml dose of a 1% solution of diphenylhydramine is given intramuscularly, and a 25% solution of magnesium sulfate with 10 ml of a 40% glucose solution is prescribed intravenously. Sodium thiosulfate, a soporific, and large doses of vitamins B_1, B_6, B_{12}, B_{15} are recommended. It is also advisable to prescribe glutaminic acid orally in 0.5-1 gram doses two to three times a day and small doses of insulin. In mild disorders of consciousness some patients turn for medical aid themselves. In these cases one should use, against the background of drug medication, rational psychotherapy.

It must be stressed once again that practically all cases of acute alcoholic hallucinoses and paranoia are absolute indications for hospitalization, since patients whose attitude to their hallucinatory or delirial experiences is uncritical may commit various antisocial acts dangerous both to themselves and others. After arresting acute psychotic symptoms and bearing in mind the peculiarities of their somatic and mental state, all patients must be given active alcoholism treatment. Some of them reject it; others, though reluctantly, agree. Experience shows, however, that unless such treatment is given, the overwhelming majority of patients eventually resume alcohol abuse.

All measures should be used for convincing the afflicted person, and even compelling him when necessary, to undergo active alcoholism treatment. Following mild forms of delirium tremens, therapeutic procedures may start after 8-10 days; in cases of episodes of medium severity, after 15-20 days; and after severe forms of the psychosis, after one to two months. One should not prescribe sensitizing treatment (disulfiram) with the staging of alcoholic tests. Disulfiram prescription may be used as supportive therapy only two to three months later. The disulfiram doses should not exceed 0.25-0.3 gram daily in combination with general roborant therapy and vitamin therapy.

A placebo that imitates ethanol-disulfiram tests with the use of 0.1 gram nicotinic acid doses three times a day is recommended. One may conduct conditioned-reflex therapy in an 8 to 12-session course with the use of minimal doses of apomorphine and emetics, which is combined with hypnosuggestive treatment. Courses of hypnosuggestive therapy consisting of 15-20 sessions also may be given at an earlier date. Supportive therapy is obligatory for all patients for the duration of 5 years.

Some alcoholic psychoses assume a subacute or protracted character from the very beginning, while others become chronic following earlier acute psychotic episodes. It is desirable that the treatment of these conditions be conducted in the hospital, although in some verbal chronic hallucinoses outpatient treatment should not be ruled out. In chronic alcoholic hallucinosis, in addition to detoxification therapy, thiol drugs, magnesium sulfate, and hypoglycemic doses of insulin are prescribed in combination with psychotropic preparations and high vitamin doses. Regulated fasting can also be used.

In subacute and chronic alcoholic paranoids psychotropic preparations such as chlorpromazine, levomepromazine hydrochloride, haloperidol and trifluperidol are prescribed. Complications are arrested with corrective drugs, like benzhexol. Hypoglycemic doses of insulin with vitamin B_{12} are also used. Some authors recommend insulin shock therapy. During such a course (one to one and a half months) sulfadiazin is administered once a week for a total of 150-200 temperature hours.

The chronic delusion of jealousy is particularly stubborn. In some patients it is exacerbated upon the intake of alcoholic beverages. Complete isolation from alcoholic beverages is crucial in such cases. Treatment with psychotropic drugs is conducted for a long time. Chlorpromazine, trifluoperazine, haloperidol in combination with diazepam, and chlordiazepoxide are used. Thioproperazine can also be prescribed.

Vitamin deficiency underlies Korsakoff's psychosis, Wernicke's encephalopathy and a number of other alcohol-related chronic psychotic disorders. Along with detoxification treatment such patients should be given intensive vitamin therapy with B group vitamins (B_1, B_6, B_{12}), PP, C, and glutaminic acid. Vitamin therapy should last two to three months. Such preparations as bromides, tranquilizers, and neuroleptics in combination with cardiacs are prescribed in parallel. After the abatement of acute symptoms it is advisable to continue general treatment (i.e., vitamins, glutaminic acid, small insulin doses, and tonics in somewhat reduced doses). Active alcoholism treatment with sensitizing remedies is contraindicated in persons after protracted alcoholic psychoses. Conditioned-reflex therapy may be given, but in small doses and in combination with hypnosuggestive therapy.

In alcoholic depressions, abstention from alcoholic beverages improves the mood and alleviates the depression. Antidepressants such as imipramine or amitryptiline are prescribed. Sleep disorders are treated by the administration of glucose with magnesium sulfate and vitamins. A good result is produced by psychotherapy, particularly hypnotherapy. In pronounced depression, hospitalization is obligatory because of the dangers that accompany suicidal ideas and attempts of the patients.

In marked disorders of mood of the dysphoric type, 0.006 gram doses of perphenazine are prescribed twice a day with corrective drugs (benzhexol, etc.). Treatment is given for three to five weeks. Diazepam, vitamin therapy, and general roborant psychotherapy are also recommended.

In stage III of alcoholism or after Korsakoff's or Wernicke's psychosis, many patients reveal different degrees of dementia. In a number of cases dementia is smoothed out and the condition improves, but in many the dementia remains and these patients become inmates of homes for chronic mental patients. Relapses of psychotic episodes may periodically occur with excitation, hallucinations or delirium. All of these symptoms are then treated by the appropriate drugs. Given the severity and diversity of such episodes, the therapy for alcoholic psychoses should be lasting and individualized.

Chapter 29

Sobering-Up and Emergency Aid

The sobering-up of a person in a state of pronounced alcoholic intoxication is essential, since it may threaten to have grave somatic consequences, mark the beginning of a drinking bout, indicate the relapse of alcoholism, or lastly, be the precursor of an impending psychotic condition.

Provided there are no contraindications, sobering-up should start with the administration of warm water, a weak solution of potassium permanganate, alkaline water (Borzhomi), warm milk with honey (125 grams of honey per 0.5 liter of milk), and 2 grams of acetylsalicylic acid also washed down with milk. Vomiting should be provoked by irritating the posterior wall of the throat until the vomit no longer smells of alcohol.

Washing of the stomach may be speeded up by sounding. A 0.3-0.5 ml apomorphine solution is administered with cardiacs. Apomorphine cannot be administered to patients in a comatose state or in a state of narcotic sleep. It is recommended to void the bladder by means of a catheter in order to preclude the repeated adsorption of alcohol into the blood. Ammonia spirits should be given for the patient to inhale. One should keep an eye on the pulse rate and respiration, and in case of deviations from the norm, cardiacs (caffeine, corasole, cordiamine, lobeline) and oxygen must be used.

In order to obtain a sobering-up effect low doses (0.5 ml) of a 0.1% atropine solution and high doses of metronidazole (one and a half to two grams) are used with the administration of the same doses two to two and a half hours later. Metronidazole will cause vomiting and aversion to alcohol comparatively quickly. Treatment with this drug, but in usual doses, may be continued on the next day. Warm baths can be given. A majority of doctors are unanimous in discouraging the use of neuroleptics, believing that they may worsen the condition, causing a precomatose or comatose state. In addition, neuroleptics cannot be used in cases of fever.

A warning sign of the severity of acute alcoholic intoxication is a comatose state. The physician must try to differentiate between alcoholic comatose conditions which come from cerebral hemorrhages that might have occurred in the state of drunkenness, and a diuretic, hypoglycemic, hepatic, uremic comatose condition. In such states hospitalization is obligatory and these patients are better handed over to intensive care units and resuscitation centers. The paramedical worker should remember that the appearance of neurological symptoms suggests the possibility of cerebral hemorrhage, and diagnosis will be assisted by spinal puncture and cranial roentgenology. When myocardial infarction is suspected an ECG is taken. In all cases when a severely drunk patient is admitted, close observation of his behavior and condition must be made and sobering up can be started only when satisfied that there are no complications.

The clinical manifestations of an alcoholic comatose condition are the following: the skin is cold, clammy; the face, hyperemic, cyanotic; there is a smell of alcohol from the mouth; breathing is irregular; the pulse is thread-like, weak; arterial pressure is steeply reduced; there are changes in the blood, such as leukocytosis, albumin in the urine, erythrocytes. With a deepening of the comatose state the tendon, corneal and pupillar reflexes diminish, muscular ataxia appears, there may be difficulty in swallowing, and respiration becomes irregular.

The comatose state is treated as follows: The stomach is washed out, a catheter is inserted, the body is warmed up and artificial inhalation of oxygen given. At the same time drugs are administered to stimulate the cardiovascular system and respiratory function. In addition to these, a saline isotonic solution is administered. In some cases spinal puncture may be recommended. An alcoholic comatose condition is most often arrested within one to four days, and intensive therapy should be maintained, with the patient kept in bed throughout the treatment.

Similarly, if myocardial infarction develops during a state of drunkenness, sobering up should be conducted very cautiously, with the patient kept strictly in bed and, when possible, under the supervision of a physician.

After completing the first sobering-up procedures it is advisable to put the patient to sleep. Amobarbital (sodium amytal) can be given in an enema. Then detoxifying therapy is prescribed, with the administration of antagonists of alcohol, such as strychnine or duplex, caffeine and other nervous system stimulants. When sobered up, patients frequently complain of poor sleep, general feeling of malaise, depression, anxiety, melancholia, tremor of the hands, sweating. All of these symptoms are characteristic of the abstinence state, which should be alleviated in order to preclude a drinking bout or a relapse of the disease. For this purpose, after 12 hours neuroleptics (chlorpromazine), tranquilizers (diazepam, chlordiazepoxide, meprobamate) and other drugs are used.

In order to provide for sobering up and the administering of emergency aid, the admission ward of drug and psychiatric hospitals, medication rooms and outpatient departments must at all times have special sets of instruments, apparatus, and medicines. They must include a minimum set of medications essential not only for ensuring the sobering up of patients, but for rendering emergency aid in severe physical conditions.

The following items are recommended for providing emergency aid: a probe, a mouth dilator, an apparatus for measuring arterial pressure, syringes (5-10-20 ml), needles for spinal puncture, oxygen breathing bags, hot water bottles, container with sterile material, catheters (male, female), potassium permanganate, 1% apomorphine solution (freshly prepared), metronidazole, ammonia spirit, caffeine, camphor, cordiamine (corazole), strophanthin, lobeline, corglykon, cytiton, blood substitutes, strychnine (duplex), glucose, magnesium sulfate, sodium thiosulfate, unithiol, dimercaprol, phenobarbital (luminal), amobarbital (sodium amytal) for oral administration or intramuscular injections, a 2.5% chlorpromazine solution, diazepam in ampules, Valium, chlordiazepoxide, and a 1% solution of sulfadiazine.

There is a method of accelerated sobering up which is most frequently used at medical sobering-up stations, especially when the patient must be sobered up quickly. The use of this method reduces the sobering-up procedure approximately by half, prevents the aggravation and deepening of the intoxication, and even improves the general status. Before applying this method of accelerated sobering up, it is necessary whenever possible to gather the anamnesis from the patient and examine him for any contraindications to the use of sobering-up drugs. One should particularly make sure that there are no infarctions, craniocerebral injuries, comatose conditions associated with diabetes mellitus, diseases of the liver or urinary system, disorders of cerebral circulation, or postepileptic states. Lastly, this sobering-up method is also contraindicated in the presence of alcoholic psychoses.

Accelerated sobering-up techniques are applied to persons in stages II and III of alcoholic intoxication. They are given a medicinal mixture consisting of corazole (0.2 gram), Phenocoll (0.01 gram), and nicotinic acid (0.1 ml). All this is mixed in 10-15 ml of boiled water. Then 10 ml of a 5% solution (500 mg) of pyrodoxine (vitamin B_6) is injected intramuscularly into the upper outer quadrant of the gluteus muscle. Depending on the patient's condition and the degree of drunkenness pyridoxine may be injected first, to be followed by the drinking of the medicinal mixture. These medicines should not be administered more than once.

As a rule, this method causes no side effects. Thirty to forty minutes later it becomes possible to speak to the patient, and one to one and a half hours later the anamnesis may be drawn up; in two to three hours there is an obvious effect of sobering, particularly if the administration of the medicine was followed by sleep.

Chapter 30

Treatment of Narcomanias and Toxicomanias

As mentioned earlier, narcomanias and toxicomanias differ from alcoholism by their clinical manifestations. Besides, each type of narcomania (morphine, hashish, barbiturite, etc.) has its own features not only in course and clinical picture, but also in biochemical changes occurring in the organism. Compared to alcoholism, the treatment of narcomanias and toxicomanias has features both common and specific to them only.

Just as with alcoholism treatment, one of the main principles in handling narcomanias and toxicomanias is treatment in stages: (1) detoxification, and general roborant and stimulating therapy in combination with the denial of the narcotic or other substance which is the object of abuse; (2) active drug treatment; (3) supportive therapy.

The main rule for treating narcomanias and toxicomanias is hospitalization, irrespective of whether the patient is in the state of the abstinence syndrome, acute intoxication, chronic intoxication, or psychosis. Inpatient treatment should be given in the drug and psychiatric institutions and, only when these are unavailable, in the general medical hospitals. The duration of primary hospitalization, according to the normative acts of the USSR Ministry of Health, is at least 60 days (Order No. 928, USSR Ministry of Health, September 23, 1976).

This Order is based on the fact that drug addicts, even when willing to undergo treatment, are always in a state of apprehension and fear of the physical and psychological effects of the abstinence condition. As a rule, these are vulnerable people who are afraid of the absence of the narcotic substance and the painful experiences, at times pronounced and severe, which they will have to face. Therefore, when beginning treatment, they quickly renege and strive by every available means to resume the consumption of the narcotic substance.

This makes it necessary to organize special departments or wards with conditions in them that would exclude the smuggling in of narcotic or other substances craved by the patients. The personnel should be well informed about the special regulations and strictly observe them. The daily schedule should provide for keeping people vigorously active, particularly in the evening, when the addicts, not accustomed to purposeful activity, are left alone with their thoughts and unpleasant sensations. They must be encouraged to join patient groups and to participate with others in work, cultural and social activities.

One should be particularly alert as to the behavior and mental state of the patients. If a dejected, torpid, low-key patient suddenly becomes talkative, vigorous and cheerful, one may suppose that he was able to attain narcotics by illicit means. The source of the narcotic substance must be sought and those who brought it to the ward should be punished.

One must be particularly attentive to the patient toward the end of the second to third week of treatment, in the period of unstable equilibrium when a recurrence of the obsessive craving for the addictive narcotics appears. In this state the patients become restless and begin to criticize treatment, or on the contrary, praise it, insist they are feeling well and wish to be discharged, alleging that they have already recovered. Some complain of headaches, poor sleep, or toothaches (characteristic symptoms) but such conditions usually pass away by themselves within two to four days.

Medication should be combined with psychotherapeutic influence. The physician, paramedical worker, and even the orderlies should constantly reassure the patients, instilling confidence in the success of treatment, firmly and convincingly revealing the harmfulness of using narcotics (or other substances), and assuring them that complete recovery is possible.

The principle of an individualized approach to each patient and prescribing the appropriate therapy for the treatment of addicts remains central. However, in every case unithiol and sulfadiazine are used for the detoxification therapy. Knowing that in narcomanias and toxicomanias the asthenic syndrome lasts longer than in alcoholism (one to one and a half months), phosphorus preparations are prescribed (0.2 gram calcium glycerophosphate tablets three times a day, 0.25 grams phytin tablets three times a day) and vitamins B_1, B_2, B_6, A, C and E.

Such general stimulants as the mixtures of Bekhterev, Sepp, Schmidt (one tablespoonful three times a day) are indicated. The recommended tranquilizers are chlordiazepoxide, diazepam, chlordiazepoxide hydrochloride, and trioxazin. All of these drugs have a calming effect and alleviate the states of anxiety and agitation, but they should be used in small doses and for short courses. The antidepressants (imipramine, nialamide, etc.) should be prescribed cautiously, since they may enhance agitation at times. Symptoms of depressions are best removed by dizaphen and amitriptiline. The use of drugs like metofenazate, trifluperidol, and haloperidol are not ruled out. They should be used in small doses, three to four times smaller than indicated in the instructions. In such cases they produce the desired sedative and hypnogenic effect, without causing grave extrapyramidal disorders and additional unpleasant sensations, like feelings of being jaded or heaviness in the head, etc.

Most of such patients, as a rule, have sleep disorders. Since normalization of sleep is not so difficult, it is advisable not to use barbamyl and other mixtures, but administer the above-mentioned tranquilizers and use such general hygienic methods as evening walks, warm footbaths, psychotherapeutic talks, hypnotic suggestion, and autogenic training. A good effect is produced by physiotherapeutic procedures, such as baths (hydrosulfuric, ordinary, salt-free) and the Shcherbak galvanic collar. In recent years the abstinence syndrome has been successfully alleviated by acupuncture.

During the first stage of therapy the patient is denied the narcotic drug. There are three methods of doing this: slow, rapid and instant. It is preferable to use the instant method, though the question is decided by the psychiatrist depending on the patient's individual features, the stage of the disease, and the presence or absence of contraindications. Healthy young people and persons with pronounced psychopathic features should be taken off the narcotic drug instantly. The same should be done when the patient's behavior reveals elements of aggravation.

The slow (step-like) discontinuation of narcotic or other substances is carried out for physically weak patients with concurrent diseases, in stage III narcomanias, elderly and old people. The first stage of therapy lasts three to four weeks, though the patient with symptoms of asthenia should be treated throughout his entire stay in the hospital.

The second stage of treatment consists of active therapy. At present no specific methods have been worked out, so that the ones mainly in use are those which are used for alcoholism treatment. Here, different kinds of psychotherapy should be regarded as the principal method of treatment, including hypnosis with suggestion of aversion and development of a negative reflex to the narcotic drug or substance abused in toxicomania, the build-up of willpower, and strengthening of healthy attitudes toward active recovery. In addition, "image therapy" as suggested by I. E. Volpert can be used. This method is a form of psychotherapy in which the patient selects for imitation the image of a person distinguished for positive attitudes who can serve as a model. The patient tries to emulate this image and modifies his own behavior depending on how the "model person" would act in a similar situation. The entire complex of the psychotherapeutic influence is fittingly called "orthopsychiatry." Moreover, psychotherapy should accompany any medication. This may include magnesium sulfate, emitine (with 0.02 gram doses in powder form once a day) and apomorphine (0.1-0.2 ml of a 0.5% solution subcutaneously).

In comparison with alcoholics, narcotic addicts undergo faster intellectual deterioration, becoming indifferent, weak-willed, withdrawn from life, and losing their jobs and skills long before admission to the hospital. Asthenia of long duration worsens these conditions. Therefore, during the second stage of treatment it is also necessary to include into the daily regimen obligatory work therapy, beginning from intermittent hours of work and gradually moving toward a full working day.

The third stage of treatment, supportive therapy, lasts a long time (five years). All this time the patients must be under strict observation of the drug consultation room, regularly visiting it or being under the observation of the home visiting medical nurse. It should be remembered that remission breakdowns and relapses are always possible, caused by repeated compulsive craving for the narcotic or medicinal drug, shifts of mood, situations fraught with mental trauma, or influences of the microsocial environment.

During this period psychotherapy is conducted, and repeated courses of conditioned-reflex, roborant, and stimulating therapy are given. The patient must be helped in finding employment and getting integrated into the workforce, and every encouragement is given to positive emotions and actions—raising one's skills, engaging in study, settling down and acquiring a family. The Order of the USSR Ministry of Health No. 388 of April 19, 1978, "On Authorizing Obligatory Minimal Treatment Courses for Persons Afflicted with Narcomanias and Toxicomanias" prescribes the following obligatory courses: during the first year obligatory visits to the drug consulting room once a month; during the second year, once every two months; in the third year, once every three months; in the fourth, once every four months; in the fifth, twice a year.

Obligatory supportive therapy is given for a period of three to four weeks in the first months upon discharge from hospital, and then in the 1st-2nd year of remission every three months, in the 3rd year twice, and in the 4th-5th years according to medical indications.

Aside from the general treatment regimens noted above, there are specific features in the treatment of certain narcomanias and toxicomanias. The most widespread among the hallucinogens is hashish (anasha, marijuana). Acute intoxication must be treated by washing out the stomach, then detoxification, general strengthening and stimulating therapy. Abstinence is shallow, unstable and does not cause severe physical or neurological changes. It is expressed in symptoms of general malaise, headaches, increased fatigability, and pains in the abdominal region or throughout the body. This state passes by itself within three to five days.

Psychic dependence lasts more than 15-20 days. During this time the hashish smoker is trying his utmost to get hashish by any means. He will cheat, steal, engage in speculation, or indulge in wild behavior. Moodiness predominates against a low-key background of irritability and anger that may lead to aggressive actions. Symptoms of mild physical dependence allows room to deny the narcotic at once. Therefore any therapy should be preceded by a kind of preparatory phase during which the addict is guided through psychotherapeutic means for deliberate efforts to recover.

The denial of the narcotic substance is followed by a prescription of a general roborant therapy: the vitamin complex of the group B, vitamin C, small doses of insulin (5-20 AU), 0.5 gram doses of phytin three times a day, and neuroleptics or tranquilizers. Subcutaneously 0.5 gram (in 0.2-0.5 mg doses) of apomorphine hydrochloride is given. After five to seven minutes, when nausea appears, the patient is given the smoke of a burning hashish cigarette to smell. After three to four sessions vomiting, through the mechanisms of conditioned-reflex connections, causes a negative reflex to hashish.

The next stage of treatment is long (two to three months). This consists of general roborant and psychotherapy for the restoration and acquisition of new positive social and work attitudes. The involvement of the patient in work situations is an obligatory component of the treatment.

In cases of hashish-related psychosis the therapeutic measures, particularly during the first stage, are of greater intensity and duration, including general roborant therapy with vitamins, sedatives, detoxification, therapy for alleviating excitation, and neuroleptics. Such treatment lasts 3-4 weeks. If no improvement occurs, insulin therapy must be initiated in order to produce 15-20 subshock or shock states. When the manic syndrome is dominant, treatment must be started with chlorpromazine and only after two to three weeks changed to insulin treatment. When dementia and psychopathization of personality occur, mild tranquilizers and glutaminic acid should be the predominant treatment.

Narcotics and addictions of the LSD type do not occur in the USSR. Narcomanias with the predominance of phenocoll (amphetamine, etc.) seldom occur, and phenocoll abuse should be treated by

the instant denial of the drug. Then detoxification and general roborant treatment is given (glucose, insulin, oxygen subcutaneously),
along with stimulating and vitamin therapy. Neuroleptics are given
in small doses.

Cocaine addiction has been eliminated in recent years. Denial of
the drug is instant, and abstinence is short-lived and relatively mild.
In case of fainting, amyl nitrite (smelling salt) is given. Ether or chlo-
roform inhalation is prescribed if cramps occur, and camphor or
caffeine for cardiovascular insufficiency. Subsequently, all types of
therapy are conducted. In view of the persistent loss of appetite and
marked weight loss, vitamins, insulin with glucose and special nutrition are prescribed.

The class of hypnotics includes soporifics, in which amobarbital
(sodium amytal, barbital sodium, etc.) is of prime importance. Acute
barbiturate intoxications frequently occur in association with suicidal
attempts. When large amounts of the drug are ingested, admission
to resuscitation centers or intensive therapy units is necessary. The
stomach is washed with a solution of potassium permanganate, and
strychnine is injected (1 ml of a 0.1% solution every three to four
hours). Depending on the concurrent somatovegetative disorders,
symptomatic remedies are also used.

In the chronic consumption of amobarbital, instant denial of the
drug may result in a collaptoid state, convulsions, or psychoses. The
abstinence syndrome takes a severe course; therefore, the method of
gradually reducing the intake of the narcotic is recommended with
parallel prescription of all types of treatment, including vitamin therapy, detoxification, general roborant therapy, stimulating medication,
and administration of neuroleptics. In convulsive symptoms antiepi-
leptics should not be given since they contain soporifics (phenobarbital); bromides, sodium borate, and diazepam should be used instead.

The class of opiates includes opium and its derivatives—morphine,
codeine, and others. A similar action is produced by some synthetic
narcotic drugs (e.g., trimeperidine hydrochloride). For acute opium
intoxication, repeated washing of the stomach, keeping the patient
warm, and the administration of cardiac medication are indicated.
Abstinence is pronounced and any methods of denying the narcotic

substance are possible, depending on the physician's strategy and the state of the patient. All enumerated methods of treatment are used. Persistent gastrointestinal disorders, particularly severe diarrhea, is characteristic of opium abstinence. This should be treated by sulfa drugs, and albutannin in enemas. Later in treatment, insulin is prescribed in small doses with glucose (40% solution) and calcium chloride (5-10 ml of a 10% solution).

Acute morphine intoxication should be immediately treated by washing the stomach, irrespective of the method by which the drug was introduced. Atropine is given. For improving respiration, lobeline or cytiton, the inhalation of oxygen or carbogen, and caffeine are indicated. In chronic morphine addiction the abstinence is pronounced and rather severe, and may be accompanied by nausea, vomiting, diarrhea, abdominal pain, palpitation, weak pulse, drop of arterial pressure, and pronounced vegetative disorders (e.g., hypersalivation, a sensation of falling into an abyss, sneezing, coughing). Patients complain of weakness and pain in the legs, tremor of the hands, shaky gait, insomnia, or sleep with nightmares. Unless there are contraindications, instant denial of the narcotic is recommended. With slower or fractional removal of the narcotic abstinence proceeds less severely but lasts longer. The principles of arresting the abstinence syndrome are the same as were described above. In cardiovascular insufficiency appropriate drugs are used, in diarrhea, astringents. Other medicines are also recommended, including ganglioblocking agents (dimecolin, pentamine), benzhexol, and trihexyphenidyl hydrochloride for alleviating vegetative manifestations. Later on, one can use apomorphine therapy as a conditioned-reflex treatment, with the patient self-injecting apomorphine subcutaneously or intravenously. At first the apomorphine action resembles the reaction following an intake of morphine, but subsequently, after the injection of morphine, it causes nausea and vomiting. The treatment of addiction to codeine, or to trimeperidine hydrochloride and other drugs with a morphine-like action, is conducted according to the above recommended patterns.

Persons abusing medicinal substances causing toxicomanias are treated, in cases of acute intoxications, by all available means for giving emergency aid; they are taken to resuscitation wards or intensive care units. In chronic abuse of these substances the basic principles of addiction treatment are followed. In abuse of medicinal drugs (meprobamate, analgetics) a good effect is produced by lithium, which is prescribed in 300 mg doses three times a day for 10-15 months. Checking up on the blood lithium content is obligatory.

Chapter 31

Methods of Breaking the Smoking Habit

The campaign against smoking (i.e., nicotinic toxicomania) should be purposeful, persistent and continuous, involving society as a whole as well as its individual members. This requires extensive organizational and educational work; in the Soviet Union it involves the "Znaniye" (Knowledge) society, the Red Cross and Red Crescent and other voluntary societies and organizations. In this connection, explanatory, restrictive, and when necessary, prohibitive measures should be taken.

Apart from active participation in broad antinicotine propaganda, the organs and institutions of the public health system bear the brunt of medical measures for the treatment of individuals. Because of the specific features of nicotinic toxicomania, its wide dissemination, the deep-rooted "positive emotions" associated with tobacco smoking, the failure to fully realize the negative aspects of using tobacco, and lastly, its peculiar abstinence syndrome, the treatment and breaking of the habit of smoking represent considerable difficulties and require special training by the physician. At present the problem is being tackled by psychiatrist-narcologists or narcologists, but because they are relatively few, it is impossible to extend all the necessary care to the large groups that need help. Therefore, these specialists must train physicians of different specialties for this work: therapists, surgeons, obstetricians, etc. Breaking the habit of tobacco smoking and treatment are carried out mainly on an outpatient basis, but in cases when this affliction is combined with others, like alcoholism or physical illness,

271

it is advisable to carry out a single plan of treatment in a hospital setting within a medical institution, which the patient needs for his main illness.

All treatment of nicotinic intoxication should be comprehensive from the very beginning, i.e., include psychotherapy, symptomatic remedies, aversiveness training, and substitution therapy. The physician decides which methods of therapy are preferable from the general complex available, bearing in mind the patient's personality, his desire to give up smoking, and somatic contraindications. Thus, the treatment of nicotinic toxicomania means influencing in a holistic manner both psychological and physical spheres.

Three methods of ending tobacco use may be applied: instant denial, rapid discontinuation, and breaking the smoking habit gradually. Treatment begins with a psychotherapeutic talk in order to provide contact between the physician and the patient and establish trust. Rational psychotherapy is conducted to explain the hazards of tobacco use and to reinforce the will of the patient toward abstention. Psychotherapy may be conducted collectively, in small groups, and individually. Self-suggestion as well as suggestion in both the waking state and under hypnotic sleep are used. Since the hypnotic state cannot be evoked in all patients, suggestion in the wakeful state is more widely used as an adjunct to rational psychotherapy.

Suggestion under hypnotic sleep may accomplish several tasks: to remove neurotic syndromes appearing in the abstinence period; to reinforce willful attitudes toward treatment; to develop a negative conditioned-reflex reaction to the smell, taste and sight of tobacco and tobacco smoke. An average of 10-12 half-hour sessions are conducted. The method of autogenic training yields good results. The patient, having learned by self-suggestion to create a state of relaxation, is capable of regulating some of his physical symptoms, particularly in the period of abstinence.

Although drug therapy is being used more widely in the treatment of tobacco smoking, it is still an auxiliary method, with psychotherapy remaining the chief treatment. Pharmacotherapy is divided into three kinds: aversion therapy, substitution therapy, and accessory or symptomatic therapy.

Aversion therapy has the task of evoking in the smoker a vomiting reaction or unpleasant sensations of taste upon using tobacco or inhaling its smoke. For this a 0.2-1 ml of a 1% apomorphine solution is injected subcutaneously. The procedure is combined with the inhaling of tobacco smoke four to five times a day for three to four days. During this period a negative vomiting reaction may be developed. An alcoholic tincture of gall nuts, silver nitrate, gallotannic acid (tannin), snakeroot solution, and young twigs of the birdcherry tree (to be chewed) are also used.

Substitution medication is based on the "competition" of some medicines and nicotine. When taking these medicines patients find it easier to tolerate abstinence. These include a 5-6% lobeline solution administered in a dose of 10-15 drops five to six times a day. Cytisine is produced as a 15% aqueous solution in ampules under the name Cytiton. Tablets containing 0.0015 gram of the preparation are marketed under the name Tabex. Lobeline is also produced in two medicinal forms: a 1% solution in 0.1 ml ampules and 0.002 gram tablets under the name of Lobesil.

In persons who have been using nicotine for many years the abstinence syndrome is protracted. During treatment there appears a repeated obsessive desire to receive a portion of nicotine. These symptoms may find expression in increased irritability, headaches, diminished working capacity, moodiness, and general physical discomfort. In such cases, even firm resolution to give up smoking and aversion or substitution therapy at times fail in preventing a breakdown of remissions. Additional or symptomatic treatment is required to help prevent a possible relapse. These remedies include sedatives, like tincture and extract of valerian root, motherwort (Reonorus), sodium bromide; tranquilizers, like chlordiazepoxide, chlordiazepoxide hydrochloride, diazepam, nitrazepam, and benactyzine; and stimulants, like ginseng root, magnolia vine seed, pantocrine, aralia tincture; vitamins A, B group vitamins (B_1, B_5, B_{15}, PP, C, E), Decamevit, and Undevit. In symptoms pointing to cardiovascular disorders, such as chronic catarrhs of the upper respiratory ways or pulmonary diseases, migraine-like headaches or other complaints, symptomatic therapy should be applied.

Tobacco smoking is combined, as a rule, with alcoholism, and this condition should be treated comprehensively. Several methods for such treatment are recommended:

1. Sudden, instant denial of nicotine. The patient should also be denied alcoholic beverages. Treatment is conducted in parallel. Nicotinic and glutaminic acids, tranquilizers and neuroleptics are administered, cytiton or lobeline injections are given for 2 weeks and, at the same time, 1-2 Tabex tablets.

2. Rapid discontinuation of smoking. At the peak of the craving for tobacco and alcohol, conditioned-reflex therapy is prescribed. Auxiliary treatment is the same. Mixtures causing unpleasant tastes in the mouth can be added.

3. Gradual denial of tobacco in inveterate smokers and persons with contraindications to active treatment of alcoholism (age 60 years and older, atherosclerosis, stages II-III of the hypertonic disease, organic lesions of the CNS). These persons are given symptomatic therapy (glutaminic acid, polyvitamins, tranquilizers, mouth washing, astringents). At the same time the number of cigarettes smoked is reduced: within 15 days the number is brought down to two to three cigarettes a day and after that they are eliminated altogether.

Detailed ways and methods of treating nicotinic abstention and tobacco smoking are described in the Methodological Recommendations issued by the USSR Ministry of Health.

EXERCISES FOR REVIEW

1. Examine the main principles of treating alcoholism, narcomanias and toxicomanias.

2. State the main principles, duration and methods of treatment stipulated in the Order No. 291, USSR Ministry of Health, of March 23, 1976, "On the Authorization of Obligatory Minimal Courses of Treatment for Patients with Chronic Alcoholism" and Order No. 388 of April 19, 1978, "On Authorizing Minimal Courses of Treatment for Patients with Narcomanias and Toxicomanias."

3. State the main methods and remedies used in sobering up,

detoxification, general roborant, stimulating and active alcoholism therapy. Delineate the specifics of their administration. Know how to carry out the basic procedures.

4. Recognize the complications and specific features in the course of alcoholism which may occur when carrying out active alcoholism therapy. Be able to render emergency aid or arrest complications with the aid of various medications.

5. Know the principles and methods of psychotherapy, autogenic training and rehabilitation.

6. Outline a plan of measures toward arresting mental disorders and further management in case of psychoses.

7. Detail the main therapy measures for narcomanias, toxico-manias and tobacco smoking.

8. Describe the role of paramedical personnel within the system of measures in the management of alcoholism, narcomanias, and tox-icomanias.

CHAPTERS 21-31 QUESTIONS

1. An alcoholic patient has been admitted to the hospital. How many days is the obligatory course of therapy, and what are the stages it must include? What document is issued for the patient's leave of absence from work?

2. A narcotics addict has been admitted to the hospital. What are the basic methods of treatment and their duration?

3. Hospitalization has taken place after a lasting drinking bout. What are the methods of therapy in this case?

4. Examination of a patient revealed a cardiovascular condition. What active therapy methods can be carried out?

5. A patient presents marked neurological complications against the background of stage III alcoholism. What should be the treatment strategy?

6. A patient is being treated for the first time. Which methods of active therapy should be recommended?

7. A patient is undergoing treatment for the second time. What

treatment strategy should be selected, and which method of active therapy is preferred?

8. Severe alcoholic intoxication is presented. What emergency aid should be given?

9. A remission has broken down. How should the patient be managed in order to restore his confidence in recovery and arrest the relapse?

10. A patient has misgivings concerning the possibility of recovery. Which psychotherapeutic methods should be used?

11. A patient complains of the desire to have a drink. What kind of psychotherapy is preferable in this case?

12. Patients after primary treatment of different duration are receiving supportive therapy at a narcological dispensary. What should be the treatment strategy during the first three years of treatment? during the 4th and 5th year?

13. A drug addict is admitted to the hospital. What are the basic principles of treatment? What are the specific features in the management of hashish and morphine addiction?

14. A drug addict is undergoing supportive therapy. What are the specific features of such therapy? What are its distinctions from alcoholism treatment?

15. A person has been abusing medicinal drugs not listed as narcotics. What should be the treatment strategy?

16. A person who has been smoking for many years is unable to break the habit on his own. What should be recommended for a self-cure in order to break the smoking habit?

17. During a remission breakdown somatoneurological complications developed. What measures should be taken?

18. The first symptoms of a psychosis (illusions, fractionary hallucinations) appeared one evening. On the next day, when visiting the dispensary, they were not present. What should be done?

19. A patient has obvious symptoms of psychosis (hallucinations, delirium, anxiety). The patient and his relatives reject hospitalization. What should be done?

20. An acutely psychotic patient has been admitted to the hospital. What observation and treatment measures should be ensured?

21. Korsakoff's psychosis has been diagnosed. What observation and treatment should be provided?

22. The acute symptoms of a psychosis have been arrested. What should be the strategy for further treatment?

PART FIVE

PROPHYLAXIS

Chapter 32

Principles of Psychohygiene and Psychoprophylaxis

Hygiene is a science dealing with the general principles of human health. Psychohygiene and psychoprophylaxis deal with questions pertaining to the strengthening and preservation of mental health. Hygiene is one of the oldest sciences; psychohygiene, however, is acquiring increasing importance in contemporary society, in our world of high speeds, scientific and technical revolution, and new, increased strains on man's nervous and mental apparatus. A product of nature, man in the historically brief period of the last one hundred years has triggered off an explosion in his surrounding life, while changing very little himself. Adaptation and compensation take place only by the mobilization of internal potentials of the nervous system. These adaptive, compensatory potentials may be inculcated and trained, so that man may, to a certain extent, regulate and actively influence his possibilities.

We distinguish psychohygiene on the basis of age, firmly believing that together with the development of the human brain and nervous system its tasks and demands undergo change; on the basis of gender, for each sex has its own peculiarities, characteristic of either women or men; and on the basis of family, sexual life, everyday life, industry and, lastly, of the sick and other special kinds which have direct bearing on alcoholism and drug addictions. Psychohygiene dovetails with psychoprophylaxis because hygienic measures, while training the compensatory mechanisms of higher nervous activity, prevent a breakdown of that activity.

Psychohygiene of age is a dynamic, uninterrupted, continuous process of upbringing and education. A person's character takes shape from childhood under the influence of parents and other relatives, friends and outsiders, and it is these influences that determine a child's development. In families with mentally sick persons or alcoholics, their negative influence on the children may be particularly deleterious. Children in such families begin to play smokers and drunkards, and even in movement imitate them. On their children's birthdays the adults, without giving a thought to it, drink a toast with them, even though the glasses are filled with lemonade (which, by the way, has an alcohol base), and occasionally, even with wine. Covertly these family celebrations inculcate drinking traditions among the children and the wish to emulate the adults.

Television programs and films may also have a negative influence in instilling drinking attitudes. Of course, one can hardly avoid depicting drinking on screen, just as it is unthinkable to deny a child permission to see films. Yet, it takes skillful upbringing to adroitly and regularly explain the meaning and dangers of drinking habits and traditions.

The teenage and youth period is particularly vulnerable. Changing in parallel with the physical development of a young boy or girl is also their world outlook and perception of surrounding reality. A process of self-assertion is emerging and this, as a rule, is accompanied both by imitation and the search of one's own road in life; therefore, it is a period of trial and error. The skillful inculcation of positive emotions and healthy attraction to books, the arts and music, to specific branches of knowledge and sports, and to lofty attachments, friendship and love is a far from easy task for parents, the school, or other institutions and organizations. But this is precisely the task of psychohygiene and psychoprophylaxis of alcoholism and drug addictions at this gentle age; it is most often a narrowness and poverty of interests, a tendency to imitate, weak will, the desire to experience new thrills, and at times, accessibility of alcoholic beverages that prompt a young boy or girl toward the use of alcohol and experimentation with narcotic drugs, which eventually may lead to alcoholism and drug addictions.

One should include among the general principles of psychohygiene the process of education, the choice of a profession, and productive activities. Very important in all these stages is the individual's compatibility with his activities, the rational distribution of mental potential and physical strength, and the prevention of stresses and strains. There are cases when such circumstances lead to the use of alcoholic beverages as people seek relief from stress and try to escape from misfortune and tension.

Psychohygiene of marriage and the family is one of the most complex problems of our time. The choice of a partner and planning one's future family life gives rise to numerous problems. In regard to alcoholism, life circumstances may turn out different from expectation. For example, a good healthy family has been started. After some time for various reasons changes occur; the husband begins to drink, gradually becoming an alcoholic. In addition, being an alcohol abuser himself, the husband may systematically entice his wife to drink with him. Being weak-willed or for other reasons she does not put up proper resistance and the family finds itself with two alcoholics at once. It is also possible that one of the partners entering into marriage is already a hardened alcoholic, so that life in the family from the very beginning becomes unhealthy. In such cases it takes a great deal of effort and patience in order to help the afflicted person.

Patient V. wrote the following while in a psychiatric hospital:

"I was born in 1940 in a small working-class settlement. Father was an egotistic and coarse man with a higher education and worked as an engineer on the railway. Mother was a simple housewife. I loved my mother dearly while rather fearing my father. So far as I remember, my father constantly drank and behaved outrageously, offending my mother and sisters, although at work he was always on his best behavior and was a good worker. I remember on my father's payday I always anticipated his return home with dread. I knew he would certainly be drunk, and would behave noisily and offend mother. Mother usually took me along and we went to visit our neighbors or somewhere else. From this 'merry life' I became a stutterer, and progress at school was poor. I was reserved and self-conscious. With difficulty I finished eight grades and went to work with my father. By that time he no longer worked as an engineer but earned money in the countryside, going from village to village. Mother had left us. It was in this period of my life, at 17, that I learned the taste of vodka. All the money we earned was spent on drink. In 1959 I was called up for service in the army.

"I got excellent marks in training and served well. I will always remember service in the army as a time when I lived a full life: I took part in social work and amateur art activities, and in general felt well in public and among people. After demobilization I got a job in a trucking establishment. There I got acquainted with a woman five years my senior. When we began living together my wife would frequently come from work tipsy. I would begin to curse, then beat her; she would cry, promise never to drink again. I loved her so much that, when commissioned for retraining as a radio operator, I refused because it meant being away from her for 45 days.

"I don't know exactly, whether it was my father's arrival from Siberia or my trip on an expedition in 1966, but I began to drink in a horrible way. I remember how I arrived home drunk from an expedition in 1966 and for the first time in my life sold my watch for three roubles. It was a gift from my wife. In the morning, when I sobered up, this shook me so much that I was unable to calm down.

"Soon I was stripped of my driving license, after which I drank still more. Once, when drunk, I got involved in a noisy altercation with a militiaman and hit him, for which I got two years' corrective labor. After serving my term, I returned home to the wife but our relations were never again the same.

"Once I learned that she was unfaithful. I packed my things and left. I began drinking again in the same way as earlier, together with my father. Again I got into a drunken brawl which resulted in two years of imprisonment.

"After I had served my term I went to live with my mother. I found a job as a welder and heard from people that my wife sent our daughter to her parents and was leading a loose life: drinking, whoring, without a job. After work I began calling on her. We did not quarrel; what was the point when each of us knew that we were not going to live together and the family was gone? It was simply a matter of being used to her, and I called on her by habit.

"I usually visited her on payday. Eventually we would shop for vodka, wine, and snacks, and then return home. Her cronies would drop in and we would keep drinking until there was no money, after which I would borrow from my sister or mother and we would drink on that money till the next payday. This went on until I was fired for drunkenness. After that I had no steady employment, hired myself out to unload railway cars, got paid in the evening and drank myself into a stupor. I was sent to a WTP, where I served a year; "served" is the right word because I had no wish to get well. All the time there I cheated the medics.

"From the WTP I returned to my former wife. I remember entering dressed in good clothes: I had some money; she didn't even recognize me. To make a long story short, I did not start looking for a job until we drank away all my money, about 350 roubles. A month later I went to work. I went on a binge on the very first payday, and did not work for four days. Then another breakdown and as a result, I am here in a mental hospital."

This example is indicative in that from early childhood the boy grew up in a grave home situation, witnessing the father's abuse and constant drinking. He grew up intimidated and silent, and started to stutter. Since the age of 17 he was on his own and began to drink. This patient was never accustomed to the constant ennobling influence of work; on the contrary, he was enticed to drink. A lucid interval came with service in the army. This was followed once again by an unfavorable family situation conducive to the development of alcoholism.

The tasks of psychoprophylaxis in alcoholism control are, on the one hand, to prevent the affliction, and on the other, to prevent remission breakdowns and exacerbations of the disease. Psychoprophylaxis includes heath education, matters of deontology, improvement of the microsocial environment, supportive therapy as well as psychotherapy. (The latter two kinds of preventive work are examined in Part Four.)

Chapter 33

Deontology

Deontology is of great importance within the system of narcological care. This is especially so because the creation of an appropriate psychotherapeutic atmosphere around the afflicted person, within his family and among his friends, is crucial for the success of treatment, which, in turn, is closely associated with problems of moral obligation and ethics. One should always remember that in carrying out his humane duty to care for the sick, the medical worker is at the same time duty-bound to influence the mental status of the patient and his relatives. He must be able to improve their morale, keep up their spirits, overcome despair, and alleviate severe psychological symptoms. Medical aid which fails to consider the total effect of the disease on the patient's entire organism, including the psychological aspects of the affliction, can hardly be considered as highly qualified. A positive attitude toward the patient and his relatives creates a favorable atmosphere that enhances the therapeutic effect on the patient. This is especially important where alcoholism, narcomania, and toxicomania are concerned, since the afflicted as well as their close relatives and friends frequently lose confidence in the effectiveness of medication. Besides, these diseases, particularly alcoholism, are often perceived by laymen as very easy to understand: "Who does not know the meaning of alcoholism and drinking?" And in connection with such a simplified attitude to the disease many deem themselves competent to offer evaluations and make decisions on complex questions connected with this affliction.

Therefore, it is the duty of the medical worker, when starting a course of medication, to attempt simultaneously to alter the attitude toward treatment not only of the patient but of those around him. This requires considerable tact: on the one hand, he must handle the patient sternly, rejecting an attitude of pure permissiveness, and on the other, must engender the good-will and sympathy of the patient and his relatives, without which he could not establish the necessary relations to ensure successful treatment. Dealing with the patient frequently makes it necessary to obtain information about many rather intimate aspects of his life, his relatives and friends. This can be achieved only by winning the patient's trust and making him believe in the doctor's good will, and in particular, that the medical worker will never divulge the information entrusted to him. Here the problem of deontology is directly connected with the question of the confidentiality.

Gaining the fullest possible information about the patient's life and illness is essential for correct diagnosis. One should bear in mind, however, that an integral approach to the study of a patient makes it necessary, even when the diagnosis is clear, to examine him in detail and evaluate the somatic condition. Even scars and tattoo marks detected on individual areas of the skin are of great importance at times. Yet, sometimes a patient states discontent and surprise that the doctor finds it possible to prescribe medications on the basis of an interview only. In such cases the patient may feel that the physician's prescriptions lack the support of a serious examination and are based on nothing more than impressions, or, particularly in the case of mental patients, that the diagnosis has been made under the influence of other, less objective persons. Deontologically, such an examination is of the greatest psychological importance because it gives the physician an additional opportunity to establish essential contact, without which it is often impossible to evaluate the patient's condition.

Obtaining detailed anamnestic information should not resemble an interrogation. When talking to the patient it is necessary to listen seriously, with a sense of responsibility, to everything the patient is saying. It is absolutely inadmissible, when interviewing and examining a patient, not to give full attention to the patient or to carelessly talk about him with other medical personnel. This insults the patient, betrays a lack of regard or interest in him, and may also constitute a breach of the essential confidential contact. Conversations on outside subjects by medical personnel or with those not taking part in the examination are also inadmissible. Quite often a casual incautious remark acquires great importance for the patient and may be the cause of grave iatrogenic complications.[7]

When talking to the patient and putting down the anamnesis one should not create the impression that he is registering everything he is being told, leave alone the fact that during the talk one should watch the patient's facial expression and listen to his voice, which frequently are very revealing for diagnosing the condition. During the examination remarks should be made cautiously. It is best not to accompany the examination with comments.

It is also of great importance, when examining a patient, to make use of relevant instrumentation. Apart from providing more precise data and validating the diagnosis, such examinations make a deep impression on the patient and his relatives, and the conclusions, suggestions and recommendations subsequently made acquire greater weight. Deontologically speaking, even when the diagnosis is clear, the use of instruments enhances the psychological effect on the patient, since he can keenly sense whether the medical worker himself believes in the therapy he is prescribing.

In this connection it becomes very important for the medical worker to take stock of his own feelings, for it takes true conviction that the care offered is really necessary and can favorably affect the patient. This is a serious matter, since some physicians and other medics deem it permissible to tell relatives, and even the patients themselves, that recovery is impossible, that modern methods of therapy are not yet effective enough, or (which is correct in principle), that success of treatment for alcoholism or drug addiction is primarily dependent on the patient's wish to get well. At the same time, an unequivocal statement of this kind may destroy the patient's belief in

---

[7] Iatrogenic = Caused by medical treatment; said esp. of imagined symptoms, or disorders induced by physicians' words or actions [Guralnick, D., Ed. (1970), *Webster's New World* Dictionary, 2nd Ed. New York: World.]

the possibility of positive therapeutic results. A flat statement to the effect that the patient can only be cured given his own wish not only strikes a psychological blow at the hope for recovery. It also embarrasses the relatives, who, knowing well the patient's lack of will, may lose confidence in the possibility of recovery. Hence, a correct strategy calls for an alternative approach.

It is common knowledge that success in the treatment of alcoholism and drug addiction depends largely on the prestige of the attending physician, on his psychotherapeutic influence on the patient, and on the relationship between the physician and other medical workers with the patient, his friends and relatives. These contacts should always be aimed at instilling belief in the actual potential of medicine. Therefore, from the viewpoint of deontology, it is inadmissible to promise that after a specific duration of treatment positive effects will necessarily occur.

In Karl Marx's *Debates on the Freedom of the Press*, he mentions that the human body is mortal by nature and that diseases, therefore, are inevitable. He thus draws attention to the fact that when falling ill a person turns to a physician and that constant medical care would make life horrible. From the standpoint of deontology, this remark by Marx sounds a special warning lest constant interference by physicians and other medical personnel in treatment of alcoholic patients be regarded as permanent psychological supervision over a "condemned" person. Here one should bear in mind that the narcological service leans in its work not only on the medical establishment but also on the social sphere (i.e., the narcological posts).

Of exceptional importance are the roles of both physician and feldsher-narcologist in raising the knowledge of persons planning to administer public narcological posts, or activists of the Red Cross and Red Crescent societies and trade unions, so that they will not inflict psychological damage either to the afflicted, or to their families. Constant educational work should be conducted with these people.

Iatrogenic symptoms may be caused not only by careless and tactless handling of the patient and his relatives by the physician and other members of the medical profession, but also by wrong attitudes and lack of understanding by nonmedical specialists or persons with scanty medical knowledge. "Not to inflict harm" is the motto of the physician, of all medical personnel and activists of the Red Cross and Red Crescent societies and other medical organizations that voluntarily assist in rendering aid to sick people. Therefore, daily work with all specialists working in the different units of the narcological service is of exceptional importance. The early identification of addiction or permanent observation should by no means make the staff involved in this process imagine they have any authority over persons suffering from alcoholism and drug addictions. Moreover, visits by medical personnel should be so organized to accommodate the wishes of patients and their relatives.

It must be stressed once again that for narcological care to be successful, not only the psychiatrist-narcologist, and feldsher-narcologist, but the workers of the narcological posts, members of the Red Cross and other public societies, by their actions, behavior, and attitude toward patients, their relatives and friends, should manifest their goodwill and demonstrate that their task is to help in providing medical care.

The well-known representative of Russian classical medicine, Mudrov (1776-1831), wrote: "Aware of the mutual action the spirit and the body exert upon each other, I deem it my duty to remark that there are also spiritual medicaments that heal the flesh. They are borrowed from the science of reason, more often from psychology—by their faculty to console the sorrowful, to quell the wrathful, to soothe the impatient, to dismay the arrogant, to embolden the bashful, to render the mysterious candid, to make the reckless heedful; this art imparts that cheerfulness which overcomes the ills of the flesh, despondency and anguish." The psychiatrist-narcologist and other medical workers must remember that the impact of the word on the mentality of the alcoholic and drug addict is of decisive importance in rendering medical aid to them.

Also of serious deontological importance is the correct use of the terms "alcoholism" and "drug addiction." To regard drug addictions as identical to alcoholism is incorrect. Apart from the fact that this is erroneous from the legal, social and medical positions, it would also have a negative psychological impact. On the one hand, drug addicts ask in such cases: "But why, if alcoholism is a narcomania and alcoholic drinks are narcotics, are they officially permitted for sale, while the acquisition of other narcotics is a punishable criminal offense?" On the other hand, alcoholics and their relatives and friends believe it wrong to regard such patients as drug addicts, justly holding that by taking alcoholic beverages they, in comparison with the addicts, are committing no crime. Such identifications also inflict serious psychological damage to the organizations of health education. Thus, in the sphere of narcological practice, deontology continues to be of deep and broad significance.

Chapter 34

Health Education

Despite universal literacy and unprecedented improvement in the population's cultural standards, a certain category of people fail to realize the truly tragic consequences of alcoholism. Screening of a large group of alcoholics and their relatives demonstrated that approximately 55% understand the problem adequately, 15% have a critical attitude toward all of the "threats by the physicians," and 30% are unable to seriously comprehend the harm of alcoholic intoxication, in other words, are insufficiently informed about its deleterious consequences.

Antialcoholism propaganda must be active and aggressive, of high professional quality and be well charged with optimism. In this connection, one may systematize the basic forms and methods of antialcoholism propaganda. Standardization of the basic parameters of this work should by no means result in rigid conformism when carrying it out. On the contrary, the introduction of certain regularities should help the numerous activists called upon to engage in antialcoholism work to know better the methods that have already been proven in practice. At the same time, the concrete content of the various forms of this work, must doubtlessly be varied, original, and interesting. Cliches here are inadmissible.

The main tasks facing antialcoholism propaganda are the following:

1. To explain the harm of taking small but systematic alcoholic drinks for they are habit-forming.

2. To demonstrate the harmful effects of systematic alcoholic intoxication on the organism's main organs and systems and their functional disorders in mental and somatic diseases.

3. To strive for the improvement of the micro- and macrosocial environment toward antialcoholism with attempts to inculcate in collectives a sensible and critical attitude to alcohol.

4. To insist that alcoholism is curable given proper temperance attitudes on the part of the drinkers themselves and their preparedness to undergo active and lasting supportive therapy.

5. To explain how moral and ethical standards are undermined by alcohol abuse, and how the breach of such moral and ethical norms results in serious problems for the individual and society.

6. To demonstrate the role and importance of separate collectives and public opinion in improving the quality of life of Soviet people.

The system of antialcoholism propaganda may be represented in the following way:

1. Ministries, departments, institutions, societies and public organizations conducting organizational-methodological work.

2. Propagandists and promulgators of antialcoholism ideas: physicians and paramedical workers, teachers and instructors, lecturers, workers of literature and the arts, of the mass media, staff members of the organs of the Ministry of Internal Affairs and the organs of justice, members of the Standing Commissions for Combating Drunkenness and Alcoholism Control, volunteers advocating a temperate mode of life, including recovered alcoholics.

3. Channels and means of propaganda: mass media, talks and lectures, visual aids.

4. Auditoriums for conducting health education: premises of cultural-enlightenment organizations, medical institutions, educational establishments, reading rooms at industrial enterprises, at housing cooperatives, work places, and television theaters.

5. Groups of listeners: staff members of the Ministries of Internal Affairs and of justice, teachers and instructors, staff members of mass media, etc. Broad audiences: school children, students of specialized secondary schools, university and institute students, office and factory workers, persons afflicted with alcoholism and their relatives, the staffs of medical sobering-up stations, of WTP and CLC.

We will now examine the individual units of the system above in greater detail.

1. Organizational and methodological work is directed by institutions of the USSR Ministry of Health and, first of all, health education centers. The central methodological laboratory is the Department for the Prevention of Harmful Habits at the Central Scientific-Research Institute of Health Education.

Health education centers study, accumulate and summarize the experience of work toward antialcoholism propaganda. They prepare methodological instructions and recommendations not only for public health institutions, but also for other ministries and departments and coordinate all antialcoholism work. The health education centers also resolve many questions of a methodological character together with the all-Union Society "Znaniye" ("Knowledge") and the Union of Red Cross and Red Crescent Societies.

Health education centers, particularly sections of the Znaniye Society, enlist and train lecturers, provide the material base for antialcoholism propaganda, including the premises as well as the films, photoexhibitions, slides and other visual aids and technical means. In most cases they are the organizers of different forms of antialcoholism work—lectures, talks, question-and-answer sessions, etc.

2. Physicians of every specialty take part in antialcoholism propaganda since every physician, to a lesser or greater degree, encounters the deleterious effects of alcohol on the human organism. The obstetrician and gynecologist know how harmful the use of alcohol is for the act of conception. The pediatrician is well aware of the physically and mentally retarded, demented children born into families where alcohol is systematically used. The surgeon frequently comes across road and industrial accidents related to alcohol abuse. The human organism undergoes deterioration before the very eyes of the internist.

Every specialist in his own way is aware of alcoholism and its harmful consequences, and this he takes up, first of all, in his lectures, talks and communications. But there are common questions that must be taken up by all specialists. This is the social impact of the problem, the role of the work environment and the public in controlling alcoholism, the harmful consequences of alcohol abuse, particularly for students and school children. Always emphasized must be the question of habituation to alcoholic beverages, i.e., stressing the negative role of systematic intake of small doses of alcohol. Health education should help to reveal new cases of the affliction.

Attention of audiences should also be drawn to the drinker's gradual diminution of a critical attitude to his or her own condition, the deterioration of the personality, the narrowing range of interests, and the impairment of the alcoholic's mental capacities and intellect. Questions of criminal law, particularly that persons who commit a criminal offense in a state of alcoholic intoxication are regarded as imputable and held responsible for their actions, also must be explained.

When speaking of treatment, medical measures should not be viewed as the only means of recovery from alcoholism. The line should be clearly drawn between habitual heavy drinking and alcoholism as an affliction. To regard all such persons as sick people would mean justifying the immoral behavior of some of them, and even giving them the benefit of a doubt as to their responsibility in the case of committing offenses. In addition, among those who seek treatment one should always make sure of their earnest wish to recover, and should strengthen and utilize it during therapy.

It must also be explained that many persons with alcoholism who sincerely wish to get rid of the disorder take active treatment and then, after completing a course of therapy, once again find themselves in the habitual circle of people who entice them again into the use of alcoholic beverages. Here audiences must be specially convinced of the need to normalize the drunkard's or alcoholic's microsocial environment, i.e., his family, his closest friends and associates.

In explaining the significance and role of the public in controlling drunkenness and in antialcoholism propaganda, one should strive to convince the listeners not to remain indifferent to the problem. It is desirable to stir the audience into an uncompromising attitude toward drunkenness, to encourage a public sentiment of scorn in regard to drunkards and their defenders, to encourage the family to vigorously join the campaign against alcohol abuse, and in case of disease, to help cure it.

Propaganda by lecture should follow two lines: One, addressing broad audiences with emphasis on health education and the overall task of improving the health of the population; the second, the holding of seminars, discussions and methodological conferences with teachers, lawyers, members of the militia, housing and communal societies, the USSR Ministry of the Food Industry, trading establishments, and with teachers and instructors of technical schools, vocational schools and institutes. The aim is to provide the specialists of other professions with elementary medical knowledge regarding alcoholism, essential not only in their general education, but for use in antialcoholism propaganda conducted by them. A large contribution to this work is expected from the teachers of schools, of specialized secondary and higher educational establishments.

Lawyers and members of the police force should be well versed in these questions. The latter come across the consequences of drunkenness and alcoholism in their day-to-day work, in medical sobering-up stations, in cases of traffic violations, and when dealing with alcohol-related offenses. The ability to effectively apply one's professional knowledge and skills to antialcoholism work is an art which has to be learned.

A substantial contribution to the overall antialcoholism drive is made by the lecturers of the Znaniye Society and by those in literature and the arts. Of great help here may be members of the Standing Commissions for Combating Drunkenness, whose organizations are set up in all strategic locations under the Executive Committees of the Soviets of People's Deputies and at industrial and agricultural enterprises. The narcological posts in industry are manned mainly by active members of the Red Cross and Red Crescent Society. These are people who are in close, daily touch with their coworkers, and who are in the position during ordinary intercourse to wage a consistent offensive against the harmful habit, by talking to the drunkards themselves, their friends, relatives and neighbors.

Persons formerly afflicted with alcoholism may and must become active propagandists. Impressive instances have been described of repentance, of an urge to recover occurring precisely after an audience of drinkers and their relatives had been confronted with a former alcoholic. One should not misuse this form of work, for a suitable speaker of this kind is not always available. Nonetheless, it should not be overlooked and must be used when appropriate.

3. The means and channels of information are so diverse that their full utilization can exert some influence on everyone. In conducting antialcoholism propaganda each of these channels should be used with maximum efficiency.

However, scientific generalization of the various forms of antialcoholism propaganda points to a rather selective impact of the relevant information and materials on different audiences. Approximately 827 questionnaires were handed out in different audiences. An analysis of the returned questionnaires indicated that in the opinion of those questioned the most telling and memorable are materials carried on wall murals or posters, demonstrated on screen or presented in talks. The poorest response is evoked by information carried in newspapers and given in lectures or papers. An in-depth study of this material showed that men and women respond approximately in the same way to different types of propaganda. Young people more readily perceive concrete and visual forms. Intellectuals also give higher marks to concrete forms of propaganda, wall murals, and "satire" showcases. Medical workers prefer films, lectures and papers. Alcoholics give the highest rating to individual talks, conversations with convalescents, and films. This indicates that antialcoholism propaganda should be carried out with reference to the prevailing audience.

The basic means, forms and channels of antialcoholism information may be conditionally divided into three groups: (1) the mass media—radio, television, cinema, newspapers, popular science literature and fiction, leaflets, collected stories, posters. Placed in the same group should be wall murals and "satire" showcases; (2) propaganda by word of mouth—lectures, skits, talks, literary evenings, debates, conferences, question-and-answer sessions, courses in health universities and schools; and (3) visual aids—slides, X-ray pictures, pathoanatomical preparations, photographs, photo series, and popular science films.

Varied forms of mass information are designed to influence large groups of people simultaneously. The lack of an individual approach is compensated for by such factors as mass character, vividness, and the capacity of such means as radio, television and films to attain a highly emotional impact. This is why very skilled specialists must be selected as lecturers, who are capable of reaching not only the minds but also the hearts of people.

When preparing word-of-mouth forms of propaganda it is extremely important to come up with striking and original titles to lectures and papers, not necessarily featuring such words as "alcoholism," "drunkenness," etc. Talks should last no longer than 20-30 minutes, held best of all during the lunch break. One should carefully study beforehand the occupational and individual interests of the organizations; this helps to make the talk interesting, referring to the individuals and concerns of the entire group involved. Lectures may be planned for 45-50 minutes, and in large auditoriums, for 60-90 minutes.

Pedagogical experience indicates that any impact on a listener is more effective when it comes from several channels, for example, by word-of-mouth and by viewing films, slides, posters, X-rays, etc. Therefore, whatever the form of antialcoholism propaganda, it should be conducted comprehensively, utilizing the varied effects on man's different senses. In addition, in a lecture it is useful to quote the opinions about alcoholism by statesmen, eminent scientists and writers. Such quotations may be used quite fittingly in the form of wall posters, but one should not overuse this method or indulge in repetition.

4. When conducting antialcoholism propaganda the proper selection of premises and their well thought out interior decoration may be helpful in enhancing the appeal to audiences. In the hall or lobby of cultural and enlightenment organizations, educational establishments, houses of culture and clubs and at industrial enterprises, lectures, papers and talks should be accompanied by the organization of exhibitions and displays of posters, books and photographs on the theme of alcoholism control or health education in general.

It is recommended to display photo exhibitions about happy childhood, motherhood, love, successful careers, and demonstrate against this background all the harmful consequences of alcohol abuse. A positive effect is also derived by moving part of the antialcoholism work directly to industrial enterprises, building sites, motor transport enterprises, state and collective farms, since this carries antialcoholism propaganda closer to places of work. Under these conditions the talks may help in frustrating drinking habits, in revealing early cases of the disease, and in organizing supportive treatment.

5. Functioning as propagandists and lecturers may be schoolteachers, instructors of secondary and higher institutions of learning, lawyers, staff members of the organs of internal affairs, of the mass media institutions, etc. To prepare them for this role they should be given the facts about alcoholism and heavy drinking as a medico-social problem and advised on methods of conducting antialcoholism propaganda among the population. Lectures, papers, theoretical conferences, and seminars run on a permanent basis with the participation not only of medical workers, but also of lawyers, teachers, etc., have proven to be worthwhile.

Explanatory work among senior schoolchildren should be carried out according to plan by teachers and school doctors. Among students of specialized secondary schools and higher educational establishments antialcoholism propaganda must be more "tough" and "undisguised." In these audiences the social evils of drunkenness, the medical aspects of habit formation, and the appearance of psychic and physical symptoms of alcoholism should be revealed. Aspects of mental degradation and impoverishment of the personality must be particularly stressed.

Students and working youth are accustomed to spend their leisure time with a glass of wine, "in a happy-go-lucky company." Such an attitude to drinking stems from incorrect upbringing, narrow interests, and inability to find worthwhile pastimes. This is why when addressing youth audiences it is not only necessary to utilize the entire arsenal of antialcoholism propaganda, but to conduct it in parallel with other forms of moral instruction.

When the main audience are factory and office workers, the approach to and organization of work with these groups should take into account such characteristics as sex, specific occupation, education, among many other factors. In a male audience it is necessary to underline the inception and development of male alcoholism. Among women one should emphasize the special features of the female organism, the lofty mission of motherhood and bringing up children, and the severity of the alcoholic disease.

Doubtlessly, people with higher education and groups of workmen will require different approaches and presentation of the material. This refers not only to educational standards, for the majority of present-day workers have a secondary, and frequently a specialized education, but rather to the different professional interests of these groups. In such cases, preliminary familiarization with the enterprise concerned, its special features and problems is highly desirable. Special concern should be shown to people having free access to alcoholic beverages, i.e., workers of the food industry (wineries and distilleries, etc.) and in trade. The harmful effects of alcohol should be spelled out carefully, consistently and forcefully among these categories.

Frequently overlooked in antialcoholism propaganda are the special features of life in the countryside and of agricultural production, when the winter months are comparatively free from labor, which, combined with inadequate opportunities for worthwhile pursuits, frequently result in greater use of alcoholic beverages and the making of hooch.

Thus, antialcoholism work with alcoholics requires constant, daily individual influence. The most effective forms are individual talks by medical workers and meetings with recovered alcoholics. In this connection, it is useful to hold get-togethers and debates on publications describing the destinies of people afflicted with alcoholism.

A certain segment of alcohol abusers are handled by institutions of the Ministries of Internal Affairs, first of all, the medical sobering-up stations. Their clients also include those who find themselves there through misadventure. But those who have been detained two or three times are the people who must be put on the medical register. An object lesson in antialcoholism should be given there to all clients, individually and in groups, by using all means of persuasion, conviction and explanation.

Recent years have seen a considerable expansion of the system of alcoholism treatment at WTP. They take care of the severest cases.

Antialcoholism propaganda at the WTP should be conducted by all workers—medical instructors, inspectors and production foremen. This is why physicians and paramedical personnel at the preventoriums fulfill the dual task of training all staff members of the WTP for antialcoholism propaganda and of carrying it out among the inmates. All means of mass and individual propaganda and visual aids should be used for this purpose. With persons undergoing treatment for the first time it must be carried out separately from those subjected to treatment repeatedly. Lawyers and teachers should be enlisted for this work, and the inmates' families and people from the enterprises and institutions where they had been previously working should be invited to make their contribution. Some persons serving a term at a CLC for committed offenses are concurrently treated for alcoholism. This is why all kinds of antialcoholism propaganda must be conducted also at the CLC.

The Union of Red Cross and Red Crescent Societies is one of the biggest public organizations, with units at every industrial and agricultural enterprise and organization of the country, and it can and must be widely used for conducting antialcoholism work. In January 1959, the Executive Committee of the Soviet Red Cross passed a special resolution "On the Participation by the Active Members of Red Cross and Red Crescent Societies of the USSR in Combating Drunkenness and Preventing Alcoholism." Under this resolution the committees of the societies were obligated to enlist their active membership for helping medical workers in dealing with those afflicted with alcoholism, conducting talks among the population about the harm of alcohol for human health.

The narcological post (at enterprises, building sites and in agriculture) is defined as the primary unit in the system of drug care. These posts are manned mainly by activists of Red Cross and Red Crescent Societies. One of the main tasks of these activists is the early identification of alcohol abusers and giving help in conducting supportive therapy. In order to enable these people to fulfil such a responsible job, they should be given constant attention and education in the sphere of alcoholism.

Antialcoholism propaganda is one of the most important forms

of improving the microsocial environment. When preparing antialcoholism propaganda the question arises of the stand that ought to
be taken by the propagandist when referring to the permissible use
of alcohol in daily life. If it is a question of pregnant or breast-feeding
women, or children who are being treated for alcoholism (the first 5-
8 years) there is only one possible stance—not a drop of alcohol. But
what about the rest? In this matter one should not be too categorical
or pose as an absolute teetotaler and "saint," insisting that no one
should ever drink any alcoholic beverages. Such statements usually
antagonize the audience and doom the presentation to failure.

There is "abuse" and there is "use" of alcoholic beverages. The
former is a vice which may evolve into disease. But how about the
latter? Maxim Gorky, the writer, upon visiting the famous Massandra
wineries in the Crimea, wrote: "I drank and rejoiced. . . . All power
to those who can make wine and through it bring the energy of the
sun into the souls of people." Louis Pasteur said in his time: "There
is every ground to regard wine as the most wholesome hygienic beverage." There even exist methods of treatment with wine—enotherapy.
They stem from the view that wine is useful as a diuretic and tonic
beverage and may be prescribed for a certain time, strictly dosed like
a medicine. However, such treatment should be under constant control, for cases are known when alcoholism was sparked off with precisely such medication. It can be said, then, that alcoholic beverages
can be used in moderation, that the matter is to know how to drink;
it is a problem of pastime, of inculcating cultured drinking habits,
and of engaging in sensible habits.

Health education work spearheaded against drug addiction is quite
different from that in alcoholism. Here public lectures and papers,
radio and television appearances, and articles in the press are cate-
gorically prohibited. Such mass forms of propaganda may produce
an adverse result, triggering an increased interest in narcotic substances and their effects. Instead, individual or group talks with persons using narcotic substances, with the parents of schoolchildren
caught smoking hashish, with teachers, and with members of the
militia and juridical bodies are recommended.

Emphasis here must be made on describing the syndrome of narcotic habituation, the state of abstinence, and methods of treatment and prevention. It is better still if this kind of health education can be carried out by a physician. Paramedical personnel may be present, and must help in detecting persons afflicted with addictions, assist in continued observations, and make home visits.

Feldsher-narcologists, feldsher-psychoneurologists and medical nurses are called upon to carry out extensive antialcoholism work. For health education to be effective the paramedical personnel itself should be well versed in the clinical aspects of alcoholism and drug addiction; they should also master some lecturing devices and the above-described requirements for health education.

Paramedical personnel should conduct talks and conversations, appear on the radio and in production settings on collective and state farms. The talks should be designed to describe facts from the life of the institution or enterprise concerned. One should not overburden them with theoretical discourses and too many figures; they should be easy to understand, simple, and contain positive criticism, good advice and good wishes. Each talk should arouse the listeners' interest, and to accomplish this, one should present films, slides, unfold an exhibition, display pictures, or simply demonstrate the points with comments.

Such get-togethers and talks should be held at any suitable time and location—in the workshop, at the work place, in a field camp, or wherever conditions are appropriate. It is desirable, apart from general talks, to engage in conversations separately with women, teenagers, and with drinkers, each time taking into account the special features of the audience.

In short, paramedical personnel should take an active part in health education work conducted by physicians: prepare the auditorium and visual aids, all the while themselves learning how to deliver lectures.

Chapter 35

The Microsocial Environment and Its Improvement

Alcoholism and drug addiction stem from a complex of social, economic, familial and biological factors. All these components are reflected, as in a drop of water, in the microsocial environment. What is usually meant as the microenvironment is a person's closest, more or less stable milieu. It includes, first of all, the parents, grandmothers and grandfathers, brothers and sisters; eventually there are husband and wife, their children and, lastly, friends and associates, neighbors, colleagues and coworkers.

All of these people, one way or another, influence those afflicted with chronic alcoholism or drug addiction by their attitudes and behavior. At the same time they too come under the influence of the drinkers themselves. It is known that the number of people constantly in touch with alcoholics and drug addicts, and interested in their fate, is on the average 7-10.

The older generation is responsible for the upbringing of their children and grandchildren. Healthy relationships, a temperate mode of life, and family traditions precluding the use of alcohol or narcotic substances are a legacy of health for the growing population. But the older generation includes individuals who breach these norms; they may, apart from their harmful influence, transfer a certain weakness of nervous organization or predisposition to alcoholism through the mechanism of heredity.

304

Take, for example, a husband and wife. At present alcoholism among men is more widespread than among women; therefore, the woman, wife and mother, more often finds herself in the role of the sufferer. Alcoholics as a rule are egotistical, hot-tempered and unable to restrain their emotions. This is why an unhealthy atmosphere pervades the family: the alcoholic alternates between fault finding, grumbling, quarreling, even beatings, tearfulness or vows of eternal love. Such chronic nervousness and strain cannot pass without trace. Things are still worse in the families of drug addicts, where their psychopathic behavior holds everyone under constant tension. Observations showed 81% of women in such families to have neurotic depressive disturbances and functional disorders of the nervous system, whereas in control groups of healthy families, only 14% revealed various deviations in the psychic sphere (and all of these had nothing to do with abnormal family relations).

Throughout the history of human society woman has been the cementing force of the family. As wife and mother, she does her utmost to keep the family from falling apart in conflict situations, at times putting up every pretense of marital bliss in order to avoid hurting the children. But this ongoing battle for existence not infrequently ends in defeat: the woman falls ill or, still worse, starts drinking herself, and in 20% of cases is the first to sue for divorce. One should not forget that the factor of heredity is also operating in the microsocial environment, and may produce physically deformed and mentally deranged children.

Although aware of the downfall of the alcoholic or addict, often close relatives (however strange this may seem), instead of admonishing and condemning the behavior of their loved one, encourage him, boast of the strength of their family, or try to cover up his unseemly behavior. In such situations, the onus of the illness again falls squarely on the shoulders of the wife who, moreover, is likely to find herself accused of being an inadequate spouse and housewife.

Children are also part of the microenvironment. While small, they are there watching, full of curiosity. In unhappy families they grow frightened, intimidated, reticent, and unsociable. They turn callous and clam up in front of teachers and age mates. Not infrequently this causes poor progress at school and, consequently, mental and physical retardation. Occasionally a youth will be bold enough to condemn his father or mother for immoral behavior and a ruined life. At times hatred overwhelms the young person who, brought up in an environment where egotism and brutality are the rule, renounces his parents and leaves home to start life on his own.

Without comrades and friends there is no society, for man is a social being and the mutual influence of the milieu and the individual is inevitable. A chum or schoolmate with whom one has grown up are persons with whom one associates for a long time. Years of study at a technical school, college or institute are irreplaceable and can be used with great benefit to oneself, spent in hard study; but it often seems that these carefree years should be spent as gaily as possible in order to have something pleasant to remember. Thus youths very easily slide down into light-hearted dissipation from which it is very difficult to extricate themselves. One may later ask: But where were the comrades and friends? Some from the very beginning always accompanied the future victim of alcoholism, others initiated him to alcohol, still others kept aloof. Thus, those who tried to render a favorable effect were often unable to prevail.

Aside from friends, different people can be encountered in a work situation. Members of one's work collective can be exacting and irreconcilable in regard to violators of labor discipline and everyday behavior. If such persons happen to surround the young man, then, influenced by their example and advice, he will be able to return to a healthy environment. But what if he finds himself in the midst of indifferent people or, worse still, in a company which holds a drinking party on the slightest pretext? Drinking goes on from payday to payday until absenteeism, ill health and mistakes bring about dismissal, and an end to the paydays. In such cases, the drunkard becomes an active disseminator of drinking habits and traditions, drawing other people into his company, thereby inflicting irreparable harm to socialist society.

Another grave problem arises when an alcoholic or drug addict, after treatment in a hospital or in a WTP returns back to his habitual milieu where drinking or the use of narcotics is routine. Still simpler situations crop up in everyday life when such a person finds himself at a party celebrating some festive occasion, say, a brithday, and he, still a patient, must attend it but abstain from drinking. He is surrounded by good-wishing people who, at times unwittingly, insist that he drink lest they take affront at such a rebuttal of their hospitality. It is well known that half of remission breakdowns are due to being drawn into drinking parties by friends and comrades, and 8-10%, by wives or husbands. These situations pose a serious question: how is a person who has been treated and abstains from alcoholic beverages supposed to live among drinkers; how is he to resist the periodic desire to resume the use of alcohol?

Noteworthy in this regard is the organization of temperance clubs with a membership of former alcoholics. One such club, "Anti-Bacchus," was founded in 1969 in the city of Tartu, Estonia, under the auspices of the narcological consulting room of the Republican neuropsychiatric hospital's dispensary department. In 1970 the Tartu Soviet of People's Deputies authorized the club's rules. According to these rules, the club is a friendly association of people who have voluntarily given up the use of alcoholic beverages, and represents a psychotherapeutic collective. Those eligible for club membership are citizens who have chosen the goal of sobriety. It unites mainly those who have been or are being treated for alcoholism. Club members take a pledge not to use alcoholic beverages, and always and everywhere to preach temperance. The club members' personal affairs are not to be divulged. At present such clubs are becoming more and more widespread.

Improvement of the social environment is a difficult, psychologically very delicate and lasting job requiring keen observation, tact, and persistence. It should be carried out by teachers and instructors at schools, secondary and higher institutions of learning, staff members of the militia, lawyers, and members of various societies and public organizations. It is the task of the medical workers, on the one hand, to provide skillful guidance in this work, identify persons afflicted with alcoholism and drug addiction, ensure their treatment, and lastly, by constant educational work, to influence this environment by promoting a climate of temperance in it. For this the feldsher-narcologist and the visiting medical nurse should establish good relations of confidence with the relatives, friends and associates of the afflicted persons. The medical worker must be a welcome visitor in the alcoholic's family.

Special tact is needed for handling children's and teenagers' collectives, which are equally receptive both to good and bad influences; being very sensitive they might easily become either helpers in this work or indifferent watchers, or even active ill-wishers. Meanwhile, the principles of goodness inculcated precisely at this age will accompany a person throughout his life, and the fostering of such qualities is the duty of medical workers.

EXERCISES FOR REVIEW

1. Give a definition of psychohygiene and psychoprophylaxis. Demonstrate knowledge of the basic tasks of these scientific trends in the field of controlling alcoholism and drug addiction.

2. Examine questions of deontology as a particular system of relationship between the medical worker and those afflicted with alcoholism, narcomanias and toxicomanias.

3. Prepare the synopsis of a brief lecture (20-25 minutes) or talk (10-15 minutes) intended for discussion in class.

4. Examine matters of improving the microsocial environment and the most rational ways of doing this work.

CHAPTERS 32-35 QUESTIONS

1. A sick person realizes that he is indulging in alcohol abuse, but rejects treatment. How should one plan explanatory talks with him in order to make him change his mind?

2. As a result of poor tactics on the part of a medical worker, a patient has lost faith in the success of alcoholism treatment. What measures should be undertaken in this case and at what levels?

3. A lecture on the harm of alcohol should be delivered to 9th to

10th-grade schoolchildren. What are the principal questions to be taken up?

4. A talk on the harmfulness of alcoholic beverages is to be held with girl students. What are the principal problems to be touched upon?

5. Schoolchildren periodically smoking hashish have been detected among the 8th graders of a secondary school. How should health educational work be organized?

6. Upon visiting the home of an alcoholic, a medical nurse finds that his wife is a drinker, too, though she tries to conceal the fact. What must be done by the medical worker?

7. It has been learned through a women's consultation clinic that a pregnant woman is using alcoholic beverages. What should be done?

8. An activist of a narcological post provided information that a patient under treatment is constantly keeping company with heavy drinkers. What measures should be taken?

PART SIX

EXPERT EXAMINATIONS IN ALCOHOLISM, NARCOMANIAS AND TOXICOMANIAS

Chapter 36

Expert Examination of Alcoholic Intoxication

The outward manifestations of alcoholic intoxication proceed according to different stages in the effects of the alcoholic beverage ingested; the form, sequence and duration of these stages depend, on the one hand, on individual characteristics and the state of the organism, and on the quantity of alcohol taken, on the other. In this connection the diagnosis of alcoholic intoxication should be based on the following:

1. study of the behavior and outward appearance of the examinee;
2. observation of the physiological functions of the organism;
3. analysis of the state of attention and cerebration;
4. study of vegetative functions;
5. coordination tests;
6. neurological examination;
7. laboratory analyses; and
8. check-up for possible symptoms of the hangover syndrome.

As is known, during alcoholic intoxication behavior undergoes changes. Some intoxicated individuals become excessively lively and merry, may shout, quarrel, or sing songs, while others seem sad and apathetic, and still others lose their sense of tact and restraint. The critical faculty diminishes, and all reactions and outward stimulants assume an excessively affective tinge.

Outward appearance also changes: intoxicated individuals most frequently are dressed untidily, lose individual objects of clothing, not infrequently look dirty and injured, with bruises, scratches, and abrasions. Thus, with the very first glance at an examinee in the state of pronounced drunkenness, his or her behavior and outward appearance provide clues for the diagnosis. In many cases there are also physiological disorders: the examinees drink a lot of water, there is copious salivation, increased diuresis, aversion to food and, occasionally, vomiting.

In addition, drunken persons present with disorders of attention, cerebration and speech. Being unable to concentrate on phenomena or actions, their thoughts leap from subject to subject, without fixation, becoming amorphous and hazy. Speech is unclear, blurred, and at times, slow. Psychic changes may reach partial or complete disorientation and even stupefaction. This can be checked by asking the examinee to solve a few problems in arithmetic, to read a text with missing letters, or to repeat a few figures (six to eight) or sentences. As a rule many will cope with such assignments poorly.

Vegetative functional disorders are expressed in copious sweating or fever, and the reddening or pallor of the skin. At the beginning of drunkenness, breathing accelerates; then it becomes slower and deeper and pupils may be dilated, narrowing with the further effect of alcohol, and dilating again in the comatose state. The pulse rate is irregular, first fast, then slow. All these symptoms can be seen by external inspection and observation.

In pronounced symptoms of alcoholic intoxication movement coordination is impaired, first of all affecting the opticomotor muscles. Rotation (five times around one's vertical axis) will produce nystagmus. The greater the intoxication, the longer it will persist. The gait becomes unsteady and shaky. The examinees wave their hands, lose precision of movements, usually fail the station test, and are unable to set rings on a rod. The writing test is very indicative. The greater the intoxication the more sweeping and illegible is the handwriting (see Figure 4a). Upon sobering up the handwriting becomes normal (see Figure 4b).

A neurological examination will reveal diminution of sensitivity to pain and of reflexes; in case of severe intoxication visible reactions to external stimulants, such as being called by name, or pricked, may be absent, and tendon reflexes are diminished.

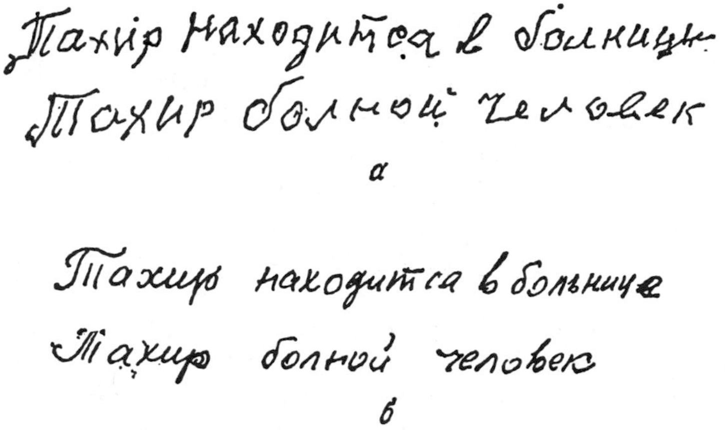

Тахир находится в больнице

Тахир больной человек

а

Тахир находится в больница

Тахир болной человек

б

Figure 4(a, b). Handwriting altered under the effect of alcohol

Of great importance are laboratory examinations and different alcohol tests. The Rapoport test is based on the conversion of alcohol into acetylaldehyde in the presence of sulfuric acid, and further into acetic acid with the reduction (and discoloration) of potassium permanganate solution as it is added drop by drop. This test is carried out in the following way: Two similar test tubes are filled with 2 ml of distilled water each. Upon rinsing his mouth with water, the examinee must make 20-30 expirations through a tube whose tip is lowered to the bottom of one of the test tubes so that the exhaled air passes through the water in it and evolves in the form of bubbles. After that, 25 drops of concentrated, chemically pure sulfuric acid solution are added to each test tube, carefully dripping the solution down their walls, whereupon 1 or 2 drops of an 0.5% potassium permanganate solution is added to the test tubes. If the exhaled air contains alcohol fumes, the solution in the test tube into which air is being blown will in the matter of 2-3 minutes turn pale pink or completely transparent. If the color in the two test tubes does not change within 10-15 minutes, this means the examinee has not used alcoholic beverages. One should remember that a weakly positive reaction may appear if medicines prepared on alcohol or ether had been taken shortly before the test. Therefore, this should be ascertained.

The Mokhov and Shinkarenko indicator tube test yields accurate results. It can be carried out even on a sleeping person, if the tube is inserted in the mouth and the nostrils are briefly compressed. Before conducting the test, one end of the tube is wiped with cotton wool moistened in a potassium permanganate solution, then both tips of the tube are sawn off and the examinee is asked to blow through it for 20-30 seconds. If the exhaled air contains no alcohol fumes, the reagent does not change color, whereas in a positive reaction a greenish ring forms. The greater the amount of alcohol ingested, the more intensive is the coloring of the ring. After drinking 0.5 liter of beer the test is positive briefly; 100 ml of wine, for 1 hour; 150 ml of vodka, for 4-5 hours; and 0.5 liter of vodka, for 15-18 hours. Alcohol content can be determined in the urine. Another test used for diagnostic purposes is a special electronic instrument which allows one to carry out expert examination of drunkenness under any conditions. It is used by the State Traffic Inspection men for examining vehicle drivers on the road. The instrument's readings appear instantly on a punched tape.

More detailed chemical examinations in a laboratory setting allow one to calculate the alcohol content of the blood and urine, which also allows the examiner to determine the approximate degree of intoxication, though the degree of intoxication may not correspond to the alcohol detected. Frequently a BAC of less than 1 cm³ per liter will not cause apparent symptoms of intoxication. The BAC for a mild degree of drunkenness may be 1-2 cm³ per liter, for average (pronounced), 2-4 cm³, and lastly, at a BAC of 5-7 cm³ per liter the degree of intoxication is deep. Although BAC findings may provide a clue to the amount of alcohol ingested, one should bear in mind the rather wide variability of this index.

In some cases the diagnosis of drunkenness has to be carried out on the next day after alcohol ingestion. In this case, expert examination can be helped by so-called residual symptoms or the hangover syndrome, expressed in headaches, nausea, low-key mood, pronounced degenerative symptoms, tremor of the tongue, fingers, etc.

The diagnosing of alcoholic intoxication may be carried out for different reasons. For example, a medical examination to determine the presence of alcoholic intoxication may be necessitated by a suspicion that the examinee was in a state of drunkenness while in the execution of his duties, or at the time of committing an offense. Therefore, the management of institutions and enterprises, and administrative, investigatory or judicial organs are entitled to send for expert examination. The expert examination should be carried out at any time of the day or night at psychiatric or narcological institutions, and when these are unavailable, at institutions of the general somatic network. The examination is conducted by psychiatrists, narcologists, neuropathologists, or physicians of other specialties. Paramedical workers should be versed in matters pertaining to the diagnosing of the degree of drunkenness and be able to prepare the solutions and other materials for conducting tests.

The results of expert examinations are recorded on a form called an "act." It indicates the surname, first name and family name of the examinee, his outward appearance, behavior, state of consciousness, orientation, memory, speech, neurological and somatic status, and the results of tests and examinations carried out. At present, the degree of intoxication is no longer determined, the act merely stating the fact of an alcoholic beverage having been used. Of utmost importance is the caution that *a paramedical worker is not entitled to draw up an act on his own; this can be done only by a physician.* However, the paramedical worker helps in obtaining the necessary information and in conducting the tests.

Expert examination of narcotic intoxication is more complex than that of alcoholism. If the examinee is being examined in a state of hashish intoxication, he presents with pallor of the skin, cold extremities, sparkling eyes, and occasionally, edema of the eyelids. There is nearly always dryness in the mouth, thirst, keen hunger, and tachycardia. Shaky gait, tremor of the hands and even of the whole body, and diminished pain sensitivity are also noticeable.

Although laboratory investigations are not specific, it is possible to detect hypoglycemia or an increase of hemoglobin (apparently due to thickening of the blood). A method has been suggested for determining the presence of hashish in washings from the fingers or lips.

Psychic disorders of hashish intoxication are characterized by confusion, disorientation, and a peculiar perception of the surrounding world. In some examinees, speech and motor excitation are observed accompanied by forced laughter, or foolish and absurd behavior. Others, on the contrary, become torpid, and immobile, as if abstracted from the world. There is moodiness and frequent disorders of perception; auditory and visual stimulants become dull and assume a gross sensual tinge, even to the extent of illusory or hallucinatory disorders. Cerebration becomes unrealistic, and thoughts flow in an accelerated tempo or are suddenly disrupted, with ample fantasies. An analysis of the examinees' behavior thus allows one to diagnose hashish intoxication. However, it is at times difficult to determine intoxication caused by other narcotic substances, each of which has its own peculiarities, and their detection is based on specific knowledge of the clinical manifestations of these particular narcomanias.

Chapter 37

Expert Examination of Ability to Work

The purpose of expert examination of a temporary incapacity is to determine the temporary loss of working ability in factory and office workers and collective farmers, which may be due to disease, injury or some other cause. In these cases a sick leave certificate is issued, which is the only document granting leave of absence from work and an allowance for temporary incapacity.

However, in order to further enhance the campaign to combat drunkenness and control alcoholism the USSR Council of Ministers ruled in an aforementioned decree (1972): ". . . that in case of illness stemming from or actions related to drunkenness, and also consequent upon alcohol abuse (injury, alcoholic psychosis, delirium tremens, chronic alcoholism) no sick-leave certificates shall be issued upon outpatient and inpatient treatment nor shall the allowance for temporary incapacity be granted." Therefore, instead of the sick-leave certificate, a special certificate (Reg. f. No. 54) is issued, certifying temporary incapacity due to alcohol-related disease or actions, and also due to alcohol abuse. This certificate is issued by physicians of medical institutions authorized to issue sick-leave certificates. The number of the certificate should correspond to its ordinate number in the Sick Leave Certificate Registration Book (Reg. f. No. 36).

Thus, when a person is afflicted by an alcohol-related mental disorder in the form of delirium tremens, hallucinosis, or Korsakoff's psychosis, or is admitted to a hospital for treatment, he is issued a document which merely justifies his failure to report for work, while denying the right to the temporary incapacity allowance. The same rules hold true in an outpatient setting; moreover, for outpatient treatment a certificate (Reg. f. No. 54) is not even issued, and treatment is prescribed for times outside working hours. Of course, in certain cases, such as pronounced symptoms of asthenia or severe reactions following therapy sessions, the special certificates may be issued.

The issue of sick-leave certificates is applicable only when alcoholism is a complication of the principal mental disease (schizophrenia, manic-depressive psychosis, etc.) and leads to the exacerbation of this illness. If the chronic course of the disease results in disruption of the organism's functions precluding the performance of professional working duties, the status of invalid is pronounced.

Medical and Labor Examination Boards (MLEB) have been organized in the USSR for determining the working capacity of persons who have suffered these or other diseases. Bearing in mind the specific features of mental and alcoholic diseases, specialized medical and labor examination boards have been set up for this category of patients. The specialized MLEB carry out expert examination only on referrals from the medical boards of psychiatric or narcological hospitals and dispensaries, and when these are unavailable, from the medical boards of medical institutions which include a psychiatrist-narcologist. The referral of patients for primary examination to a MLEB with a view toward transfer to invalid status is a responsible decision of the attending physician and the medical boards. Medical institutions are prohibited from referring to MLEB patients whose diagnoses have not yet been finalized, and who have not been given the necessary outpatient or inpatient treatment.

An MLEB can only then draw a correct expert conclusion when it has before it the materials of observation by the medical institution. Therefore, when referring a patient to an MLEB the medical board of the referring medical institution should provide the MLEB with a detailed excerpt from the patient's case history. The medical information about patients referred to an MLEB must reflect the patient's physical condition as well as functional characteristics of all detected disorders (detailed conclusions by the internist, eye specialist, surgeon, and other medical specialists).

Materials for examining the patient at his place of employment and particularly detailed data for examining the patient in everyday life are also valuable for arriving at the expert conclusion. When carrying out expert examinations the Medical and Labor Examination Boards study all the information about the patient, examine the patient himself, and when necessary, invite the attending physician, thus drawing a conclusion on the degree of incapacity which is conditionally designated by three invalidity groups: I, II, and III, where group I is the severest and III the mildest. It then defines the types of labor and jobs indicated according to the patient's health status, in other words, provides an occupational recommendation. This MLEB conclusion has the strength of a legal document, binding to all institutions concerned with the invalid's employment.

The occupational recommendation is aimed at guiding the organs of social security, the management of enterprises and farms, medical units and medical rooms as well as the invalid himself as to the kind of jobs and working conditions that should be provided for him. Therefore, the recommendation should comply with the following demands of rational job placement:

1. The character of the labor process should correspond to the invalid's functional capacities, facilitating the compensation and rehabilitation of his impaired functions and improvement of his general health status.

2. As far as possible, the job should correspond to the special and general education and training of the invalid, and his professional skills and age.

3. Working conditions should make it possible for the invalid to perform his job with the highest productivity in accordance with his personal inclinations, and consequently, must facilitate the maximum satisfaction of the invalid's material and cultural requirements.

4. The job must be selected according to the most high-skill specialties, with a view toward the further raising of production skills, particularly, for younger and middle-aged invalids.

When deciding on its occupational recommendations the MLEB

recommends various approaches and opportunities for job placement: group III invalids may be employed in diverse kinds of occupations as indicated by health status—at ordinary enterprises, at institutions, in agriculture or in their main occupation under substantially eased conditions; the return to occupational activities of groups I and II invalids, who have more serious defects, may be implemented only by altering and adapting working conditions to the invalid's capacities.

Following rehabilitation treatment, patients are frequently placed, with the assistance of the dispensary, in jobs at an ordinary enterprise or institution and, health status permitting, in their former jobs. In these circumstances the dispensary keeps in touch with the management, which on medical recommendations creates individual working conditions for the patient concerned. If the patient comes from the countryside, all of these measures are carried out within the context of agricultural production.

Invalid status in cases of affliction with alcoholism, narcomanias and toxicomanias is a rare phenomenon. Acute alcoholic psychoses do not warrant the establishment of such status at all. However, chronic psychosis in the form of a delirial syndrome in combination with degradation of the personality can be apparently assessed as a state which precludes the performance of occupational duties, and in this case, *temporary* invalidity may be pronounced. This status allows for the conducting of treatment. And, in cases of profound degradation of personality with a pronounced-mnesic syndrome (Korsakoff's psychosis), group II or even group I invalidity is pronounced.

Invalid status may be given to persons having stages II and III alcoholism with changes of personality, who at the same time have suffered a cranial injury with severe cerebral atherosclerosis, or those afflicted with schizophrenia, epilepsy or other psychic disorders which permanently impair the intellectual and occupational capacities of the persons concerned.

Group II invalidity may be established in cases of a severe intellectual defect, a pronounced psychoorganic syndrome, serious memory impairment, or considerable somatoneurological disorders (polyneuritis, cardiosclerosis, cirrhosis of the liver, etc.). Group III invalidity may be pronounced in cases of considerable impairment of skills due to organic, somatoneurological and psychic disorders, for example, epileptic seizures in a driver, polyneuritis in a fitter, turner, or impairment of memory in an intellectual.

In cases of drug addiction, group I invalidity is not pronounced at all. Group II may be given in the presence of serious organic changes of the personality, epileptiform seizures (persisting for more than six months), and group III may be pronounced in cases of profound, stable, somatic, neurological disorders, pronounced psychopathic-like behaviors, or epileptiform seizures combined with a pronounced psychoorganic syndromes, if these conditions preclude the performance of occupational duties. All of these conditions should be confirmed by hospital examination.

Chapter 38

Military Expert Examination in Alcoholism

To ensure that the armed forces of the USSR are furnished with healthy servicemen, they all pass examination by military medical boards. The boards make their decisions on the basis of a special order of the USSR Minister of Defense, which contains a Schedule of Diseases that can exempt men from service in the Soviet Army. Alcoholism, narcomanias and toxicomanias come under Article VI of the Schedule of Diseases' "Psychoses and Psychic Disorders in Acute and Chronic Infections and Intoxications."

Following psychoses related to these diseases there sometimes remain lasting and persistent asthenic conditions, pathological changes of personality, or organic lesions of the CNS. In this connection, provisions are made for treatment, and leaves of absence for health buildup are granted. In every case, favorable issues should be confirmed by an examination at a psychiatric or narcological institution. In case of repeated psychotic episodes, pronounced stable pathological changes of personality or lesions of the CNS, the persons concerned are found unfit for service in the armed forces of the USSR in peacetime and may be pronounced fit for auxiliary service in wartime.

Those considered unfit for service in the Soviet Army have symptoms of personality degradation or alcohol-related stable somatic disorders (on the part of the gastrointestinal tract or cardiovascular

system, or diseases of the liver), or present signs of drug addiction. In these cases, after repeated treatment proves unsuccessful, the boards make rulings based on the appropriate articles of the Schedule of Diseases.

However, habitual use of alcoholic beverages and narcotic substances does not exempt men from service in the Soviet Army. In individual cases in which the alcoholism or drug addictions are a secondary disease, i.e., appear as a complication of a schizophrenic process, a manic-depressive psychosis or a state of decompensation in psychopathic personalities, the evaluation of the morbid state is conducted individually and only following careful hospital check-up. Upon confirmation of the main diagnosis, release from service in the Soviet Army is effected on the basis of the appropriate articles of the Schedule of Diseases.

Chapter 39

Forensic-Psychiatric Expert Examination

Forensic-psychiatric expert examinations in the USSR protect the rights of the mentally ill and serve the tasks of enhancing socialist law and order. In the Soviet Union, forensic-psychiatric expert examination is fully administered by public health bodies and receives no fees from the interested parties, which ensures its maximal objectivity. The implementation of psychiatric expert examination is defined by a number of articles of the Criminal Code, the Code of Criminal Procedure and the Code of Civil Procedure. The organization and implementation of forensic-psychiatric expert examination is elaborated in greater detail by special interdepartmental instruction of the USSR Ministry of Health, the Procurator's Office of the USSR, and other departments.

A forensic-psychiatric examination may be appointed either in the period of the preliminary investigation, or in the stage of trial by court, and also at the time of serving a term of punishment. An examination is conducted at the suggestion of investigatory bodies or by a court ruling and, in regard to condemned persons, on referral from the administration of the institution of detention. A forensic-psychiatric examination of persons sent for expert examination may be attended by representatives of the investigatory organs and the Procurator's Office. In the case of examination of minors, counsel for the defense or other legal representatives are admitted.

An expert examination in a hospital setting of a person suspected

or indicted, but not kept in detention, requires sanction by the prosecutor. Although the right to appoint an expert examination is vested on the investigatory and judiciary organs, the right to appeal to them for holding an expert examination is granted to the defense, the defendant himself and his relatives or guardians. Thus, the organization of forensic-psychiatric expert examination in the Soviet Union already allows one during the period of investigation to detect the presence of a mental disease, and consequently, to carry out the necessary therapeutic measures.

The basic tasks of forensic-psychiatric expert examination are the following:

1. To determine the mental status and arrive at the imputability or nonimputability of persons detained or arraigned for criminal responsibility in cases where investigatory bodies or the court questions their mental health, and to reach a conclusion on the necessary medical measures of social protection regarding persons found nonimputable at the time of committing an offense or who had contracted a mental disease after the commitment of a crime.

2. To determine the mental status of persons who revealed symptoms of a mental disorder in the period of serving a term of punishment, and provide a conclusion on conducting the necessary medical measures regarding such persons.

3. To determine, when necessary, the mental status of victims and witnesses.

4. To issue a conclusion on the competence of persons whose mental health is being questioned by a court of law in a civil trial.

A forensic-psychiatric expert examination may be conducted in a hospital, in an outpatient setting, or in a court or police station, and in exceptional cases, in the absence of the examinee, from the materials of the case, and even posthumously.

Forensic-psychiatric expert examination in court, at the police station and in places of detention may be carried out by a psychiatrist-narcologist alone, or by a commission comprising several psychiatrist-narcologists of the public health organs in accordance with a decision of judicial and investigatory bodies. When an expert examiner finds it difficult to come to a conclusion about the examinee's mental health and imputability he may issue a conclusion on the need to carry out an outpatient expert examination or to send the examinee for hospital examination. Physicians carrying out forensic-psychiatric examinations at the police station, in court or in places of detention, must report on their work to appropriate public health bodies.

For carrying out forensic-psychiatric expert examinations the public health organs have created special forensic-psychiatric departments at mental hospitals, functioning on the same grounds as any other department of these hospitals (inpatient expert examination), and forensic-psychiatric examination boards at dispensaries (outpatient expert examination). A forensic-psychiatric expert examination is conducted, as a rule, by a board consisting of three psychiatrists (one chairman and two members of the board). When this number of psychiatrists is unavailable for outpatient examination, it is admissible to carry out the examination by two psychiatrists. Standing inpatient and outpatient forensic-psychiatric examination boards are authorized by higher-ranking public health organs. The duration of an inpatient expert examination should, as a rule, not exceed 30 days. When the examination board is unable to reach a conclusion within this period, it takes a vote on whether to extend the examination time.

The forensic-psychiatric conclusion on the mental status of examinees, on their imputability or competence is based on their psychiatric examination, the study of materials on the criminal case and information about the former life of the examinees, and documents and certificates about former diseases. All medical institutions (hospitals, clinics, dispensaries, polyclinics, etc.) are obligated to supply the forensic-psychiatric examination board with all information and materials it requires about the examinee (excerpts from case histories, certificates, medical analyses, etc.).

The forensic-psychiatric conclusion is issued in the form of an act signed by all members of the board, everyone bearing equal responsibility for its contents. In case one of the experts disagrees with the conclusion of the other board members, he may not sign the act, and instead submit his special opinion, which is attached to the examination act. The conclusion of the forensic-psychiatric experts is one of the important pieces of evidence in the case; however, it is not obligatory for the investigation and the court and is assessed by them. They may disagree with the opinion of the experts. When the conclusion of the examination board is found unconvincing and incomplete, and in cases of controversy between the experts, the organ of investigation or the court asks the public health bodies to arrange for carrying out a repeat expert examination, and they organize a new examination board.

A forensic-psychiatric expert can only be a person who has received a doctor's diploma and completed specialized training in psychiatry. The forensic-psychiatric expert has the right to familiarize himself with the circumstances of the case, which is essential for carrying out the examination. Soviet experts are entitled to attend the court hearings, confer with other experts, and put questions to victims, defendants and witnesses, which is of special importance when deciding the question of a temporary morbid psychic disorder at the time of committing the offense. If the request of the judiciary investigating bodies extends beyond the scope of the examiner's special expertise or the materials placed at his disposal are insufficient for making a conclusion, the examiner, in writing, informs the organ that has appointed the expert examination of the impossibility to provide a conclusion, explaining in detail the reasons for this.

A forensic-psychiatric examiner has no right to divulge materials of the investigation known to him and received during the forensic-psychiatric expert examination and reports them only to the investigatory and judiciary organs at their request. An expert is held responsible for divulging the materials of the investigation and the expert examination under the relevant articles of the Criminal Code.

Persons found by the court to be imputable are sentenced and serve their terms in the established order. Those found nonimputable are prescribed medical treatment in the form of compulsory therapy, or therapy on general grounds. Medical treatment is prescribed with account of the examinee's mental status and the degree of social danger. Treatment is conducted at special psychiatric hospitals of the Ministries of Internal Affairs if the socially dangerous act was particularly grave (e.g., murder, robbery, rape, etc.) and the examinee's mental status may be the cause of repeated socially dangerous acts.

In the majority of cases, compulsory treatment is conducted in general psychiatric hospitals. Occasionally, in cases of minor offenses, of the type of petty disorderly conduct, the medical measure may boil down to the placement of the examinee under observation of the uchastok (health district) psychiatrist-narcologist and guardianship by relatives.

The court does not rule on the duration of compulsory treatment, which is determined by the patient's mental status. Special medical boards of institutions examine all patients placed for compulsory treatment at least once every six months and lay down their opinion in a special act. If the patient's status allows for a change in the measure of medical protection and for a transfer to treatment in the general network, the board's act is sent to the court that had ruled on compulsory treatment, or to the court nearest the hospital. Only the court may decide on the question of discontinuing compulsory treatment.

Now, what questions pertaining to imputability are encountered in narcological practice? Article 12 of the Criminal Code of the Russian Federation and relevant articles of the criminal codes of the Union Republics are entitled "Responsibility for an Offense Committed in a State of Intoxication." It states:

"A person who has committed a criminal offense in the state of intoxication shall not be exempt from criminal responsibility.

"The court, irrespective of pronouncing sentence, may decide on the compulsory treatment of persons condemned for an offense, recognized as habitual alcoholics or drug addicts.

"The compulsory treatment of such persons shall be carried out at places of detention or in special institutions."

The philosophy behind the quoted Article is that a person drinks himself into a state of intoxication voluntarily, presupposing and agreeing beforehand with all the consequences related to such a state. Moreover, he is capable of realizing the nature of his actions and controlling them. In other words, persons who have committed an offense in a state of simple alcoholic intoxication, even aggravated, with possible amnesias at some moments, are pronounced imputable. The Law of the USSR of June 11, 1969, Clause 10, says: "The commitment of a crime by a person in a state of drunkenness shall be regarded as an aggravating circumstance."

Part 2 of the same Article prescribes compulsory treatment for persons found to be afflicted with alcoholism. A conclusion on this Clause is provided by medical boards, while the court determines the duration of treatment. These persons receive compulsory treatment in the medical unit of a CIC or WTP and subsequently should be placed on the dynamic registration file of a narcological institution for the duration of five years.

Case Illustration Examinee: G., age 39, indicted for murder. Being in the flat of his acquaintance and drunk, he stuck a knife into the chest of citizen A., killing the latter. From the investigation it is known that heredity was unaggravated by mental diseases. The examinee's childhood and development were normal. He finished schooling, then attended a technical school, after which he began working. Since that time he began to use alcoholic beverages, but drank moderately, seldom drinking to excess. He tolerated drinking parties poorly, with the appearance of nausea, vomiting, and headaches. In 1958 he was called up for service in the army and served well. By nature he was sociable, took part in amateur dramatics, and was on good terms with the officers. In 1962 he remained for extended service and earned a number of citations and awards. His discipline was exemplary and exacting, and he excelled in combat and political preparedness and possessed organizational ability. He coped with assignments well. He married, fathered a child, and was attentive to wife and child. He drank alcoholic beverages occasionally at parties. In 1972 he was honorably discharged and found a job.

At first he worked well but since the end of 1974 began to drink more frequently. He was no longer friendly with his colleagues, nor did he keep in touch with old friends. After work he struck up brief acquaintances with other drinkers, and more and more often came home drunk. He became rude and quarrelsome, and felt the need to drink on the morning after. He became short-tempered and irritable, and responded to reprimands from his superiors grudgingly, setting his own interests above those of others. He seldom attended work meetings and was repeatedly reprimanded for abusing alcoholic beverages. Once, when drunk, he dropped in on a friend who was at the time entertaining A. They were drinking alcoholic beverages, and after G. had drunk nearly two bottles of wine, he left for a restaurant where he drank another 250 grams of vodka, a bottle of wine, then returned to the same company. A quarrel flared up; when the examinee attempted to expel A. from the apartment, the latter brandished a knife. Irate, G. snatched the knife from him and struck him in the chest, as a result of which citizen A. died.

During the expert examination the examinee told the examiners that he never anticipated such grave consequences, did not want to commit any offense, and alleged that he did not realize what he was doing at the time. However, the forensic-psychiatric examination board found that the offense was committed in a state of habitual alcoholic intoxication and the examinee could, therefore, realize the nature of his actions and control them. At the same time, the forensic-psychiatric examination board found citizen G. to be afflicted with stage II alcoholism. The court found G. guilty of the crime committed with an aggravating circumstance (drunkenness), and sentenced him to a long term of punishment and two years of compulsory treatment for alcoholism.

Thus, persons with the diagnosis of alcoholism as a rule are recognized imputable. Seldom, in cases of profound dementia, particularly in combination with atherosclerosis, senile dementia, or cerebral injury, they may be found nonimputable. Persons who at the moment of committing an offense are in a state of alcoholic psychosis are recognized nonimputable, for example, in the state of alcoholic delirium (delirium tremens) or paranoid, hallucinosis (acute, chronic) or Korsakoff's psychosis, pseudoparalysis, dipsomania or pathologic drunkenness. In these cases, the Forensic-Psychiatric Examination Board recognizes the examinee nonimputable and he is prescribed compulsory treatment.

Expert examination of alcoholic psychoses may be very difficult since the psychopathologic symptoms may no longer be present at the time of holding the expert examination, and also because some persons attempt to simulate old psychic experiences, i.e., use their former experience, while others exaggerate the psychotic episodes present. One should remember that delirium tremens may occur already in prison after the offense had been committed, in the period of pre-liminary detention, etc.

Persons afflicted with different narcomanias and toxicomanias more often commit offenses related to the acquisition of narcotics or to the means of acquiring them. In the overwhelming majority of cases they are found imputable, and seldom found nonimputable in cases of psychotic disorders.

Forensic-psychiatric examiners have to decide on the mental status of persons afflicted with alcoholism or drug addiction who have been party to different civil-legal acts. They may have been committed in a state of intoxication or psychosis. In the former case a person is found competent, and his transaction valid, in the latter, incompetent and the transaction invalid.

In cases when the examinee has, in addition to alcoholism or drug addiction, some other mental disease (schizophrenia, epilepsy, etc.), his competence is established depending on the severity of the psychotic condition. For establishing guardianship over citizens of limited competence, the medical examination boards must determine the stage of alcoholism, the presence of a psychotic state, or degree of personality changes related to alcohol or narcotic abuse. Then the matter goes to court in the appropriate order of procedure, and trustees or guardians are appointed by special commissions of the Executive Committees of the Soviets of People's Deputies.

EXERCISES FOR REVIEW

1. Master the methods of psychological, laboratory and rapid de-termination of intoxication. Learn to use the "Pegas" electronic in-strument for determining alcohol fumes in exhaled air and to draw up acts of examination.

2. Having determined the mental status of a patient, decide the question of granting invalid status or exemption from army service.

3. Master the principal questions of imputability and compulsory treatment of persons afflicted with alcoholism, narcomanias and tox-icomanias.

CHAPTERS 36-39 QUESTIONS

1. A feldsher-narcologist has been summoned to the site of a road accident. Can he make his conclusion on the use of alcoholic beverages by the driver? If the answer is yes, by what symptoms?

2. A patient has made his first call at a narcological dispensary. Can he be given invalid status?

3. Can a patient after an episode of alcoholic psychosis be given invalid status? If the answer is yes, by what symptoms? Which group of invalidity?

4. A convalescent has not been using alcohol for five years, yet noticeable changes of personality (alcoholic-type) and neurological symptoms persist. Can he be given invalid status, and if he can, which group?

5. The diagnosis of "stage II alcoholism" has been pronounced. Can this person serve in the Soviet Army? If the answer is no, then under which Order and which Article of that Order?

6. A crime has been committed in the state of alcoholic intoxication. Is the examinee imputable?

7. An offense has been committed in the state of alcoholic psychosis. Is the examinee imputable? If not, what measures should be prescribed in regard to him?

8. An examinee has been pronounced nonimputable. In what kind of institution must he undergo compulsory treatment? For what length of time?

9. A drug addict has committed theft of narcotic substances. May he be recognized nonimputable?

10. A schizophrenic who has been abusing alcohol has committed an offense in the state of simple alcoholic intoxication. How should the matter of imputability be decided?

11. An offense has been committed in the state of acute medicinal drug intoxication (intoxication psychosis). Is the examinee imputable?

Supplement 1

Regulations and Instructions for Narcological Care

ORDERS ON NARCOLOGY

Orders of the USSR Ministry of Health: Order No. 694 of August 24, 1972, "On Measures to Further Enhance the Control of Drunkenness and Alcoholism."

Order No. 1180 of December 26, 1975, "In Addition to the Nomenclature of Medical Specialties."

Order No. 131 of February 5, 1976, "On Amendments to the Nomenclature of Public Health Institutions," Moscow, 1976.

Order No. 270 of March 18, 1976, "On Staff Complements of Medical and Pharmaceutical Personnel and Kitchen Staff of Narcological Dispensaries, Departments and Consulting Rooms," Moscow, 1976.

Order No. 928 of September 21, 1976, "On Further Measures to Step Up the Control of Narcomanias," Moscow, 1976.

Order No. 291 of March 23, 1976, "On Authorizing Obligatory Minimum Treatment Courses for Chronic Alcoholics," Moscow, 1976.

Order No. 388 of April 19, 1978, "On Authorizing Obligatory Minimum Treatment Courses of Persons Afflicted with Narcomanias and Toxicomanias," Moscow, 1978.

REGULATIONS CONCERNING ALCOHOLISM AND DRUG ADDICTION

Regulations Concerning Standing Commissions for Combating Alcoholism at Public Health Organs (Institutions), Moscow, March 11, 1976.

Regulations Concerning the Uchastok Psychiatrist-Narcologist and the Narcological Consulting Room, Moscow, March 19, 1976.

Regulations Concerning the Narcological Dispensary, Moscow, August 20, 1976.

Regulations Concerning the Feldsher-Narcologist, Assistant to the Psychiatrist-Narcologist, and the Narcological Room Manned by a Feldsher (Narcological Station), Moscow, June 22, 1976.

Regulations Concerning the Public Narcological Post, Moscow, 1978.

METHODOLOGICAL INSTRUCTIONS

Instructions on the Use of Medicinal Drugs for the Treatment of Alcoholism (Official Publication), Moscow, 1975, Issue 1.

Instructions on the Use of Medicinal Drugs for the Treatment of Alcoholism (Official Publication), Moscow, 1976, Issue 2.

Instructions on the Use of Medicinal Drugs for the Treatment of Alcoholism (Official Publication), Moscow, 1978, Issue 3.

Instructions on the Medical Examination of Inveterate Drunkards (Alcoholics) and Drug Addicts for Referral to Compulsory Treatment, Moscow, December 21, 1967.

Methods of Alcoholism Treatment of Patients with Mental Diseases Aggravated by Chronic Alcoholism (Methodological Letter), Moscow, 1971.

Clinical Aspects, Differential Diagnosis and Forensic-Psychiatric Assessment of Intoxications Caused by Hashish and Alcohol, Moscow, 1972.

Methodological Instructions on the Issue of Temporary Disability Certificates for Diseases Caused by Drunkenness or Actions Related to Drunkenness, and Also to Alcohol Abuse, Moscow, October 12, 1973.

Arresting Drinking Binges and Hangover Conditions in Chronic Alcoholics in an Outpatient Setting, Moscow, 1974.

Rapid Sobering Up of Persons in a State of Alcoholic Intoxication at Medical Sobering-Up Stations (Methodological Instructions), Moscow, 1975.

Methodological Instructions for Emotional-Stress Group Hypnotherapy for Alcoholism, Moscow, 1975.

Organization and Implementation of Compulsory Treatment of Chronic Alcoholics at Work-Therapy Preventoriums of the USSR Ministry of Internal Affairs, Moscow, 1975.

Treatment of Drug Addicts at the Specialized Department of the Berezan Neuropsychiatric Hospital, Krasnodar Territorial Health Department (Briefing Letter), Moscow, 1975.

On the State of and Measures for Improving the Registration of Persons Using Narcotic Substances (Circular Letter), Moscow, 1975.

Methods for Identifying Alcohol Abusers and the Organization of Antialcoholism Efforts at an Industrial Enterprise (Methodological Recommendations), Moscow, 1975.

Treatment of Tobacco Smoking (Methodological Instructions), Moscow, 1976.

Methods for Arresting Nicotinic Abstention (Methodological Instructions), Moscow, 1976.

Methods of Comprehensive Prognosis of Chronic Alcoholism (Methodological Instructions), Moscow, 1976.

Methodological Recommendations for the Treatment of Chronic Alcoholics, Moscow, 1976.

Clinical Aspects and Treatment of Initial Manifestations of Alcoholism (Methodological Recommendations), Moscow, 1976.

Clinical Aspects and Treatment of Severe Forms of Alcoholic Delirium (Methodological Recommendations), Moscow, 1977.

Benzhexol Toxicomania: Clinical Aspects, Diagnosis, Treatment (Clinical Recommendations), Moscow, 1978.

Arresting Alcoholic Delirium and Abstinence Syndrome by Acupuncture (Methodological Instructions), Moscow, 1978.

Alcoholism and Health Education (Methodological Recommendations), Moscow, 1978.

Methodological Recommendations for the Use of Carbamazepine in Narcological Practice, Moscow, 1979.

Narcomanias, Toxicomanias and Their Treatment (Methodological Recommendations), Moscow, 1979.

Supplement 2

List of Narcotic Substances and
Medicinal Narcotic Drugs
as of June 1, 1977

I. Narcotic Substances Prohibited for Use in Medical
Practice in Humans and Manufacture, and Not to Be
Included in Prescription Manuals and Textbooks

1. Heroin
2. Cannabis (marijuana, hashish)
3. Acetorphine
4. Etorphine
5. Lysergic acid and its derivatives (including lysergine; lysergic acid diethylamide, LSD)
6. Tetrahydrocannabinols, all isomers
7. Mescaline
8. Parahexyl
9. Psilocine, psilotsin
10. Psilocybine
11. STP, DOM
12. DET
13. DMHP
14. DMT

II. Medicinal Narcotic Drugs

1. Alphaprodine hydrochloride (struck off the State Register)
2. Amfepramon
3. Bekhterev tablets (struck off the State Register)
4. "Bisal" tablets (struck off the State Register)
5. Cocaine hydrochloride
6. Codeine
7. Codeine phosphate
8. Codterpine tablets
9. Coughing pills:
    thermopsis herb powder, 0.01 g
    codeine, 0.02 g
    sodium hydrocarbonate, 0.2 g
    liquorice root powder, 0.2 g
10. Dimenoxadol chloride tablets, 0.05, 0.015, 0.06 g
11. Dimenoxadol hydrochloride
12. Dimenoxadol hydrochloride solution, 2%, 2.0 ml
13. Dimorphan (struck off the State Register)
14. Escodol (struck off State Register)
15. Ethylmorphine hydrochloride
16. Ethylmorphine hydrochloride tablets, 0.01 or 0.015 g
17. Fentanyl
18. Fentanyl solution, 0.005% for injections
19. Glutethimide
20. Glutethimide tablets
21. Hydrocodone phosphate (struck off the State Register)
22. Levorphanol (struck off the State Register)
23. Methadone (struck off the State Register)
24. Methylphenidate
25. Morphine hydrochloride
26. Morphine hydrochloride solution, 1% and 5% for injections
27. Morphine hydrochloride solution, 1% in tube syringes
28. Morphine hydrochloride tablets
29. Opium coughing tablets for adults (struck off the State Register)
30. Opium extract, dry (struck off the State Register)

31. Opium extract suppositories (struck off the State Register)
32. Opium powder (struck off the State Register)
33. Opium tincture (struck off the State Register)
34. Opium tablets, 0.01 g (struck off the State Register)
35. Omnopon
36. Omnopon solution, 1% or 2% for injections
37. Palfium (dextromoramide tartrate)
38. Pectol tablets (struck off the State Register)
39. Pervitin (struck off the State Register)
40. Phenatin
41. Phencyclidine
42. Phenmetrazine (chlorphentermine)
43. Phenocoll
44. Piritramide
45. Piritramide solution, 15 mg-2 ml
46. Promedol
47. Promedol solution, 1% or 2% for injections
48. Promedol solution, 1% or 2% in tube syringes
49. Promedol tablets, 0.025 g
50. Propanidid
51. Reasec
52. Stomach drops (struck off the State Register)
53. Stomach tablets with opium (struck off the State Register)
54. Tablets: codeine, 0.015 g; sodium hydrocarbonate, 0.25 g (struck off the State Register)
55. Tablets: codeine, 0.01, 0.015 g; sugar, 0.25 g (struck off the State Register)
56. Tablets: codeine phosphate, 0.015 g; sugar, 0.25 g (struck off the State Register)
57. Thebaine
58. Thecodine (struck off the State Register)
59. Thecodine solution, 1% and 2% for injections (struck off the State Register)
60. Thecodine tablets, 0.005 g (struck off the State Register)

III. PLANTS AND SUBSTANCES CLASSIFIED AS NARCOTIC DRUGS AND PROHIBITED FOR HUMAN USE

1. Raw opium
2. Opium poppy
3. Opium straw, used for extracting the narcotic substance
4. Commercial morphine
5. Hemp: Southern Chui, Southern Manchu, Indian
6. Hemp pollen. Hemp resin, hashish, anasha, marijuana, hashish oil derived from any hemp variety.

IV. NARCOTIC SUBSTANCES REGARDED AS NARCOTIC UNDER THE 1961 SINGLE CONVENTION ON NARCOTIC DRUGS AND THE ORDER NO. 523 OF JULY 3, 1968, BY THE MINISTER OF HEALTH OF THE USSR

Acetorphine
Acetylmethadol
Allylprodine
Alphacetylmethadol
Alphameprodine
Alphamethadol
Alphaprodine
Anileridine
Benzethidine
Benzylmorphine
Betacetylmethadol
Betameprodine
Betamethadol
Betaprodine
Bezitramide
Cannabis
Clonitazene
Cocaine
Coca Leaf

Codoxime
Concentrate of poppy straw
Desomorphine
Dextromoramide
Diampromide
Diethylthiambutene
Difenoxin
Dihydromorphine
Dimenoxadol
Dimepheptanol
Dimethylthiambutene
Dioxaphetyl butyrate
Diphenoxylate
Dipipanone
Drotebanol
Ecgonine, its esters and derivatives which are convertible to ecgonine and cocaine

Ethylmethylthiambutene
Etonitazene
Etorphine
Etoxeridine
Fentanyl
Furethidine
Heroin
Hydrocodone
Hydromorphinol
Hydromorphone
Hydroxypethidine
Isomethadone
Ketobemidone
Levomethorphan
Levomoramide
Levophenacylmorphan
Levorphanol
Metazocine
Methadone
Methadone intermediate
Methyldesorphine
Methyldihydromorphine
Metopon
Moramide
Morpheridine
Morphine
Morphine methobromide and other pentavalent nitrogen morphine derivatives, e.g., oxycodeine

Morphine-N-oxide
Myrophine
Nicomorphine
Noracymethadol
Norlevorphanol
Normethadone
Normorphine
Norpipanone
Opium
Oxycodone
Oxymorphone
Pethidine
Pethidine intermediate A
Pethidine intermediate B
Pethidine intermediate C
Phenadoxone
Phenampromide
Phenazocine
Phenomorphan
Phenoperidine
Piminodine
Piritramide
Proheptazine
Properidine
Racemethorphan
Racemoramide
Racemorphan
Thebacon
Thebaine
Trimeperidine

The isomers, unless specifically excepted, of the drugs in this schedule whenever the existence of such isomers is possible within the specific chemical designation;

The esters and ethers, unless appearing in another schedule, of the drugs in this schedule whenever the existence of such esters or ethers is possible;

The salts of the drugs listed in this schedule, including the salts of esters, ethers, and isomers as provided above whenever the existence of such salts is possible.

Acetyldihydrocodeine	Nicodicodine
Codeine	Norcodeine
Dihydrocodeine	Pholcodine
Ethylmorphine	Propiram
Nicocodine	

The isomers, unless specifically excepted, of the drugs in this schedule whenever the existence of such isomers is possible within the specific chemical designation;

The salts of the drugs listed in this schedule including the salts of the isomers as provided above whenever the existence of such salts is possible.

Supplement 3

Regulations Concerning the Feldsher-Narcologist, Assistant to the Psychiatrist-Narcologist

1. The feldsher-narcologist of the feldsher narcological room (narcological station) is the organizer of the narcological services at an industrial, construction and motor transport enterprise and also in agriculture.

2. The feldsher-narcologist's office is the feldsher narcological room (narcological station), situated in a zone in the closest proximity to the group of patients it caters to (medical unit of industrial enterprises, medical rooms, etc.) under the direct organizational and methodological guidance of and in constant touch with the uchastok psychiatrist-narcologist.

3. The feldsher-narcologist performs the following functions:

—identifies persons inclined to alcohol and narcotics abuse among the population (factory and office workers) of the health district served, with the help of the management of the enterprise, public organizations, commissions for combating drunkenness and alcoholism control, the medical network of the medical room, and also information coming from medical sobering-up stations, voluntary public order squads, organs of the militia, etc.;

—informs the uchastok psychiatrist-narcologist about all newly detected persons inclined to alcohol and narcotics abuse;

—regularly, at appointed times, presents alcohol abusers and drug addicts for examination by the district (uchastok) psychiatrist-narcologist; only upon the establishment of the nosological diagnosis are the newly detected alcoholics and drug addicts put on the register;

—maintains dynamic observation of alcoholics in stable remission for five years, the first three years of which the patient is placed on the active registration file, and in the subsequent two years, on the passive registration file and observation; patients after WTP treatment are placed under special supervision;

—organizes the reception by the psychiatrist-narcologist of narcological patients both on the register, and newly identified persons inclined to alcohol abuse;

—implements active and supportive outpatient treatment of alcoholics as prescribed by the psychiatrist-narcologist (detoxification, general roborant, sensitizing therapy, etc.), with account of the established duration of observation and treatment during three years and subsequent passive registration and supportive antirelapse treatment for another two years; administers all kinds of treatment at the narcological station or otherwise according to local conditions and the nature of therapy;

—promptly informs the uchastok psychiatrist-narcologist about all changes in the status of patients, of failures on their part to follow the prescribed treatment and regimen;

—carries out observation of narcological patients right at work and in the home;

—organizes and plans joint work with narcological posts;

—participates in the work of commissions for combating drunkenness and alcoholism control;

—regularly reports cases of drunkenness and alcoholism at conferences with the management of enterprises, at the sessions of commissions for combating drunkenness, at factory, workshop, etc., trade union committees;

—maintains close contacts with the management and public organizations of the enterprise with the purpose of providing treatment for narcological patients, and organizes public check-ups on the observance by patients of therapeutic regimens;

—on instructions from the uchastok psychiatrist-narcologist, informs the uchastok militia officer about afflicted persons who evade treatment;

—on the recommendation of the uchastok psychiatrist-narcologist, approaches the management of the industrial enterprises regarding the job placement of those afflicted with alcoholism and drug addictions;

—together with the commission for combating drunkenness and alcoholism control, exercises tutelage (wardship) over alcohol abusers and drug addicts;

—organizes and carries out planned preventive work and health education about the harmfulness of alcoholism and heavy drinking among the groups catered to;

—holds talks about the harmfulness of alcohol among the workers of industrial enterprises of the area catered to;

—handles the operative registration documents of the narcological station: individual outpatient cards, arranged according to the different groups of dynamic observation; the registration ledger of identified cases; list of procedures, etc.;

—regularly draws up reports on the work carried out according to schedules and scope established by the narcological service of the city (district), etc.;

—takes part in all the organizational and methodological measures (conferences, seminars, etc.) sponsored by the city narcological service toward rendering narcological care to the population.

Head of the Board for the Introduction of New Medicinal Drugs and Medical Technology, USSR Ministry of Health, E. A. Babayan.

Supplement 4

"Authorized"
Deputy Minister of Health of the USSR,
A. G. Safonov
June 22, 1976, No. 06-14/8

Regulations Concerning the Feldsher-Manned Narcological Room (Narcological Station)

1. The feldsher narcological room (narcological station) is run as one of the outpatient units of the single narcological service of a city (district; region) and is fully subordinated to it as regards all organizational, methodological and medico-prophylactic questions.

2. The feldsher narcological room (narcological station) is situated as close as possible to the servicing zone (medical unit of industrial enterprises, medical rooms, etc.).

3. The feldsher narcological station is manned, as a rule, by a feldsher with special training in narcology and health education.

I. BASIC TASKS AND DUTIES OF THE NARCOLOGICAL STATION

The feldsher-manned narcological station carries out the following:

1. Active identification of alcohol abusers and drug addicts by taking into account and analyzing information received from the management and public organizations of enterprises and institutions (workshops, departments, etc.), medical sobering-up stations, voluntary public order squads, organs of the militia, public courts, local trade union committees, and commissions for combating drunkenness, and information received directly from the network of medical units.

2. Registration of all identified alcoholics only after they have been examined by the district (uchastok) psychiatrist-narcologist; persons may be struck off the register only upon the conclusion of the district narcological consulting room or narcological dispensary.

3. Dynamic observation in the course of five years of stable remission cases; during the first three years the alcoholic convalescent is on the active registration file and under observation, and is transferred to the passive registration file during the last two years; patients discharged from WTP are placed under special observation.

4. Administration of active and supportive outpatient treatment as prescribed by the psychiatrist-narcologist with account of the established terms of dynamic observation and obligatory minimum treatment courses and supportive antirelapse therapy.

5. Inspections of motor vehicle drivers and preliminary expert examination of alcoholic intoxication.

6. Planned health education and preventive antialcoholism work in the collectives of workshops, sections, etc.

7. Liaison with the commissions for combating drunkenness and alcoholism control.

8. Constant assistance to and joint measures with public narcological posts which are the support units of the feldsher-manned narcological stations in the matter of identifying alcoholics and inducing them to take treatment.

9. Measures, on the recommendation of the uchastok psychiatrist-narcologist and with the management of industrial enterprises, toward the job placement of alcoholics and drug addicts.

10. The exercise, together with the commission for combating drunkenness, of tutelage (wardship) of alcoholics and drug addicts.

II. Operative Registration Documents of a Narcological Station

I. The main operative registration documents are the following:

1. Individual outpatient cards filed according to the different groups of dynamic observation (outpatients; inpatients; those on compulsory treatment at WTP; those evading treatment, etc.), which includes: (a) visits prescribed and visits actually made to the narcological station by patients; (b) data on alcohol abuse according to information from all available sources; (c) information about all measures and treatments administered to the patient concerned.

2. List of procedures, which records all prescriptions of the physician with entries noting their timely administration; after completing a course of treatment the list of procedures is attached to the outpatient card.

3. Registration ledger of identified cases.

4. Registration ledger of health education work pertaining to combating drunkenness and alcoholism control.

II. According to schedules established by the narcological service of the city (district, etc.), summary tables are drawn up on the following totals: (a) number of registered and newly detected cases in the period under review; (b) number of patients discharged from WTP and placed on the register; (c) number of patients given active and supportive outpatient treatment according to its types; (d) number of patients sent for inpatient alcoholism treatment; (e) average number of patient visits to the narcological room (narcological station); (f) average number of visits made by the feldsher to patients at work and at home; (g) efficacy of treatment according to duration of remissions; (h) number of relapses; (i) number of health education talks and lectures about the harmfulness of alcoholism and drunkenness, etc.

Head of the Board for the Introduction of New Medicinal Drugs and Medical Technology, USSR Ministry of Health, E. A. Babayan

Supplement 5

"Authorized"
Deputy Minister of Health of
the USSR, A. G. Safonov,
June 14, 1978, No. 06-14/9

"Authorized"
Deputy Chairman, Executive
Committee, URC and RCS of
the USSR Yu. P. Ostalsky,
June 14, 1978, No. 12/1700

Regulations Concerning the Public Narcological Post

I. The public narcological post is the primary unit of the step-like narcological care system. The narcological post is organized with the purpose of maximum contact with the public in the activities of the narcological service.

II. Public narcological posts are organized at industrial enterprises, in construction and motor transport organizations and in agriculture, in housing neighborhoods and, according to local conditions, in other institutions and subdivisions. The narcological posts are manned by the activists of the Red Cross and Red Crescent Societies and citizens volunteering for work in the narcological service.

III. Members of a public narcological post are chosen from among volunteering factory and office workers, collective farmers, activists of house committees and pensioners by the committee of the primary organization of the Red Cross or Red Crescent Society on agreement with the Party organization, local trade union committee or the board

351

of a collective farm or house committee to be elected at general (trade-union) meetings.

IV. The public narcological post and its membership are authorized by the appropriate public health organs responsible for the narcological service of the district concerned. Members of the narcological post shall be admitted to service after finishing training courses. A narcological post should be served by at least four members, one of whom is appointed the responsible leader.

V. The training and retraining of members of the public narcological posts according to a program authorized by the USSR Ministry of Health and the Executive Committee of the URC and RCS of the USSR, is carried out by physicians (feldshers), i.e., narcologists, while the necessary reference and methodological literature is provided by the health education center and committee of the Red Cross or Red Crescent Society.

VI. The public narcological post operates under the immediate guidance of the feldsher narcological station and is one of its units. General guidance to narcological stations and posts is given by the narcological consulting room.

VII. The public narcological post carries out its work in daily contact with party, trade union and Young Communist League organizations, and also with Commissions for Combating Drunkenness and Alcoholism Control under the Executive Committees of the local Soviets of People's Deputies.

VIII. The public narcological post, together with the feldsher-manned narcological station and under the guidance of the narcological consulting room, draws up quarterly and yearly plans according to which it carries out its work. The working plan is coordinated with the appropriate Commissions for Combating Drunkenness and Alcoholism Control.

IX. The main tasks of the public narcological post are the following:

1. Assisting the narcological service in identifying persons afflicted with alcoholism, narcomanias and toxicomanias. Informing the psychiatrist-narcologist (feldsher-narcologist) about persons abusing alcoholic beverages, using narcotics and substances causing morbid craving.

2. Helping in inducing narcological patients who evade active and supportive therapy to undergo treatment.

3. Assisting the narcological consulting room and the narcological station in the administration of medical prescriptions and in checking up on the observance of prescribed regimens by narcological patients.

4. Assisting the narcological service in collecting information about persons afflicted with alcoholism, narcomanias and toxicomanias.

5. Assisting the narcological service in summoning for supportive therapy persons discharged from the WTP of the USSR Ministry of Internal Affairs.

6. Directly participating together with the narcological service in health education work, in antialcoholism propaganda, and in the dissemination of health education materials on the harmfulness of alcohol.

X. Regularly raising their own knowledge in the field of narcology, attending classes and lectures delivered by the uchastok psychiatrist-narcologists.

XI. The narcological post must: (a) have the decision of the appropriate public health organs on creating the public narcological posts with the names of its leader and members; (b) maintain a registration ledger of identified persons afflicted with alcoholism, narcomanias and toxicomanias and also alcohol abusers (entered in this ledger is information on visits to the registered group of patients); (c) report at least once every six months on the work carried out and state of affairs in the serviced uchastok to the commission for combating drunkenness and alcoholism control.

XII. The public narcological post reports on its work to the psychiatrist-narcologist (feldsher-narcologist) under whose guidance it operates, and to the committee of the primary organization of the Red Cross or Red Crescent Society every half year.

Chief of the Board for the Introduction of New Medicinal Drugs and Medical Technology USSR Ministry of Health,
E. A. Babayan

Chief of the Department for Health Education Work, Executive Committee of the URC and RCS of the USSR,
L. N. Galcheva

Supplement 6

List of Abbreviations Used

ACS	antireticular cytotoxic serum
ADH	alcohol dehydrogenase
ATP	adenosine triphosphate
BAC	blood alcohol content
CLC	correctional labor colony
CNS	central nervous system
DAER	disulfiram-apomorphine-ethanol reaction
DER	disulfiram-ethanol reaction
FPEB	forensic-psychiatric examination board
MEB	medical examination board
MEOS	microsome ethanol oxidation systems
MLEB	medical-labor examination board
PhyBS	phyto-biogenic stimulator
Reg.f.	registration form
URC	Union of Red Cross
RCS	Red Crescent Societies
WHO	World Health Organization
WTP	work-therapy preventorium
WTW	work-therapy workshop